Praise for othe
Marilyn J. Sore

Breaking the Chain of Low Self-Esteem

"This is a wise and valuable volume" —- THE STATESMAN JOURNAL

"Whether the reader is seeking help or simply gathering information, *'Breaking the Chain Low Self-Esteem'* is a revealing and helpful book." — THE ADVOCATE

"Dr. Sorensen is warm, media savvy, riveting and a talk show host's dream guest." — ED JOHNSON, Host & Producer, OPB

"Highly Recommended" — THE MIDWEST BOOK REVIEW

"An excellent addition to any self-help collection" — TODAY'S LIBRARIAN

"The new bible of self-esteem" — ROBERT LUBOW, M.D. **Psychiatrist, Cincinnati, OH**

"Developing a healthy self-esteem is the most valuable gift you will ever give yourself. Dr. Sorensen leads the reader clearly from confusion to clarity in how to find freedom and a new way to live." — MARY MANIN MORRISSEY, Author of *Building Your Field Of Dreams* by Bantam

"This fascinating book presents startling new insights into the experience of low self-esteem." — SANDRA K. PINCHES. Ph.D. **Clinical Psychologist, Portland, Oregon**

"Her experience, wisdom, and encouraging tone make *Breaking the Chain...* a valuable tool." — THE WOMAN'S JOURNAL

Book club rights for *Breaking the Chain...* were purchased by Book-of-the-Month Club for two of its divisions: One Spirit and Quality Paperback Books.

Audio rights were purchased by Audio Literature who produced it as an audiobook.

The Book is now available in English, Greek, and Japanese.

Low Self-Esteem Misunderstood & Misdiagnosed

"outstanding resource. Sorensen expertly guides readers in self-evaluation. Author connects with readers, has excellent writing skills, establishes warm, comfortable tone." — **TODAY LIBRARIAN**

"carefully explains... why [low self-esteem] is seldom recognized or treated seriously...This is an important book that could save lives."
— **THE STATESMAN JOURNAL**

"...candid, straight forward...an excellent book, specifically for people who've tried to seek help and found nothing useful. Highly Recommended."
— **THE MIDWEST BOOK REVIEW**

"I am a clinician and am just completing your book... I will want more training in this are as it is clear to me how misdiagnoses occur..."
— **Lisa Rathbun, MSW, CSW, OTR**

The Personal Workbook for Breaking the Chain of Low Self-Esteem

"Her open, clear approach and plain language cut to the heart of things and help readers make their way through some very upsetting realizations"
— **THE STATESMAN JOURNAL**

"Dr. Sorensen's words on developing healthy self-esteem are as wise as they are practical." — **Ed Johnson, Host & Producer, OPB**

The Handbook for Building Healthy Self-Esteem in Children

"*The Handbook for Building Healthy Self-Esteem In Children* is a fantastic resource for adults who care about children. Implementation of its practical, effective, easy-to-understand tools and methods will foster a healthy self-concept in our children that can protect them from risky behavior and help them grow into their full selves.
— **Kathy Masarie, M.D., Founder and Program Director of Full Esteem Ahead**

Available in bookstores nationwide
or at a discount through www.TheSelfEsteemInstitute.com

The Self-Esteem Recovery Toolkit

(Materials designed to help LSE sufferers continue their individual daily process of recovering from low self-esteem.)

The Toolkit is only available through the website:
www.TheSelfEsteemInstitute.com

Low Self-Esteem In the Bedroom:

How LSE affects intimacy

Low Self-Esteem
In the Bedroom:

How LSE affects intimacy

Marilyn J. Sorensen, Ph.D.
Author of:
Breaking the Chain of Low Self-Esteem

Wolf Publishing Co.
Sherwood, OR 97140

Low Self-Esteem In the Bedroom:
how LSE affects intimacy

Copyright 2004 by Marilyn J. Sorensen, Ph.D.
mjsorensen@TheSelfEsteemInstitute.com
Wolf Publishing Co.
16890 SW Daffodil St.
Sherwood, OR 97140
Phone: 503-330-2830
Fax: 503-625-1545
Website: www.TheSelfEsteemInstitute.com

Editor: Jill Kelly, Ph.D.
Cover design and page layout: Anita Jones, Another Jones Graphics
Photographer: Julie Theberge, Portraits by Design
Cover Illustration: Ardis DeFreece

Library of Congress Control Number: 2004092578

10 9 8 7 6 5 4 3 2 1

ISBN: 0-9664315-2-9
Printed in the United States

Acknowledgements

Many thanks to my wonderful editor,
Jill Kelly, Ph.D.,
and to
Anita Jones for excellent cover design and layout!

They are the best!

Dedication

To Sande

Table of Contents

Introduction

Few people develop and maintain true intimacy over the life of a romantic relationship. We see this play out in divorce statistics and in the number of times people marry or live with a partner, then dissolve that relationship only to soon begin another. We see this in the number of centers for domestic violence victims, the number of murders of one spouse by another, and the number of parents who kidnap their own children from the care of the other parent. These relationships, which at the start may have ranged from healthy to unhealthy, from casual to intimate, have completely broken down and ended in divorce or even in the death of a mate. In some of these relationships, intimacy was never formed; in others, it completely eroded as outside pressures, responsibilities, losses, and temptations entered the picture, causing these partners to change priorities and values or to become disillusioned.

Many couples form an intimate relationship while dating, especially the young who are innocent, unscathed, and unaware of the many ways that people hurt, betray, and desert one another. In their naïveté, they believe that their relationship is unique; that what they have together couldn't possibly end in anything but eternal bliss. They openly share their feelings, they spend hours getting to know each other, and they have each other's complete attention and devotion. First love feels impenetrable, like a fortress that could never be broken down or destroyed. There is nothing to interfere with this period of intimacy: few other

1

responsibilities, limitless energy, and endless affirmation for one to another all contribute to dreams of a wonderful future.

As people get older, however, even those who have grown up with healthy self-esteem (HSE) become more gun-shy. Their experience has shown them that people are fallible, that they change, that priorities change, that life is unpredictable. Once hurt, they become more reticent to share their true feelings; they become less trusting of what the other person says. Their backgrounds and past experiences provide a barrier to achieving intimacy.

Developing intimacy is even more difficult for those who have grown up in dysfunctional homes or environments; those who have been mistreated, abused, neglected, or abandoned by parents or abused or mistreated by others and who have developed low self-esteem (LSE) as a result. These people begin their search for an intimate relationship with distrust, having been hurt and disrespected in childhood. These individuals have emotional scars that haven't healed; they are confused about who they are. Inside they believe that in some way they are inadequate, inferior, incompetent, or unworthy. Everything they do is affected by this negative view of self and the self-talk that follows. They expect too much or too little, they overreact, they misconstrue the words and actions of others, they become depressed, they become overachievers or underachievers, they don't know who or when to trust, and they withdraw from social interaction.

Thus, the possibility of those with LSE developing and maintaining an intimate relationship is even more complicated and less likely than for those with HSE, for whom attaining intimacy is also difficult. There is an answer, of course, and that answer is *recovery* from LSE.

Low Self-Esteem in the Bedroom first directs readers toward an understanding of what intimacy is and what it looks like by following the lives of several individuals and couples and their struggles to develop verbal, emotional, and physical intimacy. Furthermore, it the belief of this author that physical intimacy is an outgrowth of verbal and emotional intimacy. In other words, physical intimacy cannot be established without first developing verbal and emotional intimacy, for without these two as a foundation, it is merely a sexual act, not an intimate one in the true sense of intimacy.

Second, the book clearly highlights through examples some of the many ways that LSE interferes with attempts to achieve intimacy. Third, the final chapters emphasize the absolute necessity for all LSE sufferers to go through a program of recovery from their low self-esteem so that it will not continue to obstruct their lives and their attempts to develop an intimate relationship with a life partner as well as healthy and possibly intimate friendships.

Low Self-Esteem in the Bedroom also contains notes of comparison with those with healthy self-esteem, ideas about recovery, and suggested activities at the end of most chapters. Because low self-esteem is such a complex issue, and one which most people cannot recover from on their own, Chapter 8 provides information to help readers decide if they should get into therapy, how to find the therapist they need, and what to expect from therapy.

Whether you have low self-esteem or not, you may never have experienced a truly intimate relationship and not know what it looks or feels like. This is true for many people. If you read this book and take to heart the message it delivers, you will learn a lot about intimacy that you haven't known, including how to talk to those you love and how to demonstrate your love in the gentle ways that build intimacy. If either you or your partner suffers from LSE, you will be able to distinguish which arguments originate from the insecurity and distorted thinking that accompanies low self-esteem and which ones stem from legitimate complaints and issues. You will also be able to recognize when LSE is the source of inappropriate behaviors in yourself or your partner. Along with this insight, *Low Self-Esteem in the Bedroom* will provide guidance on how to correct these problems and how to eliminate the chaotic interactions that are based on irrational thinking and fear.

The meat and potatoes book of my many years of specializing in recovery from low self-esteem, *Breaking the Chain of Low Self-Esteem,* more fully addresses the symptoms discussed in this book as well as many others and includes a questionnaire that will help you determine if you have LSE. To more fully understand how LSE forms and the many additional ways it negatively affects people's lives, I suggest you read it.

Chapter 1

What is Intimacy?

Juan and Bonita

Juan and Bonita have been married for 18 months but, for Bonita, their sexual relationship has never been very fulfilling. In fact, she is becoming angry with Juan for his insensitivity to the fact that she does not climax when they make love. Their sexual encounters last about 15 minutes, which is not nearly enough time for Bonita to get aroused and to have an orgasm. Their encounters involve minimal kissing or foreplay and no clitoral stimulation, which she has always required. When they have sex, there is silence between them, something Bonita also finds strange, though she is too shy to initiate. On the two occasions that she has tried to broach the subject with Juan, he has gotten defensive and acted hurt and angry before she could even present the problem to him. She, too, is reticent to really talk about sex or about her personal needs, precluding the possibility of their achieving true sexual intimacy.

Juan is a victim of low self-esteem (LSE) and, though uncharacteristic for most Hispanic families, he was born an only child in a home of two extremely introverted intellectuals, where ordinary life issues including sexuality were never discussed. He was alone much of the time and felt alone even when his parents were home. They were not warm and loving people but rather two individuals totally absorbed by their careers, and they let Juan know by their critical natures that he was a burden to them. They had not planned to have children but when they were faced with an unplanned and unwanted pregnancy, they chose to have the child. Soon after Juan was born, they both returned to their primary focus: their work. As a result, Juan grew up feeling unwanted and unloved. Totally without social skills, he kept to himself and did not gain the benefit of a household with siblings, company coming to dinner, family activities.

Juan is also inexperienced in the area of sexuality and ignorant of the wants and needs of women. He and Bonita met in their senior year of high school when they were assigned as lab partners. She too had come from a dysfunctional home and had developed low self-esteem. Both were social misfits and bonded to each other out of neediness, becoming close friends. Following graduation they saw each other frequently and a year later decided to get married—as much to get away from their homes as to be with someone whom they liked and who liked them—though neither knew if they were really *in* love with the other.

The few times they had had sex before marriage had been awkward and embarrassing for both of them. Bonita had had a few sexual encounters with boys she hardly knew and who had taken advantage of her neediness and vulnerability, but she had only been orgasmic when she masturbated, so she knew what it took to make that happen. Juan had never been with a woman before Bonita and was both uninformed and clumsy in his approach. He was also very self-absorbed, thinking little of what the experience felt like or meant to Bonita.

When Bonita now tries to talk to Juan about her frustration, he only hears criticism. Feeling humiliated and not knowing how to respond, Juan becomes angry and storms out of the room. Overreacting because of his low self-esteem, he inaccurately equates her words with the feelings of inadequacy he has always had about himself. He feels unable to tolerate more criticism and looks of disappointment such as he saw in the eyes of his parents. Juan has always feared that a woman would not find him worthy as a husband and a man.

Intimacy implies closeness, privacy, and familiarity. Intimacy can refer to a close and affectionate verbal and emotional relationship between friends or partners; it can also describe physical closeness in the form of foreplay, intercourse, or other sexual activity. Our focus, in this book, is to address exactly what healthy verbal, emotional, and sexual intimacy would look like within a committed relationship and how efforts to establish that closeness and to maintain it are thwarted when one or both individuals suffers from the distorted thinking patterns that accompany low self-esteem. Suggestions for changing this pattern are presented here as well.

True intimacy in a relationship is hard for any couple to achieve and even more difficult to maintain. This is especially so when one or both of the individuals has low self-esteem (LSE). The factors involved in intimacy (the need to be honest and the need to be vulnerable and open) are the same issues that activate the self-doubt of the individual plagued with LSE.

As an LSE sufferer begins to get close to someone, his fear and anxiety gradually increases, causing his negative thinking to become irrational. In the case of Juan and Bonita, for instance, Bonita may start to tell herself that Juan doesn't care about her or he would listen to her and try to solve the problem. The truth, however, is that Juan already feels inadequate and desperately wants to avoid more criticism. His avoidance has nothing to do with how he feels about Bonita; he is focused on self-protection and survival. His anxiety may push him to tell himself that Bonita is just like his parents, critical and demanding. Once these LSE sufferers have established untruthful, distorted, thoughts; they hold on to them and they act as though the irrational thoughts are true; and they attach the meaning to other disagreements as well. Consequently, once started, Bonita may approach every difficulty in her marriage with the belief that Juan really doesn't care and Juan may continue to see Bonita as being like his parents, neither of which is accurate.

As the distorted thinking grows in frequency and intensity, it may produce in the LSE sufferer a victim response that says, "She (or he) is the cause of all my stress and my unhappiness." This releases the individual from having to look at himself and how he may be contributing to the problems in the relationship. At the same time, the LSE sufferer's negativity and expectation of a poor outcome dominate his overall perspective, telling him "Nothing is ever going to change. Why keep trying? This relationship isn't going to work either." Unwilling to take a look at themselves, LSE sufferers may never get counseling or even talk about their problems because they fear they will get a negative response from the person they confide in.

The hurt feelings, anger, and resentment that surface within a deepening relationship are the result of the fine-tuned sensitivity that LSE sufferers acquired as neglected or abused children. For instance, a woman who has doubts on a very deep level, that someone could truly love her, and who fears, more than anything, that she will experience more disapproval or be taken advantage of, may easily misconstrue a look, a remark, or lack of follow-through as representing something much more profound than it is. For example, if her lover is preoccupied or insensitive due to stress, she may view a misspoken word or a remark as a purpose-fully hurtful and critical one. Then, rather than confront the situation, her LSE will encourage her to remain hurt, and in her mind, she may actually expand or exaggerate the remark as indi-cating that her lover doesn't respect her, doesn't love her, or isn't trustworthy. Once trust becomes an issue, once the LSE sufferer suspects that she is being deceived, mistreated, or taken advan-tage of, intimacy is threatened and the relationship becomes one of confusion with one or both partners under-responding (becoming passive) or inappropriately overreacting (acting aggressively or passive-aggressively). Thus, when threatened, the person with LSE tries to protect herself by either withdrawing, blaming, or indirectly punishing, anything that will shield her from having to talk through the situation, even though any one of these avoidance behaviors can be death to a relationship.

This is not to say that people who have been conditioned to think badly of themselves cannot build constructive and intimate relationships. It does mean that to be an equal partner, they must first become aware that they have low self-esteem. They must become aware of how LSE affects their thinking, their ability to respond rationally, their willingness to be vulnerable, and their inability to know whom and when to trust. Until they recognize these dysfunctional patterns and take responsibility for them, they will not be good candidates for an intimate relationship.

Jackson

Jackson, 33, single, and a schoolteacher, and Brianne, an attorney who is 36 and divorced, have been dating for two months. During this period, they have spent increasing time together hiking, cooking, watching and discussing movies, and especially talking and laughing together. Becoming more and more comfortable with each other, they have begun to share both general and personal aspects of their lives, their work, their interests, and their life goals.

As their emotional attachment grows. Brianne has tried to share her feelings with Jackson but she feels him withdraw emotionally when she does. She also wonders why her attempts to become more amorous have not brought about a more positive reaction from Jackson and why he has never initiated going further in their physical relationship than the fondling and kissing that they frequently engage in. She feels Jackson responding when he kisses her and holds her, and by what he says to her when they begin to get physical, but then he seems to find some reason to stop, either using the ringing of the phone, the fact that he is tired, or some other excuse to suggest that they call it a night. Brianne has tried to bring up the subject but senses his reluctance and hasn't pushed the issue. His lack of willingness to engage in sex and the fact that he has never married or spoken of a serious relationship makes her wonder if Jackson is gay. She finds it quite unusual that a man would date her exclusively for two months and never want to engage in sex.

As Brianne tries to analyze the situation, she realizes that most of the time they spent together when they were first seeing each other was at her initiation. Jackson was always willing and seemed excited to do whatever she suggested but he had seldom instigated anything himself. In fact, now that she thinks about it, she was usually the one to state her opinions on matters first and she had definitely shared more about herself than he did. She wonders what is going on with Jackson or between them and decides she must try to find a way to talk to him.

Jackson has low self-esteem. He likes Brianne a lot but is frightened that he might sabotage this relationship just as he has in the past. Jackson's main problem is that he has had only a couple of sexual experiences in his life and they did not go well. In both situations, Jackson was so anxious and fearful about his sexual prowess that he could not maintain an erection. In the first case, he was too humiliated to see the woman again, and the second time the woman was quite unhappy when she undressed and his penis became limp.

Jackson views these two interactions as the most traumatic events of his life and sees them as situations he doesn't think he could handle again. Not only is he inexperienced, but Jackson hasn't had a parent, close friend, or anyone to talk to about women, relationships, and sex either before or after these two encounters. He also has been unaware that he has low self-esteem; he just sees himself as hopelessly inadequate. He doesn't understand that his inability to maintain an erection is directly correlated with low self-esteem and the fear and anxiety that accompany LSE.

After the last failed attempt, Jackson resigned himself to being single for the rest of his life and made no more attempts to date or get to know the women he admired. It was only because Brianne kept asking him to do things and he so enjoyed their time together that Jackson let down his guard. Now he is in the biggest quagmire of his life; he knows that he is falling in love with Brianne, but he feels she would be disgusted and quit seeing him if she knew of his problem. Once again, his inexperience and lack of information about sex and LSE leave him with no understanding that many men have had to deal with the inability to maintain an erection at some point in their lives. Instead, he sees his inability to perform as the sign of his inadequacy.

Jackson doesn't want to break up with Brianne, but he is certain that while so far she has only gently pressed him for answers about his avoidance of more intimate physical contact, she will soon expect a full explanation.

Jackson's life is being controlled by his low self-esteem. His feelings of inadequacy and the fear of further humiliation are so strong that they prevent him from seeking help for his problem, thus eliminating the likelihood that he will develop and maintain a truly intimate committed relationship.

Molly

Several evenings a week Molly goes to one of several pubs where local bands play in hopes of meeting a man. Lonely and frantically trying to find someone to care about her, she dresses provocatively and is watchful of each male who enters the pub. Molly is quite attractive and in the months of carrying out this routine, she has made a number of contacts with men, going to their homes where the two engage in sex. On other occasions, she has had sex in their cars or even in a motel. In each instance, it has seemed to her that the man was very attracted to her and that he enjoyed the sexual activities and her willingness to do what he wanted including sexual experimentation. Yet, although each had taken her phone number, none had ever contacted her again.

Molly doesn't understand why these men don't call like they say they will, and each encounter ends in her growing desperation and despair. When the man is buying her drinks, flirting with her, laughing and talking with her, and especially when he invites her to go home with him, Molly feels cared about, almost giddy with excitement. Her hope rises, thinking that maybe this is "the one," but then gradually it dissipates as the days go by and the phone doesn't ring.

Instead of attempting to analyze the situation and maybe learn why her strategy for finding a man isn't working, Molly just continues the pattern. Instead of looking at herself to see what she could do to "be" the right person with whom a man would want an ongoing relationship, she focuses unsuccessfully on "finding" the right person. She remains depressed for a few days and then eventually returns to one of the pubs, looking for another prospective partner and becoming less and less choosy about whom she goes home with. Molly doesn't have any other contact with men and doesn't have any idea of another way to start a relationship and certainly knows nothing about intimacy.

Molly's quest to find a man to love her demonstrates one example of the self-defeating—and self-deflating—behavior of millions of women who suffer from low self-esteem and who have been saddled with the early teaching that a woman needs a man to survive and to be content with herself and in the world. Finding a man then becomes her primary goal. However, this is problematic because a person this needy is unlikely to find someone healthier than she is. In fact she is more likely to find someone who will take advantage of her because she is overly willing to please. She may think pleasing him is what will cause a man to want to stay with her, but in truth, people who do too much for others often lose the respect of those they do these things for. She is also unaware that men generally do not marry the women they pick up in bars; instead, they use these women to fulfill their immediate needs and they look elsewhere for a mate.

Many of the women who engage in this behavior of "one-night stands" with people who are basically strangers have been sexually abused as children. They are women who suffer from low self-esteem and who see themselves in a negative light. They are lonely, and they likely have poor social skills and few contacts or opportunities to meet men with whom they might be able to establish a relationship based on factors other than sex. These women often equate sexual contact with intimacy, perhaps because they were told this while they were being abused or because they have inaccurately linked all sexual contact to authentic love and affection. Either way, they are vulnerable to even the slightest show of kindness or affection, and all too frequently they respond completely out of proportion to what is happening—deceiving themselves into thinking that the man's attention means something more than it really does.

Other women who have been abused sexually, emotionally, verbally, or physically may think so little of themselves that they believe that their body is all they have to offer. They may even believe that sex is the only thing men really want from women, having heard this from their mothers or other caregivers, and unfortunately this may sometimes be the truth. The woman who believes that she has what men really want can easily delude herself into thinking that the obvious way to find a mate is to look for a venue in which she can show her willingness by dressing and acting seductively, such as a bar.

Women with low self-esteem this severe tend to not be very discriminating. Rather, they respond to the attention they receive and may hardly see the actual person. Thinking that their sexual appeal is their main attraction, many hone their skills at pleasing men sexually without even considering who or what type of men these are. Low self-esteem often causes those who suffer from it, both men and women, to feel that they deserve very little and that they should be accepting of whatever they can get, that they can't be selective. Thus thinking that they deserve little but that they may be able to offer more sexual satisfaction and variety than the man has previously experienced, these women use sexual expertise as their calling card, the feature that sets them apart from other women and one that they hope some man will be unable to resist—now and in the future.

People who suffer from low self-esteem have many irrational beliefs, and in their neediness, female LSE sufferers may convince themselves that if a man wants to be intimate with them, it means that he really cares about them; they equate sex with intimacy. They may come from a family where the parents did not demonstrate healthy communication, tenderness, sensitivity, or affection, so that they've never seen a good relationship in action. If they have never had a close relationship—and they've never observed one, they have no basis upon which to understand what emotional and verbal intimacy looks like in a relationship. And, if a person doesn't know what an intimate relationship looks or feels like, she probably also lacks the know-how and insight to establish such a relationship. (Notice, I don't say she lacks the *ability* to establish such a relationship, rather that she may not have *yet* acquired the knowledge, understanding, and skills.) Consequently, she may try to create and rely on physical intimacy in hopes that the other aspects of an intimate relationship will automatically follow. Of course, this again is irrational thinking, as verbal and emotional relationships are the foundation for building physical intimacy, not the other way around.

Jake

Jake is the editor of a big city newspaper and, as such, is well known and respected in the local political and civic communities. To the general public, he appears to be not only successful but also competent and self-assured; yet, in his private life, Jake suffers from deep-seated feelings of inadequacy and inferiority. These feelings play out most prominently in his relationship with his wife, Deidre. Doubting his ability to sexually satisfy her, Jake is irrationally jealous and often becomes enraged when he suspects that she is looking at another man or when he sees one eyeing her. This is Jake's third marriage; he drove his former wives away with his jealous and inappropriate reactions.

Jake's problem stems from his childhood: in bitterness and anger after Jake's father left them, his mother told Jake that he would never be a real man because his penis was so small. While his wives have never complained and have tried to reassure him that his penis is quite adequate and that he performs very well in bed, Jake cannot eliminate his mother's voice from his head, and he hears it whenever he engages in sexual activity. His fears play out in numerous ways, including a self-consciousness about engaging in oral sex wherein his wife would put her focus even more intensely on his penis. After a sexual encounter with his wife, he cannot control his need for reassurance, engaging in something close to an interrogation about her reactions to the experience. His wife is becoming increasingly troubled by her husband's obvious insecurity.

Jake's reaction to the engrained thoughts and memories that flood his mind is to feel out of control. Even when he has had a very exciting and pleasing sexual experience with his wife, he worries internally and externally whether he has performed adequately. His attempts to squelch his fears are unsuccessful and in his desperation to feel less anxious, he repeatedly questions his wife. When she whispers intimate words of wonder and joy after their experience, he silently questions her sincerity. Thus, Jake is never able to accept the full pleasure of the sexual encounter; instead he focuses on the negative doubts that plague him.

As is typical of all people who have low self-esteem, Jake has already accepted a negative conclusion about himself that seems set in stone. In this case, the conclusion is that his penis is inadequate and that he is less than a fully functioning man. Based on the messages he repeatedly received from his mother, he cannot find a way to alter that belief so as to accept the positive responses of his former wives and his present mate. If Jake doesn't work to overcome his low self-esteem, he may destroy yet another relationship through self-destructive behavior. Until he can accept himself and fully trust Deidre, they will never have a truly intimate relationship.

In order for those who suffer from low self-esteem to alter the behaviors that interfere with their lives and their relationships, they must first become aware that they *have low self-esteem.* Second, they must recognize that much of the negative feedback they received was not true but was based on the inadequate coping methods of unhealthy parents or other unhealthy people. Third, they must learn that that they have a thinking disorder: that they have accepted as true and built their lives upon those falsehoods that were told to them rather than deciding for themselves what is fact, truth, or based on history.

Once a person realizes that he has LSE, he can begin to understand what that means in day-to-day life, that much of what he concludes about the motives and behavior of others is distorted because it is tied to his irrational core beliefs about himself and how others view him. Once he accepts that the thinking of people who have LSE is largely distorted and once he realizes that there are behaviors commonly associated with LSE, he may be able to develop an awareness of this thinking process, including how frequently what he thinks and concludes is not based on fact, truth, or history, the real criteria for distinguishing what is— or is not—accurate and rational thinking.

In other words, he will begin to see that what an angry, bitter woman has said to a little boy, even if he is her son, does not necessarily represent the truth, nor does the fact that a man abandons his son mean that there is something inadequate in the boy. Only when a person comes to terms with the fact that he has LSE and learns what that means can he understand why he thinks as he does, feels as he does, and behaves as he does. Only then can he begin to sort out the truth, begin to see how distorted his thoughts are, and begin to alter them. All the effort he can muster to try to alleviate his fears will not help until he recognizes what the issue is that is interfering with his life: his low self-esteem. In order for family, friends, and loved ones to understand and remain detached from the irrational behavior that often accompanies LSE, they, too, must become aware of which behaviors are related to low self-esteem and why the person afflicted with LSE behaves as he does.

Many of us may understand what it means to be afflicted with low self-esteem and we may realize that dysfunctional thinking is the distinguishing factor that accompanies it. At the same time, we may be unaware of the subtle ways in which LSE permeates the entirety of a person's life and how it builds up walls that interfere with the very things that people want most. Much like electricity instantly responds to a light switch, so too, the irrational thinking that accompanies low self-esteem reacts instantly to all kinds of stimulus or behavior: an angry look, a questionably sarcastic remark, or a totally innocent statement. Hyper-vigilant out of a fear of experiencing shame, humiliation, criticism, or rejection, the person with LSE can a) hear negative responses where none are intended, b) feel rejection when it is not real, and c) experience shame in situations where those with healthy self-esteem would seldom, if ever, have a negative response. To the LSE sufferer, however, these seemingly innocuous situations are like light switches that release power; they provide energy and momentum to the irrational anxiety, self-doubt, and threat of being found out as inadequate.

The most threatening of these situations are those involving personal relationships. We highly value these relationships and most people have a dream that finding a significant other is the answer to the search for happiness. They want to build a life with him or her, maybe have a family, and have that someone with whom to share the ups and downs of life. Society also tends to be geared toward couples and families rather than singles. In fact, the first questions asked of people often include "Are you seeing anyone right now?" or "Do you have children?" or "Are you married?" creating the impression that these are the most important details of life. This emphasis is reinforced in magazines, television shows, movies, and advertisements, and the pressure to be part of a couple is tremendous. As is true of all significant events, the more importance we place on the goal, the greater the pressure is to succeed and the more frightening the possibility of failure. So, with an internal desire to be in a relationship and an external pressure to be coupled (or face being seen as inadequate), being in a relationship becomes a critical issue.

A second reason why building relationships involves so much fear and trepidation for the person with low self-esteem is that relationships are inherently unpredictable and people with LSE hate uncertainty. A large part of the insecurity of these individuals is that a) they "know they don't know" certain things that may be expected of them, b) they "don't know what it is that they don't know," c) they think most people know the things that they don't know, and d) they see their lack of knowing as a sign of personal failure and insufficiency rather than as a sign that their upbringing and opportunities were lacking. [1]

Because each of us enters a relationship with differing experiences, differing bodies of knowledge, and from differing economic, cultural, religious, and political backgrounds, we also have different expectations, dreams, and areas of expertise. Thus, the playing field is never totally level. While the person with healthy self-esteem can enter into an encounter with excitement, zeal, or at least the confidence to be able to cope and adjust, the person with low self-esteem is filled with anxiety, fear, and often unrealistic expectations. And once the person with LSE attempts to initiate a relationship and finds her efforts thwarted, she is less likely to initiate again soon. Instead, she personalizes the negative response or rejection as a condemnation of herself as a person. She tends to see things as black and white, all or nothing, unaware that this is irrational thinking and a form of rigidity. In other words, she may jump to the conclusion that there's no use initiating with anyone else

[1] Sorensen, Marilyn J., *Breaking the Chain of Low Self-Esteem.* Sherwood, OR: Wolf Publishing Co., 1998, pp. 47-52.

because if it didn't work this time, it won't work the next time either. Or, like Molly, she may go to the other extreme, repeating the same behavior rather than considering other options and admitting that her present strategy is not working.

Thus, people with low self-esteem often avoid analyzing situations or seeking help that might give them a different perspective. As a result, many of them tend not to be good at problem-solving, especially if it requires that they look at their own behavior and see their own mistakes, because they tend to interpret any misstep as a sign that they are beyond help.

A third difficult aspect for those with LSE in establishing committed partnerships is that it is in the nature of relationships to be changeable, which is disconcerting to the person who wants and who needs to feel secure. Often the person with low self-esteem attempts to control the relationship in order to provide that sense of stability and predictability, even becoming abusive in order to be in command of the situation and to keep it from changing. Or he may go to the other extreme by continually trying to please his partner, thinking that if he does everything she wants, she surely won't leave him. The partner often feels smothered when this happens or she loses respect for her mate. Both of these tactics, of course, are self-defeating and often bring an undesired result.

A fourth factor is that the person doesn't see himself for who he really is. He doesn't recognize that his thinking is distorted much of the time and that this thinking problem is at the core of his inability to succeed in relationships. He isn't aware that the reason he has been unsuccessful in relationships has less to do with who he is (which he thinks is unacceptable, even unlovable) and more to do with particular behaviors that could be altered over time with an open mind and a willingness to change. Thus, he continues to repeat the behaviors that have not worked in the past, behaviors that won't work in the present or future either.

But because the LSE sufferer is so wounded, he is unable to look at himself as able to change; rather he feels that something within himself is broken or damaged beyond repair and therefore cannot be restored. He isn't able to see that he has developed poor communication skills, or lacks social skills, or is simply repeating dysfunctional and inappropriate behavior that he learned but that could be unlearned. He already feels so negative about himself that he can't face what seems like an even more negative and shaming denunciation of who he is as a person. In this way, the practice of self-defeating behaviors continues to repeat itself with nothing changing the feeling of increasingly demoralization.

Nearly all of us desire to find someone to love and who, hopefully, loves us. The person with LSE, however, can seem much more interested in being loved than in demonstrating love. Out of her neediness, she is more often focused on what she wants and in getting her own needs met than on meeting the needs of her partner. She may also overlook her own faults or hurtful behavior while being very critical of the behavior of others. Often her attempts to please are actually attempts to temporarily appease the other person who is bothered by her preoccupation with herself and her feelings.

Carey

Carey grew up as the only girl in a family of four children. Her two older brothers were jocks; her younger brother, Joey, was a quiet boy who enjoyed reading and golf. The older boys excelled in football, basketball, and wrestling, much like their father, who was a wrestling coach. Their mother was a quiet, submissive woman in the midst of two rowdy and macho boys who were encouraged by their father to think that their athletic ability made them something special.

Together the two older boys and their father exhibited their masculinity as a form of entitlement, dominating the communication in the home and displaying an attitude of superiority towards the younger siblings. They were disrespectful and inattentive to Carey and also to Joey, whom they viewed as a wimp. Neither Carey's mother nor her father intervened on behalf of the younger children.

Carey, who was becoming more attractive as she grew up, and Joey, who was slight in build and sensitive, were perfect targets for the amusement of the older boys. Not only did their father fail to intercede on behalf of Carey or Joey, he joined in the harassment, teasing Carey about her developing figure or tweaking her breasts or bottom. When he was absent, the "jocks" took even more liberties, acting as though they were in command, bossing around their two siblings and expecting the two women and the boy to do their bidding. Once again, their mother did nothing to discourage them, simply giving Carey or Joey a shrug as if to say, "There is nothing I can do."

Consequently, Joey and Carey bonded, spending hours together reading, talking, or watching movies. While Joey had his golf, Carey became a recluse, going to school but seldom interacting with others because she felt so inadequate. She didn't have any idea how to start a friendship; she was frightened at the thought that others might humiliate her as her brothers did, and so she kept to herself. When she entered junior high school, she was further alienated from her classmates because she had no experience in relationship-building with anyone but a younger brother nor any perspective on what a healthy relationship would look like. Sadly, Carey watched as other girls developed close friendships with one another. She heard them sharing their thoughts and feelings in the school bathroom, she saw

them giggling together in front of their lockers, and she heard them
making plans in the lunch line. But Carey didn't have a best friend;
she didn't even have a casual friend.

Our view of ourselves as people whom others would want to
befriend forms at an early age. Coming from a dysfunctional
family environment where the children were valued for their
athletic prowess and for how closely they followed in their father's
footsteps rather than for who they were as people, Carey did not
meet the criteria. Her feelings weren't considered; her thoughts
and wishes went unheard; she seemed to fill only the role of dart-
board for the barbs of the older men in the family.

Once we have formed an opinion of ourselves as having less
value then others, we also feel less deserving and we may lower
our expectations. This was true for Carey, who assumed that no
one else would value her, that no one would want to be her friend.
Rather than risk rejection and humiliation, she kept to herself,
telling herself that she didn't need others.

When a child grows up with abuse, the form of dysfunction
that her self-esteem takes *always* mirrors the message of the abuse,
though it may play out in different ways. For example, if a child
is neglected, that child will feel insignificant and without worth.
Then later in life he will continually wonder if others value him,
and he will look for signs that confirm his fears thus becoming a
self-fulfilling prophesy. Also, if a child is abused sexually, that
child will often act out sexually as she grows up, possibly acting
seductive, becoming promiscuous, or using sex to hurt others. Or
if the child's abuse took the form of verbal and emotional abuse,
the child will likely become an angry adult, hurling her resentment and impatience toward others. Thus, the type of abuse she
experiences matters.

While all LSE sufferers share a belief that they are in some way less adequate, less deserving, and less desirable than "regular" people, this may play out for one in passivity and for another in aggressive behavior. Or it may take the form of overachieving for one person and underachieving for another. What is common to all people with LSE is that their response, regardless of the extreme they resort to, will be self-sabotaging and self-defeating, for once a person negatively labels herself, she then tends to act out that belief and in so doing becomes the person others have told her she is.

Jarrod

Jarrod becomes insanely jealous when he sees his wife look at another man. Though she has never been unfaithful to him, he is suspicious of any contact she has with men and constantly looks for signs that she is trying to connect with others. Unfortunately for Jarrod's irrational fears, his wife Jackie is a very extroverted, gregarious, and likeable woman. She works on many committees and fundraisers for the community and so rubs shoulders with many influential men and women. These community volunteers often have meetings over lunch or dinner or frequently meet for a drink while talking about their most pressing projects. They love to include Jackie for she keeps the process and conversation moving, she is full of ideas, and she radiates what seems to be unlimited energy.

Jarrod is convinced that he is in love with Jackie but isn't as sure that she loves him. Plagued with low self-esteem, Jarrod vacillates about how he feels about himself. At times he thinks Jackie is lucky to have him, yet more often he is unable to recognize his own

*good qualities and wonders why she is with him. Those good char-
acteristics he does acknowledge that he has seem less important
compared to those he sees in Jackie. Feeling inferior and expecting
her to leave him at any moment, he is watchful and accusing even
when the evidence does not support his suspicions. He questions
Jackie on a regular basis, wanting to know where she has been,
whom she has been with, and why she was gone so long. If a man
calls the house to talk to her, he interrogates her afterwards and
tells her he doesn't want men calling the house even though he
knows they are business or volunteer associates.*

Jarrod may well ruin the marriage he so badly wants to hold
on to if he doesn't get into a self-esteem recovery program. His
suspicions are irrational; they are not based on truth. Instead, they
are related to the fact that Jarrod saw his parents cheating on each
other when he was a child. He is afraid of being humiliated by
naïvely overlooking such behavior in his own relationship, so he
thinks he must be vigilant. His feelings of insecurity have more to
do with the fact that his parents were never available to spend
time with him because they were always busy with their social cal-
endar, working, or watching television. He was never the priority
then and he suspects that he isn't the priority with Jackie now.

When a person begins with the belief that he is less than
others (less deserving, less adequate, less competent, of less value),
his thoughts and actions will reflect that belief. Thus, because
Jarrod holds this belief, he believes that others feel the same way
about him. He even unwittingly sets about confirming it by
being watchful and then projecting his fears onto his wife. In
other words, so convinced is Jarrod that Jackie will eventually
leave him that he convinces himself that his thoughts reflect hers
rather than understanding that these thoughts and feeling are his

alone and have nothing to do with what Jackie thinks or feels. He is assuming that what he has concluded that his parents felt about him is also what Jackie feels about him. This is a huge and disastrous leap in thinking and one without a basis in reality.

Also, like many LSE sufferers, Jarrod has moments when he jumps to the other extreme and sees himself as better than he is. During those occasional periods, he becomes haughty, overbearing, and demanding. This is just another coping mechanism for the LSE sufferer, who is so hurt that he convinces himself that he doesn't deserve what is happening to him and then tries to take control of the situation to get what he wants.

Mandy and Willa

Mandy and Willa, both in their late 20's, have been in a committed relationship for three years, years that haven't been easy because they both suffer from low self-esteem. Mandy developed LSE growing up in a poverty-level home. Her parents had resigned themselves to being poor and had accepted that they would always have less than those around them: less money, fewer opportunities, lower quality clothes and material things, and a life of struggling to make ends meet.

Mandy's father seemed defeated and either unwilling or unable to do what was necessary to make a difference; her mother was angry with him and blamed him for their present circumstances and what she saw as a predictable future. She was also jealous of the more independent choices her daughter was making for her life, choices that included pursuing a career rather than taking the traditional road of marriage and children. Not only did Mandy's direction in life cast a shadow on her mother's choices, but her goals did not coincide with her mother's expectations of spending a lot of time with her daughter and having grandchildren to dote on. Thus, Mandy's path was an additional disappointment in her mother's life and she let Mandy know it by being extremely critical of her whenever that path swerved away from tradition. Though Mandy excelled in her studies, sports, and drama, she could always expect some type of criticism from her mother. Determined to live her life on her own terms, Mandy nevertheless felt that she was a disappointment to her mother and struggled between pleasing her and doing what she felt was right for herself. When Mandy realized during her high school years that she was gay, she knew she would have to keep her feelings hidden from her mother. She understood without question that seeing her daughter as gay would be the final straw for her mother. She would view this as total failure on her part and total rebellion and betrayal on Mandy's. So Mandy coped by hiding her feelings, feelings both about the rejection she felt from her mother and those related to her sexual orientation. She tried to please her mother in the ways she could, took her mother's criticism in silence, and felt very much alone.

Willa had been raised by two alcoholic parents; her older brother was constantly in trouble with the law. Arguments, angry words, and physical abuse were common in this environment; but unlike her brother who was often at the center of the chaos, Willa learned to escape at the first sign of a fight. In the beginning, she had found comfort and peace by retiring to her room, but as her brother got older, she didn't feel safe knowing that he might enter uninvited to vent his anger at her. She knew that if he did, her parents would be too inebriated to intervene, so she began to leave the house and she found a safe place in a cove of trees a short walk away. There she often retreated with a book, her journal, and her drawing pad. Withdrawing into her own world and away from the loud and crazy behavior at home, Willa recorded her thoughts and feelings, read about families and relationships, and drew what she saw around her.

Willa grew up feeling insignificant, neglected, and unloved. At school she was quiet and kept to herself. She did her assignments, but because she received little encouragement or affirmation, she did them half-heartedly and poorly. Only in art did she excel, though she didn't show her work to anyone except her fellow students and her teacher. Depressed and unmotivated, Willa went through the motions of attending and graduating from school; then, at the encouragement of a relative, she got a job at a local parts store, stocking shelves. When she began to make money, began receiving affirmation and praise at work, and received a promotion Willa began to believe that she might be able to make something of her life. She did her work and kept to herself, and gradually she began to respond to the casual, friendly attempts of her coworkers to interact.

Willa and Mandy met at the company summer barbecue, Willa as an employee and Mandy at the invitation of a gay male friend who also worked for the auto-parts store. At the time, Willa hadn't yet come to grips with the fact that she was gay, but the two young women made eye contact and knew they were attracted to one another. They talked some at the barbecue and made plans to get together for dinner the coming weekend. Their relationship developed quickly. Both were alone and wanting to be in a relationship; both were needy. Unfortunately, they had even more in common: both came from dysfunctional backgrounds and both had had little experience in witnessing a healthy committed relationship.

From the beginning, Mandy and Willa were careful to please each other and to avoid conflict. As the relationship developed, however, issues came to the forefront as they eventually do in all relationships. When Mandy was upset with Willa, she tended to be overly critical, much as her mother had been. This sent Willa into a tailspin. With fear and anxiety of her past resurfacing, she looked for a way to escape and began walking out of the tense situation and going to a local coffee shop. This infuriated Mandy; she had never walked away from her mother, no matter how hurtful her mother's words had been. Willa's walking away made Mandy feel disrespected.

When Willa didn't like something Mandy did, she kept it hidden inside herself for weeks. Then when her anger had built up, like a full cup running over, she exploded at Mandy, becoming a replica of her parents, angry and venting completely out of proportion to the situation. Mandy would once again feel devastated and scared, much like the small child and teenager who had felt her mother's cutting words.

When two people in a relationship both have low self-esteem, communication becomes even more difficult and intimacy becomes even more elusive, because both are responding not only to the present situation but also to the voices and the pain that they remember from childhood. Mandy doesn't see that she is being too critical of Willa because it is the only way she knows to address conflict or state her unhappiness. When Willa is confronted or threatened, she does the only thing she knows to cope with the situation: she withdraws and finds a place to hide. When she is angry at Mandy, Willa doesn't know what to say or how to say it; she is so fearful of re-experiencing the type of fights she witnessed as a child that she holds in her anger rather than expressing it. Then, as is typical of most people who are passive, one too many issues becomes the final straw and Willa blows up.

As with the other examples presented here, Mandy and Willa respond from a level of sensitivity that developed with their low self-esteem. Both were hurt and devalued in their developmental years when they were only beginning to form a perspective of their adequacy and worthiness; both have received more negative input than positive and both carry with them the emotional scars from these interactions. Whenever the women converse with each other, they bring into each conversation the negative memories and the strategies they each developed to cope. Neither one has learned skills for problem-solving; neither one has allowed herself to believe that her partner is only trying to improve the relationship. Instead, at the moment of confrontation, each sees the other as the enemy, just another person wanting to vent their unhappiness with them as the target.

In this way, confrontation and disagreements become huge in the mind of most LSE sufferers. They experience criticism as condemnation, displeasure as lack of caring, and criticism as a means of devaluing them. Within this turbulent storm, neither woman is able to focus on the issue at hand without bringing into the conflict their emotional scars: their distrust, their fear and anxiety, and their hopelessness. The result is chaos, more hurtful experiences, and negative results.

Darren

Darren, 46, has never been in a long-lasting relationship, though he would say that he has always wanted one. While successful in running his franchised business and respected among those he knows in his business dealings, he is afflicted with feelings of insecurity and inferiority, feelings he is unable to acknowledge and address. The main reason why Darren's relationships have not lasted is that he doesn't share enough about himself to let the woman really see him. Instead, he listens intently and tries to please by doing whatever she wants to do. On the few subjects he does discuss, Darren tends to be opinionated. He says what he believes and thinks he has a right to do so. He also strongly believes that his opinions are right and he is unwilling to consider other options or ways of looking at things. He is unaware that his relationships only go so far before the woman gets fed up and leaves because she finds him boring and extremely closed-minded.

In many ways Darren is overly polite and considerate; trying to avoid criticism or rejection, he is usually conforming and amicable in public and with people he hardly knows. When he receives negative feedback from someone he considers significant or when he feels someone important to him is disapproving of his behavior, however, he becomes defensive and unwilling to apologize. Some of these women have tried to talk to Darren about his defensiveness, but he has been too devastated by negative feedback in childhood to be able to digest new criticism. Instead, he tells these women that he is not responsible for their feelings and that they are just too needy.

Clinging to the belief that his father was a man's man and one to be admired, Darren unwittingly replicates the same rigidity that was evident in his father and that created a painful childhood. Even if Darren attempted to be open to the thought that there truly were something wrong with him, he would likely toss the input aside because to entertain the idea that his behavior was unacceptable would require that he view his father in a new and negative light. And, admitting that his father wasn't a very nice man would mean that all he had believed and based his reasoning and behavior on, was wrong. He would also have to accept responsibility for his own behavior and learn how to do treat people differently.

Actually Darren has dated several women, relationships that have lasted for several months or off and on for over several months. The women he has been with have admired many of his good qualities; they have perceived him as honest and kind, and a person of high standards, but they have also found in him a coldness and defensiveness when it comes to working out conflicts and the parts of a relationship that call for true intimacy.

For instance, when Darren was dating Sharon, she more than once confronted him about his behavior when he was tired or stressed "Darren, honey, I know you are tired tonight, but I find it hurtful that you are gruff and abrupt with me. Just because you are stressed doesn't mean you can take it out on me."

"What do you mean?" Darren snaps, "Why do you take everything so personally? You're just too sensitive."

When one of these women has asked more of Darren than he wished to give, such as wanting more time with him, he has seen this as an unreasonable demand and ridiculed her. When one of these women has complained that he seldom tells her he loves her and he doesn't give her enough verbal support and affirmation, he calls her "needy" and tells her she is leaning too much on him. When several women have asked him to help them with their various projects, he has criticized them for starting things they can't finish without needing help. Thus, just as Darren's father neglected him and made Darren feel that his needs were a bother, so, too, Darren has this same impatience and unwillingness to devote very much of his time or energy to his present significant other, unless that time is centered on him or something he has initiated.

As a result of the verbal abuse Darren received from his father, he told himself while growing up that he didn't need anyone else and he dedicated himself to becoming self-sufficient and emotionally tough, determined not to let the comments of others affect him. When he was a child, Darren's father had berated him and when Darren responded with tears, his father told him he was a wimp. When Darren could not hide the depression that he experienced as a result of this environment, his father told him to "stop acting like a child." So, to shield himself from hurt and still trying to win the approval of his father, Darren began to buy into his father's reasoning. Without actually making a conscious decision, Darren began to believe that he was stronger than those who needed affection and affirmation. He determined that he would never be called a wimp again. At the same time, he began to be critical of others and to replicate his father's behavior. When women try to get Darren to look at his behavior, he is unwilling to do so and responds defensively, "If you don't like who I am, you should just leave because I'm not going to change." To Darren, when a woman suggests that he needs to alter his behavior, she is saying that he is a bad person; he experiences her remarks as he did his father's condemning voice saying there is something innately wrong with him. Darren's low self-esteem gets activated when, in his mind, he hears comments that remind him of his father's retorts; when this happens, he gets angry inside, he won't consider the criticism, and he tries to divert the conversation from himself to the other person. By telling himself that the one confronting him is "needy" or "too sensitive," he is able to take the focus off himself and excuse his own behavior.

◆ A note of comparison with those with healthy self-esteem

Most couples have disagreements and are at times unhappy with the behavior of the other; however, in relationships where both are healthy, these conflicts are quite easily resolved because neither one is being defensive, neither one is unwilling to hear their possible offenses, and both trust that their partner wouldn't be complaining unless their criticism had merit. These conflicts can easily be resolved when the people involved are free of self-doubt about their adequacy and thus are able to see the problem for what it is. People with low self-esteem, however, tend to see any criticism as an indictment on their entire lives and their whole person.

Darren's behavior is a reaction to childhood abuse and the attempt of that child to cope with a negative situation over which he had no control. This child, who had no recourse or power to change the environment, began to build up walls to protect himself. He built his own code of conduct in order to survive, and he also erected an emotional barrier to hide behind. As a result, he became rigid and disengaged, vowing never to fully let his guard down again and viewing everyone as a potential threat to his well-being. This type of low self-esteem reaction is somewhat different from the usual response. Most LSE sufferers are constantly trying to please in order to win the admiration of others, but Darren does both. At times he tries to please; but when confronted, he becomes defensive. While all people with low self-esteem are fearful of doing the wrong thing, Darren is so fearful of having his self-doubts affirmed that he responds with behavior that is even more unusual. In his mind, if he were to accept that he had done something wrong, no matter how small, it would be an indication that he has serious flaws. This behavior fits into one of the response patterns of many who suffer from severe low self-esteem. So wounded are they that the slightest criticism sends them into a defensive mode, unable to take responsibility for their behavior. These LSE sufferers become so focused on averting pain that they only infrequently move from the confrontation to working on a solution.

Oliver

Jenny has been living with her boyfriend, Oliver, for three years. Although the two have not married, Jenny has often tried to convince him that they should. Oliver, however, has no intention of getting married. He does not trust women and thinks that once they get married, Jenny will feel so secure that she will likely no longer make an effort to please him or consider his needs. He fears that she might become lazy and addicted to soap operas, or revert to being the poor housekeeper she was in college and quit doing the cooking, or worse yet, start running around with her girlfriends and maybe meet other men. He doesn't mind that she only works part-time because he likes it that she takes care of their home, runs most of the errands, and is an excellent cook. In addition, they are able to spend most of their evenings and weekends together, watching movies and television, working on a project around the house, or going shopping for antiques, things they might not have time to do if she were working full-time. He also realizes that as long as Jenny works part-time, she is financially dependent on him and needs him and likely won't leave him.

Oliver has low self-esteem largely due to feelings of abandonment and resentment. When he was seven, his mother ran off with a co-worker leaving neither a note nor an explanation—and without telling him goodbye. Now he finds it difficult to believe that any woman would really want to be with him, and he cannot maintain a lasting trust in Jenny. When she says she loves him and wants to spend her life with him, he believes her but then his irrational thinking patterns take over and within an hour, an afternoon, or a week, his gnawing suspicions and fear once again emerge.

Oliver's mother had also cashed out the family bank account so Oliver believes that money is a big part of what women want from a man. Without realizing he is doing so, Oliver projects onto Jenny the things he thinks about his mother, as though he believes all women are alike.

His mother's abandonment raised fears in Oliver of being deserted and alone and he believes that as long as he keeps Jenny a little uncertain about their relationship, she will try hard to please him and will devote her time to winning his commitment. Oliver doesn't realize that by using this tactic to maintain his relationship with Jenny, he is actually eroding it. In time, Jenny may well decide that Oliver is never going to agree to get married and that staying in the relationship may end her dream of getting married and having a family.

Oliver's pain from the past has entered into his present relationship, totally precluding any possibility of true intimacy. Oliver is basically being untruthful. He tells Jenny he loves her but he is deceiving her at the same time because in reality, he fears she may be an opportunist, as untrustworthy, and as untruthful as his mother was.

Oliver is very insecure. From all outward appearances, his parents' marriage had seemed stable. They fought occasionally but no more than he had heard in the homes of his friends, and never with hateful words or abusive actions. Then one day, Oliver had come home to an empty house, his mother's clothes and personal belongings gone. He had called his father at work and then sat on the front steps of their home waiting for someone to comfort him and explain what was happening. When his father arrived and saw the situation for himself, however, he began to cry, so grief-stricken and self-focused that he could not attend to the needs of his son. At that moment, Oliver felt terribly alone and he vowed he would never allow himself to be that vulnerable or that trusting again.

Oliver's father became depressed and unable to cope and Oliver was sent to live with his father's brother and family, so that he now felt he had been abandoned by both of his parents. Throughout his life, he has found it difficult to trust people, especially in personal relationships or when people make promises and commitments.

Mark and Bobbi

Mark and Bobbi have been seeing each other for five years and living together the last three. Both have careers: Mark is a freelance writer for men's magazines and health magazines, and Bobbi is an author of children's books. Both come from good home environments and both have healthy self-esteem.

The two met at a weekend writer's conference where they sat by each other at the keynote address. They chatted casually before the speaker began and then settled down to listen. The speaker was boring and they exchanged glances and rolled their eyes. Soon Mark leaned over and said, "How about a cup of coffee? It would certainly be more stimulating than this."

Bobbi laughed to herself, grinned and nodded at Mark. The two escaped out a side door. In the coffee shop they continued sharing information about themselves and then became engrossed in a conversation about the love they had in common: their writing. They each shared stories of how they got started, along with a few failures and successes they experienced early on. They talked about what had led them to write in the first place and what kept them inspired. Then, they realized it was time to go to their next workshop and trotted off down different halls to hear their next speaker.

Lunch was provided in a large banquet room. Mark arrived, got his food, and picked a table where he could watch the door. Bobbi came in a few minutes later, talking with two other women. The three got their food and selected a table and continued visiting. Mark saw her come in and would have waved her over to his table if she had been alone, but he saw that she was involved in conversation.

A famous writer spoke at the luncheon and when she finished, it was announced that there was 10 minutes to get to the next workshop. Quickly, everyone rose from their seats and rushed towards the door. Mark had no chance to get near Bobbi. After the session, Mark hung around hoping to see her but he decided she must have already gone when she came around the corner. They made eye contact; she smiled and walked over to him. "You weren't looking for me, were you?" she asked flirtatiously.

"Yes, actually, I was," he said as he winked at her.

They both laughed.

"Would you like to get a drink and maybe dinner later?" Mark asked.

"I believe I would like that very much," she said, still flirting with him.

These two are establishing a healthy adult relationship based on common interests, mutual attraction, and ease in communicating. Their conversation at coffee was straightforward and open, sharing both failures and successes without hesitation or fear of how the other might misinterpret their comments. They were not trying to put on airs or be anything but who they are and they know who that is. These two people are stable, confident, earnest, and secure. Neither is thinking irrational thoughts; they are just enjoying each other's company.

They playfully flirt with each other, openly displaying their interest in getting to know each other better. Neither is overly anxious, and neither is fighting distorted thoughts or analyzing each word or action of the other person.

Low self-esteem is the primary culprit in eroding attempts to create intimacy, though few people recognize this. In both subtle and obvious ways, LSE sufferers act out the pain and confusion that lingers from their childhood. They replicate the poorly constructed and inappropriate attitudes drilled into them, they don't know whom and when to trust, and they carry with them a deep sense of foreboding that more pain is waiting for them. They are filled with fear and anxiety and have difficulty accepting life when it seems to be going well. Programmed to believe they will fail, they expect the worst; conditioned to believe they are unworthy, they are suspicious; believing they must control those around them to be secure, they become untruthful and manipulative. Yet most of these people are victims themselves, their thoughts the results of having been taught that one plus one doesn't really equal two.

They are people who have been pushed out into life with no sense of a map. They are injured and bruised. Those with LSE are people who strive to do their best, who try to be good. They are sensitive and kind, generally wanting only to love and be loved.

This book follows the lives of Jackson, Molly, Jake, Carey, Jarrod, Darren, Mandy and Willa, Oliver, and Mark and Bobbi, lives that demonstrate some of the many ways that LSE interferes with intimacy.

Establishing an intimate relationship is an awesome, time-consuming, and often difficult task. The stories here demonstrate more fully exactly how powerful LSE is and how it can interfere with the complicated process of developing intimacy by stealing the moment. For LSE sufferers, when a memory from the past floods their mind, it produces irrational and distorted thoughts about what is happening. These painful memories can come coursing into the mind at the most inconvenient moments, disrupting close and personal interaction and confusing the partner at this inopportune time. In these pages, many of the forms and faces of LSE are described, for much like a magician's tricks can create doubt about what we have seen, so does LSE cloud and confuse issues, distort reality, cause us to distrust our own perceptions and feelings, and plant the suggestion that others are unreliable and may be taking advantage of us.

The following chapter gives examples of how chaos can be created in relationships and how intimacy can be blocked because those with LSE often don't know what is expected of them in new situations, yet they don't know what it is they don't know, and they believe that others do know all of these things. Consequently they are fearful, both that they will do something wrong and that others will see their inadequacy.

Chapter 2

What You Don't Know You Don't Know

Dale and Susie

Desperate to have a man in her life, Susie 28, begins dating Dale, 39. Dale is very nice to her; and because he is trying to impress her, he manages to conceal the side of him that is also self-centered and controlling. Additionally, coming from a family where her father was the same way, Susie is overly accustomed to—and tolerant of—such behaviors so she is unlikely to spot them quickly. She doesn't realize that Dale possesses—and will one day act out—the same extremely unhealthy behavior she saw at home. Plus, Dale hasn't done anything overly offensive yet, only small things that she thinks are characteristic of men. Overlooking these problematic qualities and feeling fortunate to be pursued by such a handsome, rugged outdoorsman, Susie gladly curtails her involvement with friends and family to spend more and more time with him. She believes him when he acts disappointed that she has made plans with someone else, saying he misses her so much when he doesn't get to see her every day. After all, she reasons, when her friends were serious about someone they were dating, they, too, spent all of their time with that person.

When, after two months of dating he suggests they get married, Susie is elated and thinks her dreams of having a husband, home, and children have materialized. When Dale insists they go to Reno to get married, she is disappointed, but she listens to his argument about not wasting money on a one-afternoon event when they could put it to better use in buying the things they want. This seems to make sense so she reluctantly forgoes the wedding.

After they marry, both move out of their apartments and into a small house Dale has rented without Susie's help, saying it was a surprise. Disappointed once again, Susie nevertheless accepts Dale's explanation as something nice he was trying to do for her. She is bothered, however, when she finds out that he has signed a one-year lease on a home that is quite a distance from her family and most of her friends.

Realizing that once again he didn't consider what she would like, she tells him so, "Dale, why did you do this? This is something I wanted to have a part in deciding. You don't seem to be consider-ing what I might want. I gave up the wedding as you asked, but I didn't think you would choose our home without me or totally dis-regard me in deciding where we would live. And why did you choose a location so far from my family and friends? I don't even like this side of town. This really upsets me."

Dale is immediately angry. Instead of considering what she is saying, he reacts to feeling attacked, unappreciated, and demeaned. "I can't believe you would say that to me. All I do is try to do nice things for you. I knew you and I would have to pay for the wedding, so I thought you'd like to have the money to fix up our home instead. I spent a lot of time looking at houses I thought you'd like and all you do is criticize me. I thought that with this house being conven-ient to my work, we would be able to spend more time together. Why are you so ungrateful? I was only thinking of you."

"Now I'm ungrateful, am I?" she shouts. "How can you say you were thinking of me? How do you know what I want if you don't ask me? You don't know what is most important to me. How dare you think that you have the right to decide what's best for me. You're not my boss."

"You're being childish," says Dale, now in a rage. He raises his hand as if to strike her. Then catching himself, he lowers it to his side. His face is red and his eyes glare. "I'm your husband. I'm supposed to make the major decisions. You need to trust me to do what's best for both of us and for our future."

Susie is suddenly frightened by Dale's anger; she feels herself withdraw emotionally. She has always felt inadequate, growing up in a family that argued and yelled at each other most of the time, a home where little love or affection was ever demonstrated, where little sensitivity was shown towards each other, and where the bill-collectors were always on the phone or at the door. She had determined that her home would be one of peace and tranquility rather than a household of anger and strife. Now she sees that when faced with behavior similar to her childhood, she and Dale are reacting as her parents did, with angry words. "What is happening?" she wonders. "What is he saying about having the right to make the decisions for both of us? Who is this person I married? Have I repeated my mother's mistake? Have I married a monster like my father was?"

Susie is confused. On the one hand, Dale is telling her that she is the one who is being ungrateful, that she is the one causing the problems. "Is he right?" she asks herself. Or are my complaints legitimate?" She isn't sure, but she doesn't want to feel this bad and besides "what's done is done." Then she remembers his last words about trusting him, but she knows that right now she doesn't trust him, that he has proven how selfish he is and therefore, how untrustworthy.

Still, as she saw her mother do thousands of time, she says, "Dale, I'm sorry I've made you so angry. Of course, I know that you were doing what you thought was best. It's just that I would have liked to be a part of these decisions as they affect me too."

As the marriage continues, so do these fights, with Dale repeatedly shifting his focus from the content of Susie's complaints to feeling sorry for himself. Susie tries first to get her point across, then retreats from Dale's anger, and ultimately, feels a need to appease him and end the argument. Thus, nothing gets resolved and the issues remain the same.

Dale was raised in a family where he had to fend for himself and had to stay out of the way of his father who beat him. At 15, he had run away to the streets, eventually joining the Army. With just himself to take care of, he answered only to the military and to himself. He has never really learned to consider the wishes or feelings of others. Dale was scarred by a father who didn't want him and who had made him feel worthless. In the process, Dale became determined to get what he wanted out of life. Unfortunately, his father and the Army taught him only aggressive and self-serving ways to do that; from them, he learned behavior and thinking patterns that don't create healthy relationships and certainly don't lead to intimacy.

Both Susie and Dale have painful memories of their childhoods and both have low self-esteem. Desperate to be loved and feel normal, they are unsure of what it means to really love someone, what it would look like, or whether they are individuals that others would continue to love. Both are replicating the past: Dale by continuing the controlling, macho behavior of his father, and Susie by choosing someone with the same destructive attitudes that created her low self-esteem in the first place. Neither has

taken the time to get to know the other or they might have witnessed these self-defeating behaviors in each other before now.
Both were needy and wanted to quickly grasp something they
thought might fulfill their needs and make them whole.

Thus begins the married life of two people with low self-
esteem, with particular issues of abuse from their past charting a
course of destructive behaviors on Dale's part and overly submissive behaviors alternating with angry outbursts on Susie's. Dale is
so insecure that he thinks the only way he can keep Susie is to
remove her from all other distractions. He encourages her to quit
her job, insists on a secret wedding, and moves her away from her
family and friends as if to isolate her from input and the outer
world. Susie is so needy and so wanting to be loved and secure in
a committed relationship that she hastily marries Dale and feels
helpless from the very beginning to stop him from dominating
her life.

This relationship is going in a predictably disastrous way. In
so many relationships like this, domestic violence becomes the
end result. Unless Dale sees that he has low self-esteem and that
his actions are prompted by his insecurity and feelings of being
unlovable, he will likely become physically abusive and continue
to need to control Susie to feel secure. However, what he feels but
does not recognize is that unless Susie is with him by choice, she
will never be able to give him the sense of security he wants and
needs from her. What he doesn't realize is that he must learn to
like himself before he will believe that others can like or love him.

For her part, Susie has lowered her expectations to having a
man, any man, who seems somewhat nice and respectable.
Without getting to know Dale, she has succumbed to his wishes,
given up regular contact with her friends and family, given up her
dreams for a public wedding, and given him control over where
they live and how they live. In her need to be loved, she has given

up herself, not a very good exchange and not one that will make her happy or fulfilled.

Dale is not a bad man, nor is he a criminal. He may, however, become a wife batterer. He is already on the road to confining his wife and limiting her freedom without being conscious that he is reacting to his own insecurities at the expense of the woman he thinks he loves, and without recognizing that what he is doing is both abnormal and destructive.

Susie is not a bad person either, but she is overly submissive and carries with her feelings of inadequacy and worthlessness that make her a prime candidate for controlling men who use women to get their needs met without consideration of the other.

If this marriage continues without either one getting some insight into what they are doing and how their pasts are affecting their responses, this relationship is doomed. It may even become a full-blown violent household. If, on the other hand, each can recognize that they are responding to behaviors that trigger their feelings of inadequacy and worthlessness, their communication could be altered into something constructive and ultimately fulfilling. Then, they might have an opportunity to become truly intimate.

Most people are not aware that the presence of LSE in one or both partners can thwart the process of cultivating and sustaining intimacy in a committed relationship. Most people aren't well enough acquainted with LSE to know the innumerable ways in which LSE sufferers have been programmed to negatively and defensively respond to the present with emotions stored from the past. Consequently, most people don't associate low self-esteem with roadblocks to intimacy; instead, they perceive the behaviors that impede intimacy as personal issues due to immaturity, ineptness, and selfishness.

More importantly, most people would not recognize, even after the fact, that the problems they are having with their significant other come from the scars and memories of childhood abuse, neglect, or abandonment. Not having a thorough knowledge of the symptoms of LSE, its implications for creating conflict, and the overall emotional consequences of being afflicted with low self-esteem, they cannot come to the right conclusion. Yet, low self-esteem is undoubtedly the primary obstacle to attaining intimacy.

At a moment of conflict, the person who suffers from LSE doesn't realize that his reactions are the result of his fears being activated, he isn't aware that his reactions are likely irrational and thus distorted. Arguments and disagreements arise so fast that the LSE sufferer doesn't have time to sit back and analyze the situation wherein he might see that his or his partner's reaction is so intense because one or both of them is responding to years of hurtful behavior instead of responding to the event, word, or action that sparked the present response. In truth, the issue at hand is only a reminder of traumatic past experiences that have wounded. Now, rather than responding to the current problem, which is often of far less gravity, he responds to the severity and extent of that past experience. When this happens, his response is usually irrational and exaggerated because, in the past, the LSE sufferer was told that there was something wrong with him, that he didn't measure up. Now he feels his entire self is being condemned once again rather than realizing that this conflict is limited to this specific incident.

When LSE sufferers feel attacked, they tend to answer in kind, using global responses and accusations such as "you always" or "you never." So frightened are they by being unconsciously drawn into the past, that they make inaccurate statements that are totally out of proportion to the current dilemma. They may bring up irrelevant information, they may bring up past offenses, they may become loud and threatening, or they may make threats to end the relationship, all in an attempt to sidestep the emotional upheaval and threat to their present wellbeing that they feel.

Thus, the reaction of the LSE suffer to any type of confrontation or reprimand often propels the predicament to an impasse, producing much more devastating feelings between the couple than the situation merits. Both then walk away wondering why they bother to share their feelings at all when it seems to result in alienation rather than resolution.

Those with low self-esteem have generally come from environments where demonstrations of love, nurturing, and closeness were infrequent, contradictory, or nonexistent. And because loving, being loved, and intimacy were not modeled for—or experienced by—these LSE sufferers, they have no idea how to develop an intimate relationship or what it would be like. They may not have witnessed the give-and-take of congenial relationships at home, yet they have seen enough couples in public, in movies, and on television who look happy and connected and who are working at developing intimate relationships to make the search for intimacy their most sought-after, and most elusive, goal. Lacking experience and a clear picture of intimacy, however, they stumble along, attacking and withdrawing, offending and being offended, alienating and being alienated, usually destroying the possibility of attaining intimacy in the process.

Intimacy is the experience of feeling so close to someone that you know their likes and dislikes, their dreams and goals, their interests, their likely responses in varying situations without them needing to tell you. Intimacy is the state of desiring to share one's most personal and private thoughts, one's dreams, one's achievements and failures, and possibly even one's body while trusting that the other person will not exploit or otherwise take advantage of this vulnerability, that instead, they will hold in highest esteem and respect the trust bestowed on them. True intimacy requires that two people know each other well, rightly implying that intimacy can only be achieved over time.

True intimacy requires reciprocity; both people must be willing to share on an equal level for intimacy to be achieved. Intimacy requires a desire to please and to meet the needs of the other within reason and to the extent that the person does not have to compromise himself, his dreams and goals, or his standards and values. Intimacy implies a trust that neither partner would ever intentionally hurt the other but would instead have in mind the best interest of both partners, respecting individual differences, individual interests, individual choices, and individual goals along with the goals of the union. True intimacy requires that the couple be honest with each other. Deception of any kind makes any attempt at intimacy a farce. (For more about healthy thinking and attitudes in a relationship, see *Breaking the Chain of Low Self-Esteem*, pp 148-155.)

While intimacy also exists in friendships, friends don't have the exclusivity of commitment that people in romantic relationships generally have. Friends spend time together and then go to their own private lives and careers, maintaining independence from one another. They spend time together but may have other friends with whom they also share an intimate relationship. Friends are free to make their own decisions because their choices don't directly impact the other person in the same way that those choices would affect a partner or spouse. Friends are free to develop personal interests, take classes, spend money, travel, change jobs, etc., without the need to consult their intimate friends because their lives are separate. These decisions don't affect the relationship directly and most often don't require an adjustment in the life of the friend. On the other hand, people in healthy committed relationships usually discuss decisions ahead of time, generally consider the other person in making such a decision, and often refrain from making major changes in their lives until they have the support of their partner.

Developing and maintaining intimacy requires that the two people have sufficient time together, that they be honest with each other, that they be committed to each other and to the relationship. Healthy couples often build an intimate relationship when dating. During the infatuation stage, they are consumed with each other, spending inordinate amounts of time together, and talking and enjoying each other's companionship. Other interests are often set aside to some extent so that the couple can concentrate on each other. They get to know each other's interests, opinions, dreams, and goals. Often they experience true intimacy.

With LSE sufferers, however, even the first taste of intimacy may never occur. Fearful of their own inadequacy, one or both of the couple may hold back and not be totally truthful. Fearful that the other won't accept who they really are, one or both may be more intent on pleasing the partner and focusing on them as a way to deflect the attention from themselves. Full of self-doubt, the LSE sufferer may not even be in touch with her own feelings, may have tabled his hopes and dreams, or may not be able to envision a positive future. Fearful of rejection, the person may say what she thinks the other person wants to hear rather than what she really thinks. She may give up interests that are bothersome to her partner, all the while resenting it. She may change her routine or give up certain goals to please her partner and later become angry at both herself and the significant other. Or she may go to the other extreme and refuse to compromise on time or other interests because she is fearful that someone is trying to control her. Behaving at either end of the spectrum is equally dysfunctional.

Thus, attempts to develop a relationship and achieve intimacy are a juggling act for those afflicted with LSE, constant questions of how much do I say and how much do I reveal, how much do I compromise and how much do I hold my ground. The building of relationships and the search for intimacy present a rugged journey, full of potholes and obstacles, for those who are already unsure of themselves and who are uncertain about their prospects for being loved.

This attempt to achieve intimacy also marks the point at which the LSE sufferer needs to begin to understand himself and how his LSE is affecting his life, if he wishes to accomplish his goal. Also, once the LSE sufferer recognizes how and why his low self-esteem developed, he will also realize that he didn't cause his LSE, that having it is nothing to be ashamed of, and that he is one of millions of people who suffer from the same affliction; he is not alone.

For those who do experience intimacy, life seems wonderful and their relationship seems perfect, yet those who have been successful in forming a committed and intimate relationship often have difficulty maintaining that intimacy. Once having attained the commitment to spending their lives together, the couple relaxes and becomes more complacent. Their focus gradually returns to their jobs, to extended family demands and commitments, to community obligations, to care of their home, to their interests and hobbies, and to spending more time with their friends. Time becomes limited, communication becomes less frequent and erratic, and intimacy can be threatened or disappear altogether.

The Great Self-Sabotage

The aspect most critical to the lives of those who suffer from low self-esteem is not the type or amount of suffering they endured nor is it the degree of dysfunction that they experienced in their developmental years. Rather, the most critical and detrimental aspect of low self-esteem is the distorted and irrational view that all LSE sufferers have of the world around them, of the people in it, and of their own ability to cope and fit into that world. In other words, it is the inaccurate way that they learned to view themselves and the painful emotions that those thoughts create that present the obstacles. It is the distorted view that they have of how others see them and respond to them and how that feels. And it is that flawed thinking process that continually creates the self-doubt and self-loathing that serves as an inducement to a life-long pattern of self-sabotage.

All LSE sufferers are guilty of distorted thinking. All LSE sufferers become irrational at times, the frequency and severity of their distortions closely paralleling the severity and degree of dysfunction they have experienced. Some who suffer from LSE only do so when under extreme stress, when threatened, or when going through a situation that closely resembles a negative past event. Others who are even more sensitive and paranoid about how people view them or react to them become irrational and suffer "self-esteem attacks" more easily and more often. (For more on self-esteem attacks, see *Breaking the Chain of Low Self-Esteem*, pp. 75-90.) The problem is not so much that they engage in these periods of irrationality, but that they either do not recognize that they are distorting the truth or they do not recognize that it is happening at the time. Until they can learn that this is what they do, and until they can begin to develop awareness at the time it is happening, they will not be able to alter the reactions and behaviors they produce when they are being irrational. Instead, they will defend those behaviors and reactions, they will feel victimized, and they will continue to be unable to communicate effectively. And consequently, intimacy will continue to elude them.

The Confusion Caused by "Not Knowing"

As has been mentioned here and discussed more thoroughly in *Breaking the Chain of Low Self-Esteem* (pp. 44-53), people burdened with LSE have difficulty knowing what is normal and what is not. Even if the person recognizes that he comes from a dysfunctional background, he doesn't have any way to separate what was functional and normal behavior from what was not. He has no way of knowing what others would see as commonplace or what they might think was strange; this causes him great anxiety about the possibility of unknowingly doing the latter. Consequently, many LSE sufferers make a concerted effort to avoid situations, places, or events where they might not know what to do or what is expected; instead, they direct their energy and time to activities where they feel most comfortable, most secure, and most competent.

People with LSE avoid asking questions, getting help with their problems, or seeking advice out of fear that the other person will view them as stupid, or ignorant, or unable to make simple decisions. In so doing, they unwittingly close themselves off from information that would help them feel more normal, insights that would help them understand why they do what they do, and guidance that we all frequently need in our lives and which enables us to become better at analysis and decision-making.

This practice of avoidance prevents the growth of LSE sufferers and keeps them uninformed and lacking skills that they could easily—or through some effort and persistence acquire—if they could take the risk involved. Passing up such opportunities is self-sabotaging because it decreases our prospects for learning from our friends, acquaintances, and the environment and from enjoying new experiences. Avoidance of these situations also lowers the likelihood of our building new relationships and receiving support and affirmation.

◆   **A note of comparison with those with healthy self-esteem**

People who have healthy self-esteem (HSE) do not find it difficult to ask the advice of others. They generally have one or more friends in whom they confide, with whom they share the ups and downs of their lives, and whom they look to for direction and for sorting out their problems. They are not embarrassed to ask for input from others and they do not feel that this makes them inferior in some way; rather, they view the process as normal and something everyone does.

Jackson
Jackson is an LSE sufferer who has shut himself off from the information and guidance he needs to be able to develop a healthy relationship. Too fearful to hear the prognosis of his physical problem and too fearful to hear how severe his imagined mental problems are, he has seen neither a therapist nor a medical doctor.

Jackson is so humiliated by his inability to maintain an erection that he can't imagine how he could possibly share it with someone else, even a professional. Instead, he has avoided romantic relationships by steering clear of social contact with women. Vulnerable to the attention and the affirmation he is receiving from Brianne, however, he has accepted her invitations and later succumbed to her sexual advances.

Kissing her, holding her, and touching her feels wonderful. Jackson's heart races and he yearns for fulfillment, but each time they move toward fully undressing and what he feels will be the point of no return, a picture of his limp penis flashes through his head, and his anxiety becomes so great that he finds a way, no matter how ingenuous, to end the physical contact. This behavior, too, becomes a reason for him to feel embarrassed and disgusted with himself. He wonders what Brianne must think and feels strongly that the only solution is to quit seeing her; however, he cannot bring himself to do this.

A large part of Jackson's problem stems from his inability and his unwillingness to analyze and find help for his low self-esteem or the presenting symptom of his sexual dysfunction. Because Jackson has seen his problems as abnormal for a man his age, he hasn't had the courage to seek medical advice. Instead, he views impotency as a sign of how extremely dysfunctional and inadequate he is as a man and he thinks of himself as beyond help.

If Jackson could confide in someone or even read books about the problem, he would quickly find out that impotency is not all that unusual and that many men suffer from it at one time or another. He could also become aware that help is available and that stress and anxiety are often the source of this quandary. But Jackson feels he can't take the risk of going to a bookstore where he might find some clarity about his sexual dysfunction; he is too afraid someone would see him there and figure out why he was in that section. He doesn't dare to go to a library for the same reasons. And if he could talk himself into going to either place, he can't imagine how he could possibly select a book on the subject and then approach the cashier or librarian to take it out. He knows his face would turn red and he envisions everyone looking at the book cover with full knowledge of his problem.

In this way, Jackson's inaccurate self-assessment that he is beyond help and his perception that this physical problem labels him as undesirable and worthless have become barriers to his happiness. His fear of hearing that his inability to maintain an erection is strange and rare requires too great a risk for him to bear, and his feelings of humiliation stand in the way of his ability to get the help he needs. Thus, it's not the physical dysfunction that interferes with his life, it's his faulty thinking and his irrational fears that prevent him from overcoming it.

Brianne is a warm and effusive person and just what Jackson needs and wants in a girlfriend. Whenever she verbalizes how much she enjoys spending time with him, he beams with pride and his thoughts begin to shift from his obsession about being a sexual failure to hopeful thoughts of a different and more positive outcome. He thinks that just maybe he can maintain his erection. But when Brianne actually initiates physical contact, Jackson feels scared. Part of him wants to just enjoy the moment, but part of him hears the warning signals that he is getting too close to disaster. And because Jackson hasn't been able to share his problem with someone impersonal and professional, he certainly can't share it with the one person he wants most to impress. Instead, when they move to kissing, then to fondling, Jackson finds it hard to breathe, not because of his arousal but because he is about to have a "self-esteem attack." His only thought is "I've got to get out of here."

Jackson's behavior confuses Brianne. Finally, she decides to talk to him in hopes of finding out what the issue is. She wonders if

Jackson is not attracted to her physically although he has frequently talked about enjoying their shared activities and has openly enjoyed himself when they are together. She invites Jackson over for dinner, fixing one of his favorite casseroles. Afterwards she plops down on one end of her oversized sofa and motions for Jackson to sit at the other end where they can face each other. Jackson sits down slowly; he knows what is coming.

"Jackson, we need to talk," begins Brianne.

Jackson swallows and nods but says nothing. "Do you find me attractive?" she asks.

Taken aback, Jackson quickly replies, "Of course I do. I think you are beautiful, Brianne."

"Is there someone else?" she asks. "Have you recently been hurt or is there someone else you are interested in?"

"NO!" Jackson blurts out at a high pitch. "There isn't anyone else."

By now Jackson's anxiety is so intense that his jaw hurts from clenching his teeth. His stomach is churning and he thinks that he may be sick. He looks at the floor and becomes silent.

Brianne looks at him with concern and confusion. "What is going on?" she wonders out loud.

"Look, this is a mistake," Jackson says, close to tears. "I just can't do this."

Before Brianne can respond, Jackson is on his feet and heading for the door.

"Wait," she implores but without turning around Jackson says, "I just have to go," and he walks out the door.

As Brianne watches, Jackson runs to his car and then sits there with his head down. She considers going out but, instead, stands and watches until he finally starts his car and drives slowly away.

Fortunately, Brianne is a mature and stable woman. She has seen people in pain before and recognizes that Jackson is experiencing some extraordinary anguish, though she doesn't have a clue as to what it might be.

As is typical of those with LSE, Jackson has difficulty communicating personal information such as feelings, fears, and issues, because he views himself as less worthy than others. Inside he believes that no woman will ever accept him as he is; no woman will ever stay with him or ever have respect for him if she knows of his sexual deficiency.

Jackson's fear of finding out how truly dysfunctional he may be blocks his willingness to get help, to get information about his difficulty. It also rules out the possibility that he can confide in Brianne. In this way, his LSE precludes the likelihood of achieving intimacy in their relationship. Instead, his behavior and lack of communication are the initial building blocks of a wall between them. Ultimately, if Jackson cannot face his problem and seek help or begin to confide in Brianne, their relationship will almost certainly deteriorate and end. While the specific details differ from situation to situation, LSE sufferers exhibit similar behavior to Jackson's as they self-sabotage.

Molly

Molly doesn't know much about relationships—at least healthy relationships—but even more problematic, she doesn't realize that she doesn't know much about how they function. Surrounded by equally dysfunctional and needy people, Molly, too, has had no one to talk to who might cast new light on what constitutes a good relationship. Nor does she realize that her obsession with finding a man is due to her view of herself as inadequate and, as such, in need of a man to take care of her. She doesn't see anything wrong with her method of searching for a male partner. Additionally, Molly does not recognize how needy she is; she doesn't recognize that her desperation to find a man makes her less appealing as a steady girlfriend or potential mate.

Molly has three friends remaining from high school with whom she spends time; two are women and the other is a man. All are single; the male is alcoholic and unemployed. None are educated beyond high school. One of the women has been raped, the other has had an abortion because she hadn't used birth control; both work for minimum wage. Molly has a secretarial job and makes more than the others, a fact that rankles her friends. At times they pester her to pay more than they do towards their mutual activities.

At least once a week the group goes out to a movie, shopping, or dinner. These four people socialize together not because they enjoy each other's company but because they are desperate for companionship and because the behaviors they witness in one another are so similar to what they each experienced at home that they accept them as normal. In other words, they are all so accustomed to being treated poorly that they not only accept the likelihood of it happening but they also mistreat one another. They are sarcastic with each other; they are jealous of anything good that happens for one of them; they ridicule each other. From time to time, two or more of them gang up on another in the group, intentionally leaving the person out of the plans, then feigning ignorance as to how and why he or she was snubbed.

None of these four feel good about themselves. None of them comes home from an evening together feeling supported, affirmed, or encouraged. And because they have not experienced much positive attention from others, this is all they expect—and all they get.

Occasionally, one of them has a date or at least a one-night stand with someone met at a bar or a dance. In the past, they bragged to the others about these experiences, but after many such relationships end as quickly as they started, the members of the group no longer feel they have anything to boast about.

One day in the lunchroom at work, Molly is approached by Howard, a consultant for her company, who asks if he can take her to dinner. Molly is excited; she has never had anyone ask her out on a real date. The only men she has spent time with were those who happened to be in the same bar.

Molly has interacted with Howard from time to time about shared work projects, and he has always been friendly and considerate. Still, she wonders if she should be so pleased about the date, since he is balding and overweight. She wonders if other women would accept his invitation or if they would be embarrassed to go out with him. Molly is finally able to dismiss these thoughts since she sees the date as an opportunity to do something different and she has always perceived Howard as a nice man. She doesn't expect anything to happen beyond this date.

Molly is a typical LSE sufferer. In her dysfunctional home, she was not taught what makes up a healthy relationship, nor were those behaviors modeled so that she could see them in action. Consequently, Molly doesn't know what constitutes a relationship, what the important characteristics are that she should look for in a potential mate, or how to meet someone who might make a good partner. She only knows that she wants to find a man to be with and that she is willing to do most anything to find and keep one. She daydreams about what the man will be like, but she also thinks she can't be too picky. In fact, she would be happy just to have a man in her life.

That night Molly shares with her friends the details of Howard's invitation and her date with him; she shares her perception of him as kind and friendly and she also tells of his receding hair and chunky body. Upon hearing the description, the other women become cruel and sarcastic.

"Why would you go out with a fat man?" one of them asks.

"That's disgusting," says the other.

"Won't it seem like you're dating an old man since he has no hair?" adds the first.

"Hey, it's a free dinner!" chimes in Dan, the male in the group, conscious of money since he has little of his own.

"I didn't say that he had no hair," responds Molly, "His hair is just receding somewhat." Nevertheless, Molly is confused. She doesn't know what to think. Are her friends just jealous? she wonders. They certainly are being cruel. Or are they right?

Molly and her friends have never spent time talking about the merits of the men they have slept with because none of them has ever dated one person long enough to know much about his character, his attitudes, or his standards. Thus, when Molly gets negative feedback from her friends about her upcoming date with an overweight balding man, she is confused. She wonders if there is merit to their criticism. She has no one in her life whom she can trust to give her truthful, mature guidance. Molly suspects that she and her friends are all dysfunctional in some way, but she doesn't know just how abnormal they are. She knows that there are many things she doesn't know, and so she isn't sure if what she knows is accurate or inaccurate.

The old adage "Birds of a feather flock together" applies here. LSE sufferers have a knack for finding each other, quite possibly because they have lowered their expectations about the quality of people who would be attracted to them or want to spend time with them. So they settle for less satisfying relationships than they otherwise might have. On the other hand, many people with LSE don't recognize what constitutes a quality person and may put more emphasis on outward appearance than on internal substance. Furthermore, LSE sufferers are often too fearful to initiate relationships with healthier people who, they suspect would easily recognize their shortcomings. Finally, LSE sufferers often lack the social skills to attract people who are healthier and who would, therefore, make better friends and partners.

Jake

One Saturday morning Jake's wife rolls over and wraps a leg and an arm across his body. As does so, she feels his muscles tighten, though in no other way does he acknowledge her approach. The night before, Jake had been quiet and she knew he was upset. They had come home from dinner together at an expensive new restaurant where they had enjoyed excellent food and drinks. Unfortunately, the waiter had been very attentive to her and had all but ignored Jake. She had tried not to respond to the attention because she knew Jake would be jealous, but he had still become quiet and had refused to talk about it. When she tried to bring it up, he had become angry, snapping at her, and then he had gone to bed.

Jake is confused. He is also miserable and tired of feeling angry, knowing that within hours or days his anger will turn to guilt. He has experienced this pattern hundreds of times and he hates it; whenever this happen he feels unbelievable rage toward his mother for creating this anxiety about his manhood by continually referring to his small penis. After all, he was only a small boy at the time. Still her words haunt him and create the self-doubt that he agonizes *over. He wonders why his wife is with him when so many other men are obviously attracted to her. He sees that she enjoys the attention; he thinks that she tries to hide it, but it's apparent that she brightens up whenever it happens. (For more on the Anger-Guilt Cycle, see **Breaking the Chain of Low Self-Esteem**, pp. 208-209.)*

When these incidents occur, Jake feels as if he is shriveling up inside. He feels panicky, desperate, and instantly depressed. He knows that he is overreacting, but he doesn't know what to do differently. He doesn't know how much of what he senses is actually true, and he doesn't know how others would handle this problem. He only knows that he finds it difficult to fully enjoy their sexual intimacy and their relationship. He is so full of self-doubt that he cannot focus on the positive aspects of their time together and he cannot relax and trust his wife's commitment.

Again, we see how a man afflicted with low self-esteem is affected by his distorted thinking, thinking that puts a negative spin on normal circumstances. Instead of being proud of his wife and the attention she gets from others, he personalizes her response to mean that either she doesn't love him or that she, too, see him as inadequate and would rather be with someone else. When they have sex, he feels better for a while, knowing that she readily engaged in sex with him, but he is also apprehensive that she may be faking her response to some extent because she knows how unsure he is of himself. Thus, his feelings of security are short-lived, and he goes back to ruminating about whether he can trust her and whether she will leave him.

Jake has never talked to anyone about his self-sabotaging thought patterns—he doesn't know if they are normal or not. At times he thinks that he is acting irrationally, but at other times he thinks just the opposite. He is aware that he doesn't know how to control his reactions, that he doesn't know what to do differently or how he could think differently. He doesn't know if others deal with such problems or how they would handle them if they did. Jake has no idea that his paranoia is due to low self-esteem. He doesn't know that his extreme reactions are entirely due to his mother's cruel remarks with wherein she implanted in Jake's psyche that he is abnormal, a belief that he cannot dispel and that affects his ability to be at peace with his relationship and with himself.

Carey

By the end of her last year of junior high, Carey had become an angry girl. She felt that she didn't deserve the treatment that she was receiving at home, and she blamed both her mother and father for allowing it to happen. She decided that she would have to take charge of finding a way to fit in at school, and so she spent the summer before high school reading magazines about make-up and the current trends in clothes and hairstyles.

One thing that Carey did have was an adequate allowance from a mother who tried to compensate for the other unhealthy aspects of their home life by spending money on her two younger children. At Carey's bidding, she spent many afternoons accompanying her daughter to the mall while the girl experimented with new hairstyles, got manicures, tried on clothes and shoes, and selected makeup and accessories. She denied Carey nothing, though she often raised her eyebrows when she looked at the price tags or heard the final bill at the cash register.

When high school began, Carey thought she was ready, but her transformation did not translate into immediate friendships as she had anticipated. Her attempts to make conversation with other girls at her locker or in class were often met with short responses at best and stares at worst. "What is wrong?" she wondered. "Why don't they like me?"

She watched the other girls at school and wondered what was so different about her, what it was that caused them to dislike her. She had thought that as she developed physically, as she dressed in style and looked like the other girls, they would think of her as one of them, but that wasn't the case. The other girls always seemed so happy while she was so miserable. She wondered why she couldn't seem to make friends and what it would take to be accepted. She wondered why they didn't seem to even notice her in spite of the fact that they knew she was intelligent, a good student, dressed like everyone else, and had become quite attractive.

Sometimes Carey wondered what the lives of the other girls were like but she couldn't imagine it. She had no idea what other families did at home or if their home life was any different from hers. She didn't have any idea how they interacted with each other or if it was unlike what she has experienced. The only thing she did see as different was that her teachers, both male and female, treated her with more respect than she received at home and several complimented her on the changes she had made over the summer. The teachers listened attentively when she asked questions, responded appropriately, and offered support and affirmation for her efforts, acknowledging her academic achievement. Several of the teachers had asked where she planned to go to college and encouraged her to do so.

Although the girls at school did not seem to respond to the changes Carey had made in herself and her appearance over the summer, the boys did notice! In fact, at first, they were quite drawn to her, to this person they had hardly noticed and who had blossomed since they last saw her. But as with the girls she wished to befriend, Carey didn't know how to respond to the boys who approached her. She was always overly anxious and fearful of rejection, and as a result, so self-absorbed that she was unable to relax, smile, and make small talk. She was so eager to please that her intensity permeated the immediate environment, radiating a neediness that quickly repelled most of her interested suitors. On occasion a boy waded through this river of intensity and asked her out, but these attempts to socialize usually ended in disaster, with Carey feeling terrible and the boy avoiding even talking to her again.

For Carey, not knowing and not knowing what it is that she doesn't know becomes a nightmare, in which, try as she may, she doesn't have the insight to understand what she needs to do differently to make friends, what it would take for the boys to want to spend time with her. She hates sports and has purposely avoided any interest because of her loathing for her older brothers and father so she is unable to converse with boys about sports. She hasn't had much experience in interacting about specific issues with males, again because of the behavior of the males in her family, so she doesn't know what to talk to them about. An introvert who is intellectually advanced beyond most of the boys who do ask her out, and with no practice in casual communication, Carey isn't a great date. She doesn't know what to talk about, doesn't know how to joke around, and is on guard, wondering how the boy will treat her and scared that he won't find her interesting or fun to be with.

Carey is tense and miserable. She doesn't realize it, but she is so tense and her facial expressions are so serious that she appears unapproachable. Filled with anger, she is sharp-tongued and can be abrasive. After all, this is the type of language she has been accustomed to at home her entire life and she assumes it is the norm. Additionally, her fear of "doing it wrong" and being rejected adds to the other pressures that result in behaviors that sabotage her goal of building a relationship.

Jarrod

Because of his low self-esteem, Jarrod doesn't know how to respond to his wife's obvious popularity, and he doesn't know if another man would respond differently under similar circumstances. Furthermore, Jackie doesn't help. Knowing that Jarrod is insecure, she is nevertheless insensitive to his wishes that she not have drinks with men after work, that she not take calls from ex-boyfriends, and that she not accept invitations for the two of them to parties given by any-one she has dated. He doesn't know if other men would accept these activities, and he gets confused when Jackie tells him that he doesn't have the right to tell her who she can and cannot spend time with.

Because she does these things, Jarrod does not fully trust her and he tends to become anxious whenever she comes home later than expected. In his mind, Jarrod begins to imagine that Jackie is being wined and dined by someone who not only finds her a great business woman, but who also is responding to her attractiveness and her gre-garious personality. Furthermore, because as an introvert he doesn't see himself on her level socially, he believes he would not be invited to these parties if he weren't Jackie's husband. He thinks that her friends see him as boring, that Jackie does as well, and that she must find these other men much more exciting and desirable. If he comes home and Jackie is not there yet, he begins to wonder where she is and he begins to fantasize about where she is, who she is with, and what she is thinking, always coming to the conclusion that her behavior and thoughts are negative towards him and more positive towards someone else. Pressure builds within Jarrod though he determines that he will not say anything.

Then Jackie comes in the door, smiling broadly and obviously bubbling over from her day, stirring up thoughts within Jarrod that she never seems to be that joyous after spending time with him. Feeling jealous that she seems always to have a better time without him, his resolve to be quiet dissipates quickly. "So, what have you been up to?" he asks with irritation in his voice.

"Oh, I just came from a meeting with John, Amy, and Stan," Jackie replies.

"A meeting or was it happy hour after work?" asks Jarrod.

"What does it matter?" replies Jackie. "It's all the same thing."

"Well, did you forget we were going out to dinner tonight?" asks Jarrod sarcastically. "Or were you having such a good time that you forgot?"

"I didn't forget," snaps Jackie, "Stop acting so insecure. You're being such a wimp. It's only 6:30. I'll be ready to go in a few minutes."

"I'm not being insecure," barks Jarrod, feeling ridiculed and hurt. "Why do you say such things to me? I bet you don't talk to John and Stan the way you do to me."

"Oh, so that's it! You're upset that I had a drink with my friends? Why are you always so paranoid? I really get tired of your petty jealousy. What is the matter with you?"

"There isn't anything wrong with me," snarls Jarrod. "It's you that has something wrong, always wanting to spend time flirting with different men."

"That does it. You are really sick," sneers Jackie. "I haven't been flirting with anyone, and furthermore, if you don't like it that I enjoy the company of the men I work with, you can just leave. I don't have to put up with this anymore."

From there the conversation deteriorates further until they both stomp out of the room to get space from one another.

Jarrod is, indeed, insecure. He has low self-esteem and is very introverted; he doesn't like to socialize in groups especially when he doesn't know the people very well. His wife is a social butterfly and an extreme extrovert. Consequently, most of the guests they entertain come from Jackie's business activities, so that Jarrod often feels out of place with little to contribute to their conversations, and most of the parties they are invited to involve large group situations that are uncomfortable for Jarrod.

Jarrod's insecurity alone could lay the foundation for his need to be watchful and even distrusting of his wife's actions, but coupled with Jackie's unwillingness to compromise on some of the issues that bother him and her refusal to acknowledge that his feelings and wishes might have merit, Jarrod becomes suspicious. Furthermore, her sarcastic and often ridiculing responses heighten his paranoia and trigger the feelings of worthlessness that accompany his LSE.

Confused and angry, Jarrod jumps to protect himself, both by trying to defend himself and by pouncing on Jackie with accusations and irrational remarks, the exact opposite of what is needed to create intimacy. Repeatedly, their arguments become chaotic and emotionally destructive, after which both are reluctant to have a conversation.

When two people are unwilling to acknowledge the issues each has and when they are unable to consider how their behavior impacts the other person, communication breaks down and relationships suffer. Many people would not find it palatable to have their spouse socializing or even working with past partners, but Jackie's reluctance to look at and to discuss this concern with

Jarrod causes him to feel that she is hiding something from him, that she is wanting to keep her options open. If she were to give some credibility to Jarrod's uneasiness and even agree that she will only interact with ex-boyfriends when business requires it, Jarrod would more likely believe in her commitment and loyalty and thus be more secure. Jackie, however, is an independent person who has been successful when she is in full control and without limitations and she isn't willing to give in to Jarrod's requests. She thinks that his insecurity is his problem and not something she should have to change her life to help him with.

Mandy and Willa

Mandy and Willa love each other very much, but they have found it difficult to transform their love into healthy, consistent behavior toward one another. Neither knows what is wrong, why they so often get into big blowups when there is the smallest disagreement or misunderstanding. At one point, Willa decides to visit a library to look for help and finds a book that thoroughly explains low self-esteem. Afterwards, she initiates a discussion with Mandy about what she has read and encourages Mandy to read the book as well. Willa strongly expresses her concerns that their backgrounds have left them both with low self-esteem. She tells Mandy that she fears that their personal issues are going to destroy the relationship unless they both try to understand how their respective childhood memories are impacting their present interactions. They each agree that they will do something to work on themselves, Mandy less enthusiastically than Willa, who decides to go to a support group for women who come from alcoholic homes and to check out possibilities for therapy. Mandy reluctantly commits to go to therapy.

Willa finds her new group very informative, inspiring, and helpful. At meetings, each woman has an opportunity to share and Willa quickly sees the similarities in the stories of the other women and her own experiences growing up in an alcoholic home. She marvels at the ways in which the more senior participants have altered their attitudes, their behaviors, and ultimately, their lives. The group emphasizes looking at oneself, rather than blaming someone else, and Willa becomes inspired to focus on her own responses rather than blaming Mandy for their relationship issues.

Setting a goal to work on her low self-esteem is a challenge in and of itself. Willa interviews several therapists and finds that they do not really have a plan for overcoming low self-esteem; instead, they tend to work only with the symptoms: the depression, the anxiety, the anger, etc. This is not what Willa wants; she wants to attack her problem head-on.[2]

Mandy enters into therapy with a woman who was recommended by a friend. Like Willa, she is not aware that few therapists specialize in working with low self-esteem issues and that even those who do often have little background, education, or experience in doing so. As her therapy progresses, the therapist focuses entirely on Mandy's childhood: the specific incidents, feelings, and confusion that she experienced; the therapist seems to believe that simply understanding her childhood pain will translate into automatic changes to Mandy's perspective, attitudes, and behaviors. Mandy finds this therapy painful, and she wonders why she is subjecting herself to this misery. She is skeptical that she will learn anything form this person that will change the course of her life. She doesn't see that she is learning anything practical that might enable her to be a better partner to Willa. Frustrated with the lack of progress, she quits therapy, never considering that another therapist might do a better job of guiding her to overcome her LSE.

Here again, we see the dilemma of those with low self-esteem who don't know what they need to know or where to find the

---

[2] Sorensen, Marilyn J., *Low Self-Esteem Misunderstood & Diagnosed*. Sherwood, OR: Wolf Publishing Co., 2001.

needed information and guidance. Both Mandy and Willa realize that they have problems, but for a long time they don't know that LSE is the core issue for both of them and the underlying reason for their poor communication and destructive behaviors. Without knowing why, their relationship is being controlled by lingering feelings of inadequacy, insecurity, worthlessness, and anxiety. Both become upset when current words and actions mirror those experienced in childhood and trigger the negative feelings that accompanied those experiences. When this occurs, both tend to react to the magnitude of the earlier situation, which produces an overreaction to the present one, creating confusion and chaos and causing their discussions to disintegrate.

Willa has more insight into their problems than does Mandy and after reading a book on self-esteem feels certain that both she and Mandy suffer from it. After a discussion in which they agree to individually seek help, Willa is fortunate to find a group that steers her in the right direction while Mandy is further frustrated when she doesn't find competent assistance.

Darren

Darren is always considerate at the beginning of a relationship. Whether it's instinctual or something he just thinks is expected while dating, he goes out of his way to try to please the woman in whom he is interested. Perhaps he believes that a man is supposed to wine and dine a woman as a way of expressing his manhood. Whatever the reason, Darren has enough social skills and motivation to act in ways that women find appealing and that attract them to him. Only after the relationship becomes more consistent and expectations build does Darren start to become less available, seemingly less willing to compromise, and more rigid. To the woman he is dating, it appears that the closer they get as a couple, the more he does what he wants, putting his agenda first and without consideration for his woman friend. Unconsciously, however, Darren becomes more fearful when they start getting close. He believes it is at this point in the relationship that they expect more from him than he is capable of giving, that they expect him to share in ways he has no experience, and that women don't seem to stay around once they get to know him better. His experience is that the closer they get, the sooner they run away from him.

Darren doesn't know how to build a relationship and becomes fearful when others want him to share his personal ideas, opinions, perceptions, and especially his feelings. He realizes that he in inadequate in conversing on a level deeper than facts, but he hasn't the slightest idea how he would change this. When women criticize him, he reacts defensively by directing criticism back at them and by using many of the same words and phrases his father had used to excuse himself and blame others for any unpleasantness. Unlike many who suffer from low self-esteem, Darren is not aware that he doesn't know the difference between what is normal and what is not; he doesn't realize that the examples displayed by his father and his adoption of his father's behavior and attitudes are not conducive to the maintenance of healthy relationships. He just thinks that he doesn't choose the right women and wonders why so many females are so contrary and demanding; his mother was certainly not like that.

Darren does know that he is insecure and that he feels uncomfortable much of the time; he acts out these emotions and reactions and is unhappy as a result, but he doesn't have a clue as to why this is or what he does wrong. He doesn't understand why women seem to like him when they first meet him but soon start complaining and criticizing him. Unwilling to consider the validity of these complaints or even listen to them, he remains the same and moves from one short-term relationship to another, continuing the self-sabotage.

Lacking sufficient affection, nurturing, and support while growing up, Darren has become frightened by demonstrative behavior and fearful of closeness, including personal communication. However, Darren isn't aware that he fears something good and necessary; he just automatically avoids what he is uncomfortable with. He saw the relationship of his parents, but he isn't conscious of a desire to avoid replicating what he saw and experienced because he doesn't know what would replace it. He has nothing else with which to compare it; he knows of no relationships that he would like to emulate.

Darren watches other men in an attempt to glean some insight into what they do when they are with women, but, of course, all he sees is their overt behavior and not what he most needs to know. So, as is often the case, Darren does what he knows, rather than questioning his lack of success and looking for ways to do it differently. Ironically, "like father, like son" becomes an accurate description for Darren and a formula for his failure.

Sadly, many people who suffer from low self-esteem aren't aware they have it, They haven't been able to—or even realized a need to—analyze their childhoods and, therefore, they haven't understood that much of what they saw, heard, and learned at home was outside the norm of appropriate and acceptable behavior, ideas, and attitudes. LSE sufferers have had to expend most of their energy coping in a frightening and unpredictable world. Most of them haven't had the motivation or inclination to figure out why they are as they are, or they haven't had the inner strength to seek the resources that might have directed them to see the big picture of what has happened to them and why they now live and react as they do. Then again, many have sought help from therapists who have ignored their low self-esteem issues while addressing only their symptoms. As critical as it is that these people suffered in their early environments and developed LSE as a result, so, too, are the consequences of not identifying that truth, not recognizing that the environment was dysfunctional so that they can become aware of the need to relearn the basics of being a healthy individual is equally important. Once a person realizes that the environment that formed his reasoning and thinking was abnormal, he can more quickly move from guilt, self-doubt, and self-admonishment to growth and learning.

Oliver

As a result of his abandonment issues and LSE, Oliver becomes manipulative and dishonest with Jenny. His mother had told him she loved him and then had left him. His father had been there for him until his mother left, and then he had been unable to put his personal grief aside so that he could attend to Oliver's needs. The son has concluded that people are really only interested in fulfilling their own needs and in getting what they want; therefore, they cannot be trusted. He sees no reason to expect Jenny to be an exception. Consequently, Oliver reacts when Jenny talks about wanting to get married.

"Why are you always pushing for us to get married?" Oliver asks Jenny. "Why can't you be content with our relationship? I feel you are pressuring me all the time."

"I love you, Oliver. I want to spend my life with you and I want to have your children. I would think you would see that as a positive thing rather than a negative one."

"Well, if you really loved me, you would understand that I'm busy at my work and that I don't need more stress right now."

"But, Oliver, there will always be stress in our lives. I'm talking about a life's commitment, not the ongoing stress of a job."

"Oh, I see," says Oliver, "What I think is important is insignificant to you. Only what you think is important is what really matters."

"No!" responds Jenny in frustration, "That's not at all what I'm saying. Why do you do this? You deflect the conversation in another direction. You change the subject."

"Oh, so now that I don't say what you want me to say, you accuse me of changing the subject, of 'deflecting the conversation'? Isn't it just that you don't want to hear what I think? Isn't it just that you don't want to hear what I feel?"

"No, Oliver, that's not it at all. I do want to know what you think and feel about getting married. I don't understand why it is that you can't just address your feelings. It feels to me like you aren't being honest with me."

"Now I'm not being honest? And you want to talk about marriage? Why do you want to talk about marriage if you think I'm dishonest?"

Jenny stares at Oliver in total confusion. "How does this happen?" she wonders. "How do our conversations become so convoluted and feel so crazy?"

Oliver was devastated after his mother left and was emotionally shattered when his father all but disappeared as well. He decided that there must be something wrong with him because good parents who are nice people don't just walk away from their children. From his point of view, he had only two choices of how to understand what had happened to him: either he was so unworthy that his parents didn't want him or they were terrible people and he would probably grow up to be just like them. Neither option placed him in an enviable position, certainly not one that would make him a desirable partner. So, when Jenny tells him she loves him, Oliver thinks, "Yeah, sure. She says that now, but I'd better watch my back as I can't trust that that's true." To protect himself from eventual abandonment by yet another person he loves, Oliver refrains from making a commitment to Jenny and tries to maintain some emotional distance. He hopes to keep her always wanting more from him and thus to prevent her from getting too comfortable in the relationship. In order to avoid discussing his true feelings, he becomes defensive and manipulative, erroneously placing the focus on her in a negative way.

Intimacy and deception are incompatible; the latter is self-defeating for a person who wants to love and be loved. Oliver deceives Jenny by refusing to tell her what he is really feeling. He claims he cannot discuss the issue of marriage with her because he is too stressed by his job, when it is his distrust of all women in-cluding Jenny that gets in his way. The negative views he holds from being abandoned by his parents are the real obstacles to his willingness to have an intimate conversation. In this way, low self-esteem and the faulty thinking that results from it control the relationship, and as dysfunctional and irrational thinking takes precedence, it removes any opportunity for intimacy, which is based on openness and truthfulness.

Oliver's fears and self-doubt, though unspoken and unrealized, sabotage his desire to have a healthy, close relationship with Jenny. But Oliver doesn't know that his thinking is flawed, that he has over-generalized, using one incident, admittedly severe and traumatic, as the basis for his lack of trust and his inability to be vulnerable. If only he could talk to Jenny and share his reluctance to commit, if only he could talk to her and discern what her values are, and if only he could take the risk of being truthful and forthcoming, Oliver might be able to tackle this problem in a more constructive way. He might also begin to realize that it is his fear and irrational thoughts about who *he* is that creates his reluctance to commit. However, he doesn't know what he doesn't know, and he doesn't know how to look at the situation differently; he is reacting out of his unhappiness and his experience.

Not knowing, not knowing what we don't know, not knowing how or what to think differently, and accepting that it's okay not to know are all common to—and problematic for—the person who has LSE. This lack of knowing inhibits growth and keeps the person imprisoned in her distorted thinking where she is unable to see other possibilities, unable to learn how to determine whom and when to trust, and where she is unable to change, all of which are a recipe for chaotic relationships with disastrous endings. In all likelihood, this dysfunctional behavior will end with Jenny leaving the relationship and Oliver once again feeling abandoned.

Mark and Bobbi

Mark and Bobbi have dinner and begin seeing each other three or four times a week. After three weeks, they also become sexual. Both have had other sexual relationships, so establishing physical contact is not new or awkward. Bobbi has been practicing birth control for years and Mark regularly carries condoms, so both act responsibly sexually.

When they undress each other, neither one is embarrassed. They don't expect bodies to be perfect, but they admire what they see. They love the entire sexual act, including kissing, fondling, dispensing with clothes, skin-to-skin contact, caressing, touching each other's genitals, oral sex, and intercourse.

When engaging in sex, they freely and uninhibitedly explore each other's bodies and talk about what they like. Playfully they establish a game in which each one labels specific behaviors as being on a scale of 1 to 10. When Mark kisses Bobbi's neck she moans and says, "9" or when he kisses her toes, she pulls away giggling and says, "Oh, that's a 5; it tickles too much."

Both are sensitive to what the other likes and finds stimulating or just pleasurable. Both are concerned that the other feel satisfied when they finish. Afterwards they savor the moment while cuddling in each other's arms and then talk about other things. Thus their sexual relationship is enjoyable, fun, and fulfilling.

For these two people with healthy self-esteem, their sexual interactions are the finale of the intimate relationship they are building. This part of intimacy came after they had experienced verbal and emotional intimacy.

Unlike the sexual relationships of couples where one or both suffer from LSE, this sexual relationship is open, free from guilt or embarrassment, and enjoyable for both partners. Those with LSE usually have significant difficulties in this area of their relationship. For instance, due to their insecurity, many LSE sufferers feel too self-conscious and reticent to let another see their body. Others feel uncomfortable and embarrassed with the sounds that often accompany sexual interactions and remain as quiet as possible. Some are so anxiously focused on pleasing the other person that they cannot relax and enjoy the experience themselves. Many uninformed males with low self-esteem do not respond well to the complaints or directions of their female companions who are unable to be orgasmic and who want to explain what they need their partner to do differently. Many female LSE sufferers feel too insecure to complain or even make suggestions. The person suffering from low self-esteem is often too entangled in their feeling of inadequacy to be able to enjoy a sexual relationship.

◆ **A note of comparison with those with healthy self-esteem**

Those with healthy self-esteem do not lug around the negative baggage of abuse, neglect, and abandonment that those with LSE carry with them everywhere. Those with HSE are generally not constrained by fear of another's reactions or by self-doubt concerning their adequacy and self-worth. Instead, they feel free to ask for help and guidance, they find it easier to accept criticism, and they generally recognize the need for—and benefit of—seeking and receiving feedback.

Those with healthy self-esteem more readily recognize what they know and admit what they don't know without feeling that not knowing is an admission of an abnormal limitation. They are more likely to know what they know and have an idea of what they don't know. If they recognize that others know something that they don't but wish they did, they find ways to get the information or skills they want. People with healthy self-esteem don't feel bad that there is much they don't know. They see that what they don't know is what they haven't been exposed to or haven't yet learned; they don't see it as a condemnation of their adequacy or competence.

While low self-esteem is not the only factor that interferes with the building of healthy relationships, it is the primary one. Certainly immaturity, narcissism, and mental health problems are additional factors that might affect the likelihood of two people being able to form and sustain a quality relationship. Simply put, however, LSE that is untreated probably negatively affects and eventually destroys more budding relationships than any other cause. This makes it all the more important that people recognize that they or their partner have LSE, that the sufferer be willing to admit to "not knowing" and, consequently, to take steps to find information, develop skills, and to seek help, if necessary, to recover from it.

RECOVERY

When a child is raised in a dysfunctional home, she has no way of knowing that this is so. She has nothing with which to compare it. Furthermore, within that dysfunctional family she may see that when others are present, such as when there is company, a birthday party or a barbecue, that her parents' behavior changes—they act better toward each other and toward the children. She also understands from what her parents have told her that there are certain things you do and say when no one else is around that you do not do and say when outsiders are present. Consequently, even when she experiences the homes and behaviors of her friends, she doesn't know but that they act entirely differently when she is not there. So, she has no way of knowing what is normal and what is not. She may not question whether her family is normal, or she may see the dysfunction but be too embarrassed to tell anyone or to get feedback about the health of the environment in which she lives, a "Catch-22."

Those who have not grown up in a chaotic family environment and who have not experienced the mixed messages, constant criticism, anger, bickering, name-calling, bitterness, and unwarranted explosions that are frequent in these homes cannot begin to comprehend the stress, the emotional turmoil, the confusion, or the disruption to maintaining one's equilibrium that is caused by this lifestyle. And while coping in this situation would be difficult for the most mature and healthy adult, the trauma is many times multiplied for the child who has yet to form an emotional foundation upon which to build. The child has no power: no power to leave, no power to change the circumstances, no power to even protest. The child is the victim, the adults the persecutors.

This is important to reiterate because a big step toward recovery is recognizing that "not knowing" and "not knowing what it's normal to know or not know" is not an indication of a person's worth or competence but is, instead, a sad reminder of where she has come from, of what she has missed out on.

In other words, "not knowing" doesn't say anything negative about the person who doesn't know just as getting burglarized or raped isn't the fault of the victim. Therefore, if you don't know something, try to separate yourself from feeling guilty that you don't know because it isn't your fault. You didn't fail to learn these things because you weren't paying attention or weren't smart enough to learn it. Your "not knowing" comes from not being adequately taught, appropriately guided, or presented with healthy models. Once you realized that you were behind in what you knew, you likely withdrew from the race to fulfill your dreams. This, too, is not your fault because in your attempts to cope, you have done what we all do: you have tried to stay safe because your experience showed you that bucking the system was too great a risk to your emotional and/or physical wellbeing.

While the task before you—of attacking this problem rather than continuing to avoid it—is not an easy one, it is necessary for your future. The first step is to forgive yourself, to place the blame where the blame should be—not on yourself but on the circumstances and people who erected, structured, and managed the dysfunctional environment you grew up in, or the people who molested or otherwise abused, neglected, or abandoned you. This doesn't mean you have to hate these people, toss them out of your life, or never speak to them again, though in some cases you may choose to do so. Rather, the purpose of placing blame where it belongs is that until you do, you will blame yourself and remain stifled rather than motivated to do what you must do to learn what you don't now know. Of course, this isn't as easy as it sounds, but the principle is that simple: you didn't learn what you needed to at an earlier age, you are behind, you have the capability to learn, you must now take action to do so. This is the task before you. This is what you can do. Make a plan. Take a step forward. Open your vision. Soak up information. Seek out feedback. Read. Get counseling if you can afford it. Take advantage of every opportunity. Push yourself to do what's difficult to do. Start today.

QUESTIONS TO CONSIDER / THINGS TO DO

You will need to have writing material and pen for this section; it appears at the end of chapters 2-7. For best results, write down your responses rather than just thinking about them as some questions build upon the earlier ones. Also, you will later be able to review your answers as you move through the book.

The author is aware that while some of you may want to concentrate on these pages, others will not and it is suggested you do what you feel works best for you. You will benefit greatly from this book whether or not you answer the questions or do the exercises.

1. In what situations have you found yourself uncomfortable lately? List these. Leave space after each situation to add more information.

2. What was it about these situations that made you uncomfortable? Was it a new or unusual situation? Did you know any or many of the people there? Was anything unfamiliar expected of you? Write down your answers.

3. Were you in any way at the center of attention or was too much attention focused on you? Again, write down your responses.

4. Are you aware of things that you know you don't know that interfere with your life? If so, list the areas in which you think this is true.

5. Can you think of any ways you can get information or help in learning what you don't know? Write these down.

6. Can you think of anyone who might be available and knowledgeable and whom you would be comfortable consulting about the information that you don't know?

7. If not, do you know anyone who could possibly direct you to the resources that you could use to solve your problem and get the help you need?

8. Have there been times when you have been asked to do something, go somewhere, or participate in something and you have refused because you felt you didn't know what would be expected, what would be required, or whether you would fit in? List these.

9. How did you feel afterwards when you declined the invitation out of fear that you might not know enough and might embarrass yourself?

10. What is your experience about getting help when you've needed it? For example, have you ever needed help with a project, needed to learn to do something new around the house or at work, or just needed to ask a basic question but were too embarrassed or too fearful of rejection to ask?

11. Are you aware that most people know some things and don't know others and that no one knows everything? Do you realize that there is nothing wrong with needing to ask for help but that the real problem is needing help and being too fearful to ask for it?

12.   Determine that you are going to take small steps toward correcting this problem of not knowing and avoiding what you think that you don't know.

13.   Choose one area of your life that you would like to alter regarding this avoidance pattern and list all the possible things you could do to get information, talk to someone, or find resources for working on your issue. For instance, would there be information at your local library? Is there a particular friend, relative, counselor, or instructor that you feel you could trust and with whom you could discuss your dilemma? List the least threatening to most threatening and set a goal to do one step this week.

Chapter 3

Fear of Trusting

Melissa and Scott

Melissa and Scott met on a hike with a group of singles. They talked and laughed during the trek, and while sharing a fallen log at lunch, they found out that they had a lot in common, including their enjoyment of camping and backpacking. When they got back to the city, Scott asked Melissa if she'd like to have a drink with him. Nervous to be alone with him, Melissa refused, using an excuse that she had plans for the evening.

A week later Scott called Melissa, whose phone number was on the hiking list of participants, and asked her out to dinner. At first, she was taken aback and asked Scott how he had gotten her phone number. When he reminded her of the list she had signed, she then relaxed and agreed to meet him for dinner. They met at a pizza parlor and again had a good time talking, laughing, and sharing experiences and information about themselves. The evening ended with Scott walking Melissa to her car where he kissed her tenderly and told her good night.

Scott continues to pursue Melissa with invitations to movies, dinner, and sporting events. He is quite mesmerized by Melissa and thinks that she may be the woman he's been looking for. After about a month, he suggests that he would like to make dinner for her at his home. This makes Melissa uncomfortable and using some excuse, she refuses. A month later he asks again and this time she agrees. The more time they have spent together, the more comfortable she feels with him. In spite of her fears, she is quite smitten with this man and is excited by the effort he is putting forth. She wonders if this is an invitation to move their relationship to the next level and the thought excites her. Still, she wonders how she will respond if it is.

After a scrumptious dinner, the two clean up the kitchen and then Scott suggests they sit in the living room. He puts a new CD on the stereo and sits on the couch facing her. For a few minutes they talk about the music and what they each enjoy, and then Scott leans toward Melissa for a kiss. As her lips meet his, he slips his tongue into her mouth. As her tongue touches his, he moans and begins to kiss her more deeply. His hand moves to her waist and then upward until his palm cups a breast and Melissa flinches.

Scott pulls back and says, "Are you okay?"

Melissa says "Yes," and Scott again kisses her deeply. Melissa moans as well. They move closer together as Scott kisses her neck and her ears, and covers her face with kisses. With his face covering hers, Melissa is begins to feel like she is smothering. As his mouth covers hers again, she is aware he is getting more excited. Gently, Scott begins to unbutton Melissa's blouse when suddenly her hands pull his away and she says, "No!"

Startled, Scott jumps back. "What's wrong, Melissa?" he asks.

"I can't... I don't... I can't do this. I can't breathe," says Melissa, gasping.

"Why?" asks Scott, confused, "What do you mean? What did I do?"

"I just don't want you to see me," cries Melissa. "Oh, I'm so embarrassed."

"Did I do something to scare you, Melissa?" asks Scott.

"No, no, it's not you, Scott. It's me. It's me, Scott. I have problems. I'm fat."

"What are you talking about, Melissa? You're certainly not fat. In fact, you look great," says Scott. "I've seen you in shorts and you have great legs."

"I'm sorry," sobs Melissa. "It's just me. I feel fat."

"But you're not," pleads Scott, "Did someone tell you that you were fat, Melissa? Who was it?" he asks angrily. "Because it isn't true."

"No, no one told me that. They just... they just... Oh, I don't know. It's just me. I'm sorry."

"Listen," says Scott. "We can turn the lights out or we can stop. We don't have to do anything more until you feel comfortable. I won't push you and you don't need to be frightened. It'll be okay."

Buttoning her blouse, Melissa says, "You may be right, Scott. I just don't know. I'm so embarrassed and I'm so sorry to do this to you. I should have known better. I should have known I couldn't do this."

"Melissa, I think I'm falling in love with you. We can work this out."

"I need to go now," replies Melissa, "I need some time to think about this. I've got to go home. I'm sorry, I'm so sorry." She grabs her coat and without looking back walks out.

Scott walks to the door and sadly watches her leave. He wonders if he will see her again.

Melissa has low self-esteem and is fearful of people, especially men. She is not only cautious but also frightened by—and suspicious of—the attention of a new acquaintance. Then once she relaxes and begins to enjoy her new relationship, her LSE kicks up in a different way; she is reminded of a past traumatic event that has led her to hate herself and to focus on herself as a fat person. Though untrue, when Melissa looks in a mirror, she thinks she sees a fat body. She cannot see herself as she really is because even more powerful than the image in the mirror are the words of the three boys who abused her and called her fat while doing so. Melissa's view of herself as inadequate translates into a visual distortion wherein Melissa cannot see her body as it is and cannot rationally compare it with other women's bodies like hers, bodies that others would agree are very nice.

When Melissa was a sophomore, she was molested by Frank, a neighborhood boy who she thought was a close friend, and by two of his buddies. After a football game she had gone to get hamburgers with Frank. While there, Frank's buddies invited him and Melissa to join them in their car. The two had been drinking and offered some to their companions. Frank took one and then another; Melissa refused altogether. As the three boys drank, they got boisterous and drunk and Melissa became nervous. She asked them to take her home, but Frank's buddies only laughed. By this time Frank was too drunk to see what was happening. One thing led to another and they drove to a secluded place where the three boys raped Melissa.

When they dropped Melissa off a few blocks from her home, she had run into the house sobbing hysterically and immediately told her parents. Knowing their daughter as they did and seeing the condition she was in, they knew she was telling the truth and called the police. The trial that came later was a travesty. Frank and his friends pleaded innocent and brought in other boys to testify that they too had had sex with Melissa while stating that she was always a willing participant. Melissa's life was never the same. She became withdrawn, quiet, and fearful, unable to trust that any man was truly interested in her as a person. She had always been somewhat heavy, but now she became obsessed with her weight and appearance; no matter how much weight she lost, she still saw herself as fat.

Before the rape, Melissa had planned to go to college and study to be a biologist; afterwards, she chose to study computer program-ming at a local community college so she could live at home. Her family was very supportive; they encouraged her to get therapy and to be as independent as she could, while letting her know that she was welcome to live there as long as she wanted to. During her sec-ond year of community college, Melissa began dating occasionally but never let a relationship develop beyond kissing and fondling. Most of the time she socialized in groups such as the single's hiking club. A year later, that's where she met Scott.

When Trust is Broken

When a child is repeatedly mocked, reprimanded, criticized, and ridiculed, or if she is abused, neglected, or abandoned, she generally has one of two emotional responses: she either becomes fearful and hurt with her anger suppressed or turned inward, or she becomes fearful, hurt, *and* overtly angry. Both children will have lost their ability to trust others or to know when to trust and who to trust. If nothing intervenes to alter this abusive pattern of behavior or to help them get a different perspective about themselves, two things also can happen. The person who experienced the fear, pain, and anger turned inward will be left with constant feelings of depression, shame, and guilt, plus a sense of hopelessness and helplessness. These feel-ings may negatively affect her motivation, her ambition, her willingness to take risks, her ability to trust others, and her belief in her ability to succeed at tasks that others feel adequate to tackle. Her tendency, instead, will be to avoid what is new and unfamiliar or what looks daunting.

Telling a child that she is inadequate or severely mistreating her is a good way to break her will. Or when a young person is subjected to molestation as Melissa was, she is unable to cope with this horrific injustice and is left with her spirit damaged, believing for some reason she must have deserved this treatment or that in some way she caused it. Thereafter, she will view herself as less worthy, as less deserving, as less adequate, and as truly limited. Fearful that others will view her in the same way, she will avoid risks that might reveal her limitations and she will lower her overall expectations of life. Even the view she has of herself in a mirror will be affected; she may see herself as fat when she isn't; she may see herself as ugly when she is attractive or even beautiful.

Some LSE sufferers make poor choices because it's easier for them to imagine that someone equally dysfunctional might be attracted to them than to think that a more successful and respected person would find them worthy. On the other hand, many people with low self-esteem hold out for a relationship with someone who is so far above them intellectually, socially, and economically that they would not fit into that person's life, nor would that person consider them a potential partner. They so badly need the prestige that goes with having a beautiful or successful partner to enhance their feelings about themselves that they sabotage the possibility of having a relationship with someone more suitable.

People who've been abused have many ways of coping, most of which prove to be self-sabotaging. Until they develop an understanding of what has happened to them, who is to blame, and how it has distorted their view of themselves, they will continue to behave in ways that are self-destructive and that deny them the very things they most want in life. Sadly, this is now the state of millions of people, who do not understand their dilemma and who cannot find the help they need to correct it.

For instance, many LSE sufferers who have been abused have internalized the treatment as deserved or have inaccurately equated sex with love have a slightly different problem. Such is often the case with children who have been molested by relatives and friends who told them that the abuse was a form of love and affection. Wanting attention but unsure of whom to trust, when to trust, or how much to trust, they readily place their trust in strangers or acquaintances. In their need to find someone who truly cares about them and values them, they often place their faith in anyone who shows them positive attention or affection. As a result, they become the targets of users and manipulators, while they shy away from those who are more respectful and healthy because they feel unequal and uncomfortable and because these healthier people don't as readily show affection to new acquaintances as do those who manipulate and use others.

Jackson

Saturday morning finds Jackson bleary-eyed because of lack of sleep, embarrassed about his behavior the previous night at Brianne's, and depressed about the thought of losing her. He is miserable but doesn't know what to do to change the pattern. He is too fearful of rejection to confide in Brianne; he thinks that if he were to do so, it would surely be the end of the relationship. Still, he tells himself, the damage has been done and he has probably already ended the relationship by walking out on her without an explanation. Full of grief, shame, and remorse, he asks himself if he could possibly take a chance this once, if he could approach Brianne and trust her enough to tell her the truth. He has never confided in anyone about his problem even though two women have witnessed his limp penis at an inopportune time, but then he has never been as smitten as he is with Brianne. He thinks she comes as close to being the woman of his dreams as he could ever imagine finding. Filled with despair, he pours himself another cup of coffee, runs a hand through his hair, and collapses into a chair.

Just then the doorbell rings. Wondering who could be on his front porch at 7:00 on a Saturday morning, Jackson considers not answering, but then he rises slowly and moves through the dark living room to the door. Once there, he turns the lock, pulls open the door, and finds himself looking into the tired face and concerned eyes of Brianne.

For a second they just look at each other while Jackson fights his impulse to close the door. Sensing his fear and noticing how haggard he looks, Brianne quickly begins to talk. "Jackson, I don't know what the problem is, but I'm sure we can work this out. Can you just trust me enough to tell me what's going on? I love you, Jackson."

Jackson stands there with tears welling up. Then his chin drops to his chest, and his hand rises to cover his face.

"Jackson, may I come in?" Brianne asks softly.

Jackson hesitates, then steps back, opening the door wider in invitation. Brianne opens the screen door and walks in, taking Jackson's hand as she does so and gently guiding him to the sofa. She turns, walks back, and closes the door and then comes to sit facing him. Jackson avoids eye contact by looking at the floor.

The two sit quietly for a few seconds. Brianne tries to collect her thoughts while Jackson's mind races and his heart pounds. He wonders if she can hear it and then thinks how strange it is to be thinking of something so stupid at a time like this.

Brianne reaches for Jackson's hand and begins to talk. "Whatever it is that you are afraid of, Jackson, I'm here with you. I'm not going away. I love you. You can tell me what it is. Please give us a chance. Please talk to me."

Slowly Jackson raises his head. He looks into Brianne's eyes and says, "Brianne, I love you too. You are all I've ever wanted. There's no one else I'd rather be with, but I have a p-p-problem." *He is stuttering now.*

"What kind of a problem, Jackson? What is it that you can't tell me? Are you married? Are you in trouble? What is it, honey? You have to tell me."

"No, no, it's nothing like that," *replies Jackson.* " I," *pausing, he takes a big breath and starts again,* "I-I have a physical problem."

"Are you sick?" *she asks.*

"No," *says Jackson. He pauses once more, his head again lowers, his eyes leave hers.* "It's a sexual problem," *he mumbles.*

"Jackson, it's okay; you can tell me. I'm here with you. Maybe I can help. Please tell me what it is."

"I can't perform right. I can't maintain an erection," *says Jackson in a whisper, barely audible.* "I'm impotent."

Moving closer to him and looping her arm inside his, Brianne asks, "That's not so unusual. What does your doctor say?"

"I haven't seen a doctor," *Jackson responds as he begins to sob.* "I'm too embarrassed. It's so humiliating."

"Oh, Jackson, it's okay. I've heard it happens to a lot of men at different times in their lives and for lots of different reasons. We just have to get you to a doctor or maybe a counselor. We just have to talk and try to figure out who you could see."

"Don't you find this disgusting?" Jackson asks. "Don't you find me a disappointment? Repulsive?"

"Of course not, Jackson. Why would I? We're not teenagers. I understand that people have their difficulties. I don't expect you to be perfect. So, you have a problem. Next year I may have one. That's just life. That doesn't change how I feel about you. Would it change how you feel about me?"

"Well, no," says Jackson, "It wouldn't. I love you. I'd love you no matter what."

Brianne reaches out and lifts Jackson's chin, then bends forward to kiss him lightly on the lips, then more deeply.

Jackson's heart flutters at the taste of her tongue in his mouth. "Did this just happen?" he wonders. "Did I just tell her and now she's kissing me? Is this for real?"

Jackson and Brianne have just shared a moment of intimacy. Jackson has bared his soul and Brianne has responded by being open, receptive, sensitive, and loving. Jackson has allowed himself to be as vulnerable as a person can be and Brianne has acted in kind. Both have declared their love for each other as they've moved to a new level in their relationship, one of in-depth honesty, transparency, trust, and togetherness.

In this instance, Jackson has been able to move beyond his fear and low self-esteem largely because of the sensitivity of Brianne, who shows herself to be a loving and nonjudgmental partner. In a very tender moment, she has communicated to Jackson that he can trust her with his truth, with his problem. He, in turn, is able to accept her offer of acceptance and, for the first time in his life, has truly shared a very deep concern with someone he loves. This is an experience of intimacy, of loving, of closeness, of honesty, of vulnerability. This is what we all strive for.

✧

Molly

Molly goes out with Howard, and she has a great time. They eat at a nice restaurant that is new to her, and they talk and laugh throughout the evening. Afterwards he takes her home, politely walks her to the door, and thanks her for a nice evening without so much as expecting a kiss. That, in and of itself, is so unusual and unexpected that it surprises her, though it also feels good to Molly. She feels respected.

Still she wrestles with Howard's appearance and the feedback she receives from her friends. He seems very nice. He is kind, humorous, and intelligent. She knows the company has hired him as a consultant for many years, so they evidently value and respect his work, but does she really want to spend time and to be seen with a fat man? After some thought, she decides not to be concerned about it since men never ask her out a second time, even when sex is involved. Besides, she rationalizes, he probably isn't really interested in her since he didn't push her for any physical payoff for the dinner.

The following morning Molly calls her friend, Dan, and shares with him the details of her evening. When she talks to him individually and without the influence of the women in the group, he listens to her and gives her feedback from a different perspective than the one she gets from the women. Plus she doesn't feel that he competes with her the way they do, and she finds that his comments aren't as hurtful as theirs are.

Describing what they did and talked about, she tells Dan about the evening spent with Howard. She speaks of her perceptions of him as an honorable man, one who doesn't expect anything in return. Then she asks him what he thinks of Howard's weight problem and balding head. Dan hesitates and then tells her that while appearance is all important to some people, it isn't necessarily that critical for others. As far as he is concerned, appearance is of some significance but what is most important to him is how loyal and truthful the person is. Molly listens and asks a few questions, all the time remembering that Dan's last two lovers left him and she wonders how much credence she can give to his words. Are loyalty and truthfulness the most important things? Are looks and appearance next in line? Can she trust that what Dan says is an indication of what is right? What about how the person treats you? Where does that come in?

Molly has a date for lunch that same day at the home of her sister and husband, who are having a birthday party for their toddler. This means, of course, that other members of her family will be there, which she dreads. The family always give her the third degree about whether she is dating and when she is going to get married. Most of the time she doesn't have any information to give them and that is embarrassing. She wishes they would just leave her alone or take an interest in her job or other activities. Why do they always have to put her on the spot about her personal life? The more she thinks about it, the angrier she becomes and the more anxious she feels about going to the party.

Once there, her expectations are more than met as she receives the usual grilling. Finally, she relents and tells one sister that she was out on a date the night before, hoping that will shut them all up. She realizes her mistake immediately as the barrage of questions become more incessant. "What's he look like? Who is he? What does he do for a living? Where did you meet him?" Her family has long thought that she is just too picky. Her two sisters found men and married them even though these men are lazy good-for-nothings in Molly's mind. So when the questions continue, "Is he a banker? Is he 6' tall and handsome? Is he rich? Is he a doctor?" she isn't surprised. Her family members are really into money even though what little they earn runs through their fingers like sand.

"So tell me," her mother asks, "what does he do for a living?"

"He's a consultant hired by the company I work for," Molly replies.

"Just a consultant?" asks her mother. "Doesn't he have a title?"

"He's self-employed and does consulting, Mother. It's a good career."

"He can't be very well-to-do then, I suppose."

"No, Mother, I don't think he's rich and besides he has two daughters," offers Molly tiredly.

"I do hope he's not married?" snaps her mother.

"Of course not! He's divorced, Mother. He's been divorced for three years."

Her mother's next question was also predictable. "What does he look like?"

"He's about average height, I guess," says Molly, "or a little bit below average."

"Oh, he's short," spits out her mother. "Is he good-looking at least?"

Wondering why her mother is always so bitter and rude and why she never comments this way about her sister's two jerk husbands, Molly replies, "I think he's nice-looking. You might not."

"What does that mean? Is he ugly? Is he deformed or something?" her mother is relentless.

"No, no, no, Mother. Why do you have to do this? What does it matter what he looks like? He's a nice person and besides I've just had one date with him. Who knows if we will continue seeing each other?" Then after a short pause, Molly adds angrily, "If you must know, he is a little overweight, just like all of you."

Instantly, laughter breaks out in the room. "Oh, he's fat, poor, and saddled with two kids," one of her sister's husbands shouts above the noise. The laughter gets louder. They've always seen Molly as thinking she is better than they are; they resent the fact that she hasn't made many of the poor choices that they have made, though they won't admit it. Now they will celebrate the fact that maybe she isn't faring so well after all. Maybe she will have to settle like they did.

Molly is devastated, and her legs hardly hold her up. She stumbles to the back bedroom and picks up her coat from the bed and puts it on. Pausing for a moment to pull herself together before facing them, she stands erect, squares her shoulders, and without another word heads straight for the front door.

"Where are you going?" asks her mother as the laughter subsides and everyone's eyes turn to the two of them. "Don't be silly, Molly. You're just too sensitive. We're all just joking. Don't take everything so seriously. That's part of your problem; you always make a big deal out of nothing. Don't act like a child; come back in here and stay for the party."

Molly stops in her tracks, turns and glares at her mother, and then lets her eyes span the room of faces, hatred and despair written on her face. Her mother's face becomes red, and Molly turns and walks out the front door and to her car, her posture stately.

She feels them watching her out the window. She gets in and, without glancing back, drives away. "Why is it always like this?" she sobs quietly to herself. "Why do they hate me so?"

Molly has no one that she can trust with whom to talk about personal issues, no one who doesn't have an agenda or hang-ups of their own. Dan tries to be her friend, but he too has many problems. How can she take the advice of a person whose own life is in shambles? Molly doesn't have any friends who seem stable, together, and happy. She can't trust her coworkers, her family is consumed with anger and bitterness over their own failed lives, and her friends are having as much difficulty as she is in fulfilling their lives.

As is often the case with those whose lives are chaotic, the lives of those with whom they associate are equally chaotic. These people have few opportunities to hear opposing viewpoints, to be challenged to do or think differently, or to be inspired by the successes of others close to them since their social contacts are struggling as much as they are. And if a person has LSE and is relegated to that quality of companionship, feedback, motivation, or openness to change, it is extremely difficult to acquire new friends who might encourage a new perspective.

Molly doesn't know what to think, who to believe, or what to do. Is she somehow lowering her standards to date a heavyset, balding man? She doesn't think so. After all, don't men usually lose their hair when they get older? And thinking about the people she knows, hasn't she seen their weight fluctuate over the years? Hasn't hers gone up and down to some extent? Is this what's really important? Molly is terrified of making a mistake. She doesn't want to have people laughing at her. Still, she thinks, the people at work speak highly of Howard. In fact, she's never heard anyone say an unkind word about him.

Finally, Molly decides that she will just wait and see what happens. She won't be influenced by others, especially those whose lives are in shambles, as she has in the past. She will see if Howard invites her out again, although she doubts he will, and she thinks that will take care of her dilemma. And, if perchance he should ask her for another date, Molly muses, she will go and see how she feels about it.

❧

Jake

Jake feels as if he is at the end of his rope. He is so fearful of losing Deidre that he is driving himself crazy. He finds it difficult to concentrate on his work because he is consumed with wondering where Deidre is, who she's with, what she's thinking. He recognizes that this is a familiar pattern, which distresses him all the more. His lack of trust and fear of rejection have ruined two previous marriages and countless other relationships, and he admits to himself that if something doesn't change, he will destroy this one too. And at this point of desperation, Jake decides to seek help. He also decides that he will trust Deidre enough to confide in her, something he has never done with the other women in his life.

That evening, Jake suggests that they get take-out at their favorite Chinese restaurant and spend a quiet evening at home. He tells Deidre that he needs to talk to her about what's going on with him. Once home, they open the boxes of food, fill their plates, and sit down at the table facing one another.

Deidre notices how serious and drawn Jake looks, but she says nothing. She doesn't know what's coming and wants to let him talk in his own time. Jake takes a few bites while looking down at his food, then swallows, lifts his eyes to meet hers, and begins to talk.

"I think I need to see a therapist. I think I need help. I don't like the way I'm acting or the way I'm treating you and I know it's my problem, but I just don't know what to do about it. I'm thinking that I should find a psychologist to see." Jake looks beaten and tired.

Deidre reaches across the table, takes Jake's hand, and says quietly, "I love you, Jake. I hate to see you so miserable, so I want you to know that I support you in your decision to go to therapy. I want you to be happy."

Jake feels moved by Deidre's response. She hasn't ridiculed him, hasn't indicated any negative feelings about his declaration, and has said she will be there to support him. After he has admitted to his need for help, she has reiterated that she loves him. He feels closer to her than he has for a long time.

Then he continues talking, "I know that my problems stem from my childhood, but I don't understand why I can't just forget the things that happened. After all, I was just a child then; I'm an adult now."

"Jake, I want to thank you for trusting me enough to talk to me about this. And, if it would be okay, I would like to share with you some thoughts that I have."

"Okay," says Jake, nodding at her.

"Well, a few weeks ago, a friend of mine confided in me that she has low self-esteem and that she was working by phone with a psychologist in another state who specializes in self-esteem recovery. The things she told me she was learning were fascinating and she told me about a book that her psychologist had written. I asked if I could read it because I think I experience low self-esteem at times myself. Anyway, I read the book and think you might find it interesting too. Do you think you'd be willing to take a look at it, maybe read the first chapter and see what you think? I found out it's really a common problem for both men and women."

"It's disgusting to think I might have low self-esteem," Jake replies. "Only weaklings have low self-esteem. How could I have accomplished what I have if I had low self-esteem?"

"That's a myth, Jake. What I've learned is that many people who are extremely successful in their lives have low self-esteem. And, it's nothing to be ashamed of if you do have it. I won't think less of you. I love you and just want you to be happy. Won't you please just look at the book?"

"Okay, I'll read the book. At this point, I'm open to anything. In the meantime, Deidre, I'm so sorry for the way I've been acting. I don't want to hurt you. You are so very important to me. I love you."

"I know that, Jake, and we can work this out."

Jake feels relieved. He has admitted to having a problem. And it's not that Deidre didn't already know it, but she didn't react negatively. She didn't get sarcastic. She was very tender and very supportive. She didn't ridicule him like his mother would have. Deidre was very different from his mother, and she didn't think less of him if he had issues he needed to work through. He wishes he had trusted her sooner. He wishes he had been able to accept that he had a problem sooner instead of blaming her.

While those who experience anger early on often become overachievers as a result of their motivation to prove themselves, these angry LSE sufferers find it difficult to trust others and tend to constantly evaluate the motives of others. Fearful that others might try to use or manipulate them, they are quick to see the deceitfulness in others, and at times they even imagine deception and dishonesty where none exists. Overly watchful and vigilant, they interpret the verbal and nonverbal behaviors of others by their own standards or based on the behavior of others who have hurt them in the past. But because people do and say things for many different reasons, this judgment of the intentions of others by the LSE sufferer is not always accurate, and it can lead to misunderstandings and alienation.

Jake is beginning to recognize that his fears have prevented him from trusting the person who loves him most. He wonders if others would have responded in the ways he has if they had received the same messages that he did from his mother. He wonders what others would think of him if they knew how jealous and possessive he has become. They respect him in business, but they don't see what he experiences within himself or how he acts in his personal life with the woman he loves.

Deidre has never thought that Jake was perfect; instead she has seen how defensive he gets at the slightest suggestion that he has a problem and how jealous he gets when other men show her even minimal attention. She has been hurt by his interrogations and his constant doubts about her loyalty. She is elated that Jake is now willing to look at himself, and she desperately hopes that he will find some answers and guidance in altering his suspicions and lack of trust in her and in her love for him. She knows she has given him no reason to distrust her, and she has long recognized that this must be something from his past, something he hasn't felt he could share with her, something traumatic that has caused him to be so cautious and suspect.

She is encouraged by Jake's willingness to talk to her, though she knows it is likely the result of his desperation and sense of helplessness and hopelessness. Still, whatever it has taken, she thinks, to bring him to this brink of change was necessary. She is just sorry that he has had to be so miserable before he could take steps to help himself.

Carey

Carey graduated from high school with excellent grades and a scholarship to a major state university. Even though she hadn't fared well socially, she had applied herself intellectually. Despite the fact that she was somewhat depressed most of the time, she had been driven to prove her worth to herself and others and she had excelled in nearly everything.

After high school, Carey convinces her mother to give her enough money to move to the city where the university is so that she can get a summer job which she does, with a company that cleans offices. This is hard work and includes night and weekend hours and low pay, but Carey does well and begins to respond to the friendly people with whom she works. At first she is too reserved and fearful to say much, but her coworkers are accepting, down-to-earth, and friendly. They laugh a lot and after a few weeks, Carey finds herself joining in with the chatter and with the fun. For the first time in her life, Carey feels she fits in, though she rationalizes that people in other situations wouldn't treat her with such respect and kindness. At first she only sees her new friends at work, but before long they ask her to join them for breakfast follow-ing their night shift. Delighted by the invitation and determined to make a life for herself, she accepts, even though she is nervous doing so.

Carey is 19 years old and has had very little social contact in her life. Her father and older brothers had had their jock friends and activ-ities, and her older brothers had dated some, but as a family they had never had company other than her grandparents and they had seldom gone anywhere except to watch the boys' athletic endeavors. Carey wasn't involved in school activities, she hadn't had a group of friends she went out with, and except for the movies she and Joey attended and the times she went to the mall with her mother or out to eat with her parents, she hadn't experienced much. Even their vacations were only to visit relatives, mostly older aunts and uncles and grandpar-ents, so she hadn't had many opportunities to be around other children. All in all she has led a very sheltered and uneventful life.

With that history, Carey is nervous going to the restaurant the first morning. She feels awkward in her movements, not knowing where to stand while they wait for the hostess to seat them. She doesn't know which chair to take or what to do first. Mostly she remains quiet and watches what everyone else is doing and then tries to follow their lead. She wonders if they notice or can tell how uncomfortable she is, but they seem not to pay attention. They are just a group of nice people, talking and laughing, upbeat and respectful of each other. They are also polite and include her in the conversations, bringing her up to speed about things with which she couldn't be familiar.

Carey waits until two people have ordered and then orders the same thing. When she doesn't know what to do with her hands and can't think of anything to say, she sips her water. Then when she realizes they might see her hands shaking or that she might spill it, she puts the glass back down. When the others ask her questions about herself, she mostly gives one-word answers. She isn't used to people being interested in her and she isn't accustomed to sitting facing others while being asked questions about herself. When it happens, she feels everyone's eyes on her, waiting for her response. Additionally, she feels uncomfortable revealing anything about herself or her thoughts for fear that they will see that she doesn't have much to contribute.

This group spans all ages; Carey is the youngest and the oldest is a woman about her mother's age named Bernice, who is the crew manager. Bernice is especially nice and seems to take Carey under her wing. In the days that follow, she always makes sure that Carey is included in their plans and she begins to initiate spending time with Carey apart from the group. She invites Carey to attend a play with her; another time she calls and suggests they catch a movie. Gradually, Carey begins to become more comfortable in different situations, all because Bernice exposes to her to so many different opportunities. She invites Carey to her apartment for meals, including times when her two grandchildren are there, but it isn't until she can tell that Carey is getting more comfortable that she includes her in Sunday dinner with her daughter and family. Knowing that Carey doesn't have much money, Bernice makes the excuse that she just loves to cook and always makes enough for an army; then she sends leftovers home with Carey.

Bernice is a very caring woman. She has raised her own children without help from their father and she has done a very good job of it.

When she first met Carey, she saw in the girl much of the pain she had experienced when she was young and when her husband ran off with a fellow junkie. Gradually she begins to share with Carey about her own past and to gently nudge Carey to talk about her home life. Carey loves the time she spends with Bernice and loves to listen to her, marveling that she can talk so openly about her past disappointments and her struggle to raise her family. As a result, Carey gradually begins to trust this woman in a way she has so far only trusted Joey. As she opens up to Bernice and slowly reveals aspects of her past, she is surprised and relieved to feel the compassion and support from this woman who has fulfilled the role her mother should have. Bernice listens and empathizes; she helps Carey see that the messages she has received that painted her as inadequate were inaccurate and understandably painful. Carey then begins to realize how her view of herself and her neediness played into attitudes at school that didn't attract others but instead repelled them. From this she gathers the truth about herself: that she isn't incapable of making friends; rather she is just a product of her environment and has acquired a lot of bad habits, a lot of misconceptions, and an insecurity that has been visible and uninviting. This is Carey's first taste of intimacy with another adult.

In the fall, Carey begins classes at the University. Taking the minimum number of hours and still keep her scholarship, she is nevertheless kept busy with her studies and her night job. Carey thinks this is just as well, because she still doesn't feel comfortable interacting with her peers. She prefers to limit her socializing to Bernice and her family and her coworkers.

Nine months after Carey starts her cleaning job, Dirk, a nephew of Bernice's, asks her out on a date. Carey is at first excited, then scared. How much the scars of her past will affect her future will soon be tested in her new relationship with Dirk.

Learning to trust others and to trust herself is a formidable task for Carey, who has trusted no one except Joey. She is reticent, but gradually, as she learns what to do in new situations and as she experiences the respect and consideration of her coworkers, Carey begins to develop the ability to trust.

Given the support, guidance, and love of a mature adult, Carey is able to repaint the picture she has had of herself as a misfit. Given the opportunity to meet others on an equal basis as coworkers and experiencing their acceptance, Carey responds appropriately and begins a new life in which she is respected and treated well and in which she grows and blossoms. Her low self-esteem is not overcome, but it is in repair. How well she will be able to transfer her new confidence and new skills into a romantic relationship is yet to be seen.

Jarrod

Jarrod's plan to refrain from attacking Jackie and his commitment to avoid arguing with her doesn't last long. Part of the reason is that he does nothing except make a decision. He doesn't figure out what he will do in place of his present behavior, what he will say if he doesn't react in anger. Also, he doesn't consider possible times or situations in which he may be tested. Furthermore, he hasn't had any time to practice and he doesn't know that it may take several false starts before he can put his plan into action.

Furthermore, neither Jarrod nor Jackie realizes that Jackie also has low self-esteem. An overachiever who has been extremely successful in organizing community and charity functions, she thrives on attention and power as ways to quiet her inner negative voice.

Consequently, she is defensive, and rather than hearing Jarrod's words or responding to his hurt feelings, she only hears criticism and the resumption of that inner voice telling her that she is a bad person. Jackie has learned to cope with and dispel these condemning thoughts by denying any connection with Jarrod's accusations, yet she yearns for affirmation and praise to dispel her negative self-statements and self-doubt. She knows her social and volunteer contacts like her, but she also knows that it is in their best interest to cultivate an ongoing relationship with her as she has much to offer to their work. Jackie needs constant involvement in activities and to be surrounded by people to keep her spirits up, but she knows that it all comes down to business and productivity. Jarrod is the one she would most like affirmation from, yet she sabotages that through her defensiveness and insecurity.

Now recently retired from her community and charity responsibilities, Jackie feels somewhat lost, like a sports star who is no longer in the limelight. She is having trouble adjusting to the letdown of being without the daily demands for decision-making, the influence she wielded, and the acclaim she received daily. Feeling this loss, Jackie tries to hold on to what she once had and makes herself available as a volunteer consultant. Any criticism from Jarrod about her unwillingness to let go of past relationships or to transition into building a life outside the limelight is frightening to Jackie. Achieving has been her life, what she has used to feel competent and worthwhile. She doesn't know how to relate to Jarrod as a wife or a woman without feeling that she is competing, and when she has competed with men in the past, she has always felt superior. Now, without her title and position, Jackie actually feels less adequate than Jarrod, a position she hasn't experienced before; without her power, she wonders why he would want to be with her. His criticism of what's so important to her causes her to feel panicky. What would she do if she lost him and was without both her work and her husband? The thought of being alone is her worst fear.

Jackie moves through the stages of fear, defensiveness, anger, panic, and more fear. Often after these angry moments with Jarrod, she leaves the room, starts to feel alone and fearful, and then reconsiders her behavior. She wishes she didn't always react so cruelly to Jarrod's complaints and tells herself that he just wants a closer relationship with her, that he too craves the security of their relationship.

Then, with regularity she looks for Jarrod to apologize and makeup, not with the idea of resolving their problems but to remove her fear of being alone and to regain her sense of security. To do this, she cuddles up to Jarrod and initiates sex. This show of affection and invitation of sex momentarily lessens Jarrod's anger and quiets his fears. He responds slowly at first, consenting to her advances as she begins to undress him and slips off her blouse and bra.

Once they are both naked, Jackie leads Jarrod to their bedroom and pushes him down on the bed. Still conscious of what has caused her amorous mood, Jarrod barely participates, wanting her to prove her sincerity. Jackie proceeds as though she doesn't notice, determined to engage him in what always works to end their fights—sex.

First kissing his face and neck, she slowly moves down his body, taking his penis in her hand as she does so. Jerrod groans and Jackie knows her efforts to appease him are working

When they were finished, they were both relaxed and happy. Sex has always been good between them, bringing feelings of closeness and safety, even though both would have to admit that the relationship was based more on fear and they use sex to feel more secure.

People often confuse sex with intimacy, thinking that if someone is willing to engage in sex with them that that person must love and be committed to them. Unfortunately, this is not necessarily true. People have very different motives and perceptions about sexual interaction. Some use it to get their own needs met, some use it insincerely to get what they want, some withhold it to punish or to manipulate others. And while any sexual experience may appear to be an act of intimacy, true intimacy requires that the couple not only be willing to be sexual but also to engage in the sexual experience as an act of mutual affection and without ulterior motives.

Unfortunately, those with low self-esteem are easily duped in the area of sex because they so badly want to feel that they have a close and reciprocal relationship, that they have someone who truly cares about them. In their desperation to experience the love that has eluded them, these LSE sufferers readily accept any sexual interaction as an authentic show of affection. Even when those with LSE question the loyalty of their significant other, they allow sexual interaction to temporarily quell their fears. They may even engage in sex when they don't particularly want to or accept the advances of their partner when they know it's manipulative because they have convinced themselves that sex is the ultimate sign of intimacy.

True physical intimacy occurs when two people are open and honest and are entering into sexual behavior willingly and for the purpose of pleasure, rather than to cover up the feelings that remain after a disagreement. Couples often have intimate sex once an argument has been resolved and they feel close again, but intimacy cannot function as the means to the end. It's not a mechanism that can be used to produce authentic emotional closeness; closeness must come first. The sense of closeness that people experience when they have had sex for the wrong reasons doesn't last long; then the individuals have to either face the problems that exist or deny them.

Mandy and Willa

In her facilitated support group, Willa is learning that she is personalizing much of what Mandy says, that emotions from her past are being triggered by Mandy's words and behavior. She is gaining insight into how her reactions are less about Mandy and more about her unresolved feelings from the past, specifically from her childhood. She begins to see how she is getting hooked by responding as though Mandy were one of her alcoholic and negligent parents rather than her loving partner. She is determined to change the ways that she responds to criticism and complaints from Mandy, deciding she will try to listen and consider what Mandy has to say rather than get hooked by her past and overreact.

Mandy is frustrated. She doesn't know what to do differently but decides that she won't fight with Willa anymore. "After all," she tells herself, "Willa really loves me and is not trying to control me or remold me as my mother has always tried to do. But without a specific plan of how she will respond differently, without more insight into what is happening to trigger her defensiveness and her anger, and without daily attention to her past resentments, nothing is likely to change.

A week passes and Mandy comes home from work frustrated about some interactions that took place there. She feels that her supervisor is picky and criticizes her unnecessarily. Just as she felt she could never quite please her mother, Mandy feels she can't seem to satisfy her supervisor. She works hard and knows she does a good job, but all she gets is grief for her efforts. After looking at the mail, she decides to start dinner and has everything on the stove when Willa walks in with a tantalizing-smelling pizza and a wide smile.

Mandy sees the pizza and snaps at Willa, "Why didn't you tell me you were going to get a pizza? I have dinner on the stove."

Determined not to take the bait and overreact, Willa responds,
"Well, we can eat the pizza tonight while it's hot and fresh and save
your meal until tomorrow or we can eat what you've fixed and save
the pizza. It doesn't really matter."

"Of course it matters," spits out Mandy, who is feeling once again
like she has done it wrong, "Everyone knows pizza is best when it's
warm out of the oven. I notice that was your first suggestion too," she
says angrily.

"Hey, I didn't mean it that way. It doesn't matter to me. Really, it
doesn't," says Willa sincerely. Setting the pizza on the table, she walks
over to the stove. "Mandy, it was really nice of you to go to this work to
make dinner; it looks really good. Why don't we have this tonight and
save the pizza for tomorrow?"

Willa's response confuses Mandy. Normally, by this time things
would have gotten out-of-hand because the smallest issues have in the
past become huge fights. She feels slightly embarrassed. "Why does it
matter which meal we eat?" she asks herself. We were both just trying
to be nice, after all.

"Okay, let's just eat the piazza," says Mandy in a voice that indi-
cates she is giving in. "It really does smell good and now we have dinner
for today and tomorrow, so I guess that's a good thing." Mandy isn't
willing to let Willa fully off the hook.

Mandy and Willa have developed a routine way of disagreeing
that usually burgeons into a destructive fight in which accusations
are made and feelings are trampled on, causing their fragile trust
to erode. Willa, however, has made a decision not to engage in
this type of interchange if she can recognize what is happening
before she participates. She is trying to avoid getting ensnared by
statements that trigger negative memories to flare up, distorting
her perception of the present. She is trying to look at her present

interactions with Mandy for what they are, words spoken between two people who love each other but who are also affected by their pasts and their daily lives. She is determined to be more respectful towards Mandy, more sensitive, and less reactive.

This is a good strategy and one that could change the dynamics of their relationship if they only give it a chance and if Willa can manage to stay on track. At this point, she has more insight than Mandy, and one of them has to break the pattern so each of them can slow down and not react so quickly, so irrationally, so negatively, and so dramatically.

Darren

Darren is not only fearful of relationships, but he is fearful of life. He is good at his work and is respected by his coworkers and those who don't know him well, but he is often thought of as boring by those who know him best. He does all the necessary work to maintain his home, his job, and the basics of living, but he has no interests that set him apart from someone else. He attends movies, goes out to dinner, brings in take-out, rents movies, and attends community functions. He watches a lot of television and listens to music. He attends the local high school basketball and football games and an occasional track or wrestling meet, but he has no male friends and so attends most of these events by himself. He is lonely but won't admit it or seek out counseling.

Darren is too fearful to engage in any new interest; he feels too vulnerable to try something that could be difficult and prove embarrassing or could possibly end in failure. He seems unaware that most people try one thing for a while, then give it up and do something else, but they don't feel like failures. They may take a couple of classes on refurnishing furniture and then start to work on a dresser that they may or may not finish. If they do finish it, great; they have a nice piece of furniture to keep, sell, or give away and they have a feeling of accomplishment. Or if they take a class but never put it to use, they can still feel good that they learned something new and not feel embarrassed about having done so. Later they may decide to take a class on pruning their fruit trees, or join a hiking club, or take golf lessons. But Darren doesn't trust himself; he doesn't trust his abilities; he doesn't trust that others won't ridicule him if he doesn't do well; he doesn't trust that he can be successful.

None of these endeavors means the person is going to do these things the rest of his life; they are just steps in growth through which we each learn and expand our lives, our interests, and our knowledge. Darren, however, sees all of this as too threatening and a waste of time. He is an LSE sufferer who, because of his fear and anxiety, has become rigid and uninteresting, thus lessening the possibility that he will ever form an intimate relationship. He will not take a class unless he thinks he is going to make good use of the information, probably for the rest of his life. He is fearful that he cannot do what will be expected of him in the class or activity. He is rigid, fearful, and doesn't know what's normal. Furthermore, he is bright but doesn't know it, he has talent but is too fearful to use it, and he has little encouragement to live his life differently. He has succumbed to the feelings and characteristics of those who suffer from low self-esteem, settling for less than is possible, and playing it safe.

When a person engages in opportunities, he grows socially. When he avoids participation in anything beyond his normal work and home routine, however, he becomes stiff and awkward in social settings. Thus, as with any skill, the more we practice, the better we become. But how do we get to the point of trying these new activities, learning these new skills, or interacting with people beyond casual conversation if we don't trust our ability to hold our own in these situations? This is Darren's dilemma.

Many LSE sufferers become lethargic and remain under-achievers, too fearful and depressed to attempt changes in their lives that might prove to be mistakes and that might make their lives even worse than they are now. Desperate to protect themselves, they become rigid and closed to different perspectives and new possibilities; this then elicits more criticism for the lack of progress in their lives. As if stuck in a time warp, their lives change little over the years as they stick to what is familiar.

Oliver

As the months and years go by, Jenny's friends listen to her dissatisfaction with Oliver's unwillingness to make a commitment to marriage and the future, and they encourage her to leave him. Jenny loves Oliver, and she realizes that he struggles with the whole idea of trusting someone after his mother deserted him and he then suffered the loss of his father to depression. Oliver has never had a relationship with his father since he went to live with relatives, though his father has since recovered and has tried to reunite with him. Jenny wonders if he ever forgave his parents, if he could then learn to trust again. She decides the time has come to confront him with her decision to leave him if he doesn't make some changes.

After the dinner dishes have been cleared away that evening, Jenny tells Oliver that she would like to have a talk with him. Oliver gives her a puzzled look and then says, "Okay, what is it?"

"Let's go into the living room where it's more comfortable, Oliver," Jenny says, leading the way. Once there she looks him in the eye and softly begins, "Oliver, you know how important it is to me that we get married and how much I want to have a family. Well, we haven't discussed this for a while, so I wonder if you are any closer to wanting the same thing or if you don't want to ever get married. Or maybe you don't want to marry me? And, before you respond, I want you to know that it's time for us to make a decision about this. I love you, Oliver, but I'm prepared to end this relationship if you don't want to marry me. That isn't what I want, but I'm not getting any younger and we have been together nearly five years now. It's time to do something."

"Well, it sounds as if you've already made up your mind to leave," says Oliver defensively. "Isn't that what you're really saying, that you're going to bail out on me?"

"That isn't what I said, Oliver. Don't twist my words. I want to stay with you, but I can't do it if you can't make a commitment to our future. You have to take some responsibility here, too."

"Oh, so now I'm twisting your words," says Oliver, veering off the subject. "If you have such a negative view of me, you should leave." He can't believe that he hears himself almost pushing her out the door.

"Don't do this, Oliver. We need to be able to face this issue. I know you have difficulty trusting. I know you don't want what happened to you and your father to happen to us, but I'm not your mother and you aren't your father. We are very different people and we wouldn't do what they did. I believe in you, Oliver. I want you for my husband, but you have to decide what you want. Do you want to lose what we have here, what we've built together?"

"No, but I can't stop you if that's what you want to do," replies Oliver.

"It isn't what I want, Oliver. What I want is for you to make a commitment. I want to marry you and I want to know that you want that too."

"I don't want to talk about it right now," says Oliver angrily. "You know I'm under a lot of stress at work. Why do you bring up these things when I'm already overwhelmed? Give me a break, will you?"

"I'm sorry, Oliver. But there never seems to be a time that's good for you. You always have a reason why it's not the right time."

"Well, this sure isn't it," he shouts as he rises and leaves the room.

Oliver is defensive and tries to blame Jenny, suggesting that she is insensitive to his needs when the real problem lies with him. He is avoiding conversations about important issues about which he is anxious. Oliver is fearful of his ability to make decisions, especially one that might include a permanent commitment. He doesn't trust that he will make the right decision or that he will be a good husband and father. He doesn't trust Jenny either. He has tried to only make decisions where he thought he could predict the outcome, and he has stayed at a job that is below his qualifications and abilities to be safe and not make a mistake that he will regret later and have to live with. So fearful of following in his father's footsteps is Oliver that he has become a master of excuses as to why he isn't in the right frame of mind to discuss important issues, especially those that deal with marriage and commitment.

Mark and Bobbi

Neither Mark nor Bobbi enters this relationship with unusual trust issues. Mark has seen in his work the ways people can try to take advantage of others and, of course, he knows that these people exist. He has had other relationships that have been good for a time but that have not lasted for a variety of reasons, including a relationship in which the woman person was seeing an old boyfriend at the same time she was supposedly committed to Mark. But Mark holds no bitterness and none of these relationships was ever all that important or depressing to let go of.

Bobbi has been hurt in a relationship by a man who turned out to be dishonest. She had cared a lot for him, but the relationship ended before it was six months old and she hadn't invested too much into it. She has also had other relationships that didn't work out, but she thinks of that as just being how life is. She doesn't personalize it to mean anything negative about her.

Both Mark and Bobbi pay attention to the words and behavior of each other, but neither started out being overly watchful or suspicious of the other's motivation. If one of them felt the other had lied, they would be very concerned; if one of them felt the other was manipulative, they would likely recognize it and confront it. They would see these behaviors as significant red flags and would likely break off the relationship rather than suffer later on. At the same time, they both are trustworthy, sensitive, and caring, and each recognizes these good qualities in the other.

Because people with low self-esteem have difficulty knowing who and when to trust, they often trust those who seem to take a personal interest in them, who flatter them, and who show them affection. These LSE sufferers place their trust in the person who is outwardly nice to them, which has little to do with whether the person is trustworthy. Instead, if the person responds to a need they have, they see that person as someone to trust.

Others with LSE don't trust anyone. They are suspicious, thinking everyone is out to get them, to ridicule them, or to use them. This person may outwardly act as though he trusts the other person but remain hyper-vigilant at all times, watching for signs that the partner is not trustworthy and often distorting what he sees.

◆   **A note of comparison with those with healthy self-esteem**

Trust is not as big an issue for most people who have healthy self-esteem, for they more easily recognize in others those behaviors and attitudes that are manipulative, disrespectful, and dishonest. Coming from environments where people were open, direct, and trustworthy, they more readily recognize the people who purposefully plot to take advantage of others and those who are honest and trustworthy.

Those with low self-esteem usually come from very different backgrounds, some where social skills were not taught or modeled, some where anger and sarcasm were the main means of communication, and some where parents could not be trusted to do what they said they would or even to protect their children. Furthermore, many LSE sufferers come from backgrounds where love and affection were not demonstrated and where they received little or no support, encouragement, or guidance, leaving them with only their own perceptions and with no adult to consult for verification.

People with HSE generally trust their own perceptions and opinions but often get advice from others when they are uncertain. This form of checks and balances usually prevents them from making serious mistakes or from trusting the wrong people. Without tragic events in their backgrounds that trigger overreactions like those with LSE, people with healthy self-esteem are generally able to make commitments with only a normal amount of anxiety. They are less likely to manipulate or to use others for their own purposes.

People who suffer from LSE don't often have a good support group upon which to rely for help in making decisions or thinking things through. Often the people they consider to be their friends are as dysfunctional as they are and don't give advice that is helpful or wise. Thus, the LSE sufferer not only doesn't know whom to trust but he doesn't have the resources to help him figure out if someone is trustworthy.

RECOVERY

Children develop LSE as a result of unmet needs during a critical period in their lives when healthy development requires that they be consistently affirmed, encouraged, told they are loved, and treated with respect. When this is not the case, these children question whether they are loved and begin to doubt their worth and competence. They grow up confused about whom and when to trust. When parents neglect them or abuse them, these children may withdraw from life in an effort to feel safe. When parents abandon them, they feel alone and without direction or purpose, and when parents model inappropriate behavior, they don't learn right from wrong.

When children encounter one or more of these abnormal behaviors in their early years, others are often able to recognize their lack of development. They may look and act frightened, hesitant, and unwilling to communicate or participate. Unfortunately, this often makes them the target of those peers who like to tease, harass, and embarrass other children. Additionally, their behaviors may seem strange to adults, who a may treat them as though they are weird or even mentally ill. Piling abuse on top of abuse is more than these children can handle, often causing them to retreat into silence and inactivity so that they stop taking risks in life, and where they do whatever is necessary to protect themselves. This results in retarding their personal growth and limiting their abilities and potential.

To recover from low self-esteem, we must first become aware of what it is, how it developed, how it affects us, and how it is now causing us to sabotage our own lives. This step of becoming more aware is absolutely crucial since we must know what needs to be changed before that change can occur.

Awareness requires information. Information can be gained through feedback from experts in the field, from those who've already gone through the recovery process, and from books and workshops that explain the complex details of low self-esteem. Unfortunately, while there are many books in print that deal with the subject of self-esteem, few of them indicate that the writer understands LSE or even believes that it exists as anything more than a symptom of other disorders. Additionally, many of these resources give poor or simplistic advice. Some suggest that low self-esteem can easily be altered in an unrealistically short time, and some think that low self-esteem forms at various times in life. These are all incorrect. Low self-esteem forms in childhood and is a thinking disorder in which those who suffer from it have a distorted view of themselves. Fear and anxiety are the main features of low self-esteem, and they affect everything the LSE sufferer does or says. Consequently, there is no quick fix for LSE. However, recovery **is** possible. Be sure that when you seek out information that takes these facts into account. If you seek a therapist, be sure you see someone who agrees with these facts.

QUESTIONS TO CONSIDER / THINGS TO DO

1. In what situations have you felt fearful or anxious lately?
    List these and leave space to add more information under
    each one on your list.

2. What do you think happened (the triggers) that caused
    you to feel fearful or anxious in each of these situations?
    Write these down.

3. When you think of each of these situations in which you
    now recognize that you were fearful or anxious, can you
    think of similar ones from your childhood that likely
    produced these fears in the first place? List these under
    each of the situations you wrote down for question #1.

4. If you can see the connection between what happened in
    your childhood and the situations in which you are now
    fearful and anxious, can you see how you may be over-
    reacting due to lingering pain from the past?

5. If this is so, can you see what a more appropriate reaction
    to the present situation might be rather than the over-
    reaction that is tied to the past? Write down what you
    think a more appropriate reaction would be.

6. Do you have difficulty trusting people? Who are the
    people you have the most difficulty trusting? List them.

7. Have you found yourself trusting the wrong people or
    not trusting those who later proved that they were
    trustworthy?

8. What criteria do you think you draw upon to make your decisions about whom to trust?

9. For instance, do you tend to trust those who are nice to you, who flatter you, or who want to spend time with you, or do you have some other measure for deciding whom and when to trust?

10. Can you think of situations in your childhood that have affected your ability to know whom and when to trust? Write these down.

11. Can you think of ways that you can separate your thinking about trusting today so that it is not a reaction to your past but rather is a response only to what is happening in your present life?

12. One by one, take the situations where you have made mistakes in whom and when you trusted and list the reasons you trusted this person in one column and the information that you had that should have created distrust in you in a second column.

13. Determine from this point on that you will watch for red flags, signs, and clues that a person is not to be trusted, and that you will act upon your suspicions or that at least you will talk to someone who might be able to give you reliable feedback. If you practice this guidance, in time you will be able to trust your own perceptions.

Chapter 4

Depression
and the Inner Voice

Mitch and Gary

Prone to depression and the distorted thinking that is the most prominent feature in all LSE sufferers, Mitch knows that his moods have taken a toll on his 3-year relationship with Gary. He also knows that while Gary has tried to be patient and understanding of his depression and irrational suspicions, he is becoming less tolerant of these episodes, which last for hours or even weeks.

Mitch has tried various medications that seem to help some, but he has been unable to find one that completely takes away his depression without also causing unacceptable side effects, such as hair loss, blurred vision, nausea, and headaches. What neither of the men know is that Mitch's real problem is low self-esteem and that depression and negative thinking are only the symptoms. For this reason, the medications can only give partial relief from his problem.

Here's how Mitch's low self-esteem plays out in their relationship: He feels unlovable and doubts that Gary can really love him. His self-doubt leads him to be hyper-vigilant and suspicious, and to distort what is obviously the truth. When Gary says he is going to play basketball with friends, Mitch wonders if that's where he is really going. When Gary says that the group went to a restaurant afterwards for a sandwich, Mitch imagines a quite different scenario. When Gary is late coming home from work, Mitch's inner voice goes into high gear, worrying that he has found someone else. Thus, without any substantial reason for not trusting Gary, Mitch works himself into a frenzy, convinced that he is going to lose his partner.

Each time Mitch fantasizes about a particular possibility, he becomes depressed, irrationally convincing himself that his ponderings are true. These are all examples of distorted thinking, wherein a person has certain fears, then conjures up stories that give credence to those fears, then endorses those stories as though they were fact. As the LSE sufferer goes through this process, his thoughts accelerate and become even more irrational. What's more, his fears increase and his heart races.

When this happens, the person is suffering from a self-esteem attack, and while suffering such an attack, he loses his ability to differentiate truth from fantasy. All LSE sufferers have self-esteem attacks, though the frequency, severity, and length of these attacks depend on the severity of their low self-esteem and how critical they view the threat to be.

So fearful is an LSE sufferer of being abandoned, rejected, humiliated, or demeaned that they often misread the verbal and nonverbal behaviors of others. Prior to and during the self-esteem attack, they may imagine that a person is manipulating them when they are not; they may imagine that he is laughing at them or being unfaithful when they are not, and they may imagine that she is rejecting them when they are not.

Obviously, when one partner is this fearful and suspicious, intimacy is not possible. Only when the person with LSE becomes aware that his problem stems from his past rather than from the present, can he begin to understand and correct this destructive pattern. Only when Mitch can see that his insecurity has to do with those specific incidents that formed his low self-esteem and the view he has of himself as inadequate, can he begin to separate his distorted thoughts about Gary from thoughts that are rational and factual.

The Inner Voice

Each of us has a voice in our head that talks to us every waking moment of every day. This voice produces not only involuntary thoughts but consciously derived ones as well, so that after a meeting, the voice might say, "Hey, that went pretty well. I think she liked my ideas. I think she may hire me to do this work for her." Or it says, "Wow, that was close. I almost took that guy's rear fender off. I'd better focus on what I'm doing here or I'm going to have an accident one of these days." Or "I sure feel fat in this outfit. I must have gained 10 pounds." Or "Sally wasn't very friendly today. I wonder if she's mad at me. What could I have done to offend her?" Or "How embarrassing! I can't believe I made that remark about Bill right as he was walking into the room. What must he be thinking? What a jerk I am! And I could tell he heard because of the way he looked at me. Boy, am I in trouble now!"

Then depending on how we feel about ourselves, our level of self-esteem, we will either forget about it, think about it and come up with a solution if we think it's necessary, or chew it over and work ourselves into a state of agitation, discouragement, or even despair. Those with the healthy self-esteem will likely forget about it or look immediately for a solution; those with low self-esteem will beat themselves up and become upset and only later look for a solution or not look at all.

We can't turn off the inner voice for it will always be with us. It will always be recording our thoughts and, like a printer, spitting them back out again. We can, however, learn to control our thoughts and thus our inner voice and the resulting emotions. First, we must recognize that as an LSE sufferer, we are prone to distorted thinking. Second, we must learn to sort out what is irrational and untrue from what is fact. Anyone who suffers from this problem can do this, but it takes time and diligence to master the technique; there is no quick fix.

Distorted thinking leads to misunderstandings, arguments, distrust, hurt feelings, fear, and anxiety. Such thinking can destroy budding relationships or cause long-standing ones to erode. Irrational thinking leads to negative emotions and overreacting; such thinking is not based on what is true. It is never a good thing but rather an extremely destructive tendency. Certainly, distorted thinking blocks all attempts at intimacy, for trust and rationality are necessary ingredients of a close and intimate relationship. (For more on the inner voice, read *Breaking the Chain of Low Self-Esteem,* pp. 167-190.)

The inner voice is very powerful; it is the captain at the wheel steering the feelings and actions of all people, but it is particularly troublesome for those with LSE. For instance, self-doubt is the result of Mitch's negative inner voice telling him, throughout his life, that he is unlovable. Additionally, his inner voice suggests that since Gary is becoming frustrated with his depression and episodes of irrational suspicion, he is probably out trying to find a new partner. The more Mitch mulls this over, the more likely it seems. He is now hooked into the thought and doesn't even consider that it might be an irrational one. If he were to tell this to a friend, that person might be able to point out to Mitch that there is no evidence to support his thoughts and he might be able to see the truth. Without anyone around to point out what is happening, however, and without any other resource to help him dispute the inner voice's claims, he accepts what he hears. He buys into the suggestions of the inner voice and believes it as though it were proven fact: Gary is looking for someone to replace him.

What makes it difficult to be in relationship with an LSE sufferer is that we have no idea what their inner voice is telling them. We may be sharing a conversation with them that we had at work while at the same time their inner voice is negatively critiquing what we are saying. We may be acting friendly towards someone while their inner voice is telling them that we are being unauthentic and that we are really mocking them. We may ask them for a favor while their inner voice is telling them we are manipulating them. Thus, we never really know what they are thinking or why they respond as they do and unfortunately, they are often too fearful of looking crazy or of offending us to tell us.

Jackson

Jackson has suffered from depression most of his life. His inner voice has told him how inadequate he is, how no woman is ever going to stay with him, how he is always going to be alone. He has felt helpless and hopeless to change the direction of his life.

When a person's inner voice is constantly negative about himself, it creates self-doubt and a form of self-flagellation. He becomes fearful that anything he does will end in failure. When this incredible amount of anxiety actually results in a malfunction, as in Jackson's difficulty in maintaining an erection, the devastation only serves to create even more anxiety, plus reluctance to attempt anything similar in the future. This has been the case with Jackson, who felt himself sinking deeper and deeper into despair until he met Brianne.

Additionally, because his inner voice has told him that his sexual dysfunction was highly abnormal, he was too embarrassed to research the issue, seek help, or talk to a friend, any of which might have provided information and a healthier perspective, easing his mind. Thus, his inner voice has continued to fuel runaway thought patterns that have only become more irrational and more self-destructive.

While this is true for Jackson, we see that with the understanding, sensitivity, and support of someone who cares about him, Jackson is able to finally confide in Brianne. Her response quiets his negative inner voice, replacing it with one that is more hopeful and accepting of him and his problem. With the love of one sincere person, Jackson's view of himself begins to change, enabling him to see that everyone else doesn't view him or his problem in the horrific way that he has. Without hesitation, Brianne responds with maturity, seeing a physical problem that can likely be corrected and supporting a person who is worried and hurting because he has been greatly affected by the problem. She neither feels nor indicates any repulsion or lack of compassion. In fact, she is relieved to know that this is the issue rather than that Jackson is married or in trouble with the law or doesn't love her.

So, while the inner voice can cause heartache, disillusionment, and dysfunctional behavior in an LSE sufferer, it is important to note that this voice *can* be altered. Unfortunately, however, the person suffering from low self-esteem has for so long believed his anxiety-producing negative self-statements and words of caution that he cannot do it on his own. What is needed is a therapist, loved one, or other support person who can give this wounded individual the sound reasoning and the sensitivity and caring that he didn't receive as a child, guiding him to look at himself and his options in a less distorted way and giving him hope and courage to do what is necessary to help himself.

Molly

The week following the party at her sister's, Howard once again approaches Molly at work and asks her if she'd like to do dinner and a movie on Saturday. Pleased that he has asked, she smiles at him and says quite seriously, "Yes, I would like that." Howard then asks her for her phone number saying that he will call one evening this week to discuss what movie they might both want to see and where she'd like to eat. Again Molly is pleased that he wants to make these decisions together.

At the same time, Molly feels very conflicted. Her inner voice reminds her of how her friends responded and her family ridiculed her. In fact, she has been depressed since the family fiasco. At the same time she is delighted with the attention and respect she is receiving from Howard. Pondering the situation, she decides that she may be at a point in her life when she should get some professional help. She has a feeling that she may be at a crossroads that is too important to leave to an uninformed and careless decision. She also realizes that she has no one in her life who is stable and whose opinions can be trusted.

Molly sets up an appointment with a psychologist. Once there, she can't believe her ears as she freely begins sharing her pain and unhappiness. Like a waterfall, the words gush out over the precipice and freefall to the bottom. She talks and talks about her life: her social group, her critical mother and her passive father, her jealous sisters, her disappointments, her loneliness. Now through therapy and books, Molly begins to learn that her lifestyle, attitudes, and reactions are really the result of low self-esteem. Finally, in this safe place, she can ask for help, listening with rapt attention to the feedback she receives and beginning to develop a different picture of what her life is really like as well as a glimpse of what it could be.

As Molly begins therapy, her relationship with Howard continues. She enjoys talking and laughing with him, and she can feel herself relaxing with him. Her admiration for him is growing. He is unlike any man she has known. Unlike her father, her brothers-in-law, or her friend Dan, he is thoughtful, sensitive, energetic, generous, and witty. Gradually their conversation moves from casual subjects to their opinions, ideas, and perceptions. Molly is surprised that she feels open to share her thoughts without fear of ridicule or reprisal. (For more on the five levels of communication, the highest of which is intimacy, see **Breaking the Chain of Low Self-Esteem***, pp. 146-149).*

To this point, there has been little sexual contact. Howard has not initiated anything beyond kissing and handholding, which Molly also appreciates, as it says to her that he is more interested in her as a person and companion than as a sex object, She is beginning to see Howard as quite a remarkable person.

As the time spent with Howard becomes more frequent, it also involves longer periods of time. One Sunday they spend the entire day together, driving to the beach, having lunch overlooking the ocean, walking hand in hand on the sand, and taking off their shoes to wade and splash in the waves. Later they browse through the shops, eat salt-water taffy, and reluctantly head home.

"What a wonderful time I had today, Howard!" Molly exclaims. "I don't know when I've had a better time."

Beaming at this, Howard chimes in, "Me too. You are so much fun to be with. I love the time we spend together."

Now it is Molly's turn to be pleased with the compliment, "Thank you, Howard, I really enjoy being with you too."

They drive on in silence, both deep in thought and filled with joy. To herself, Molly says, "I really like Howard. Is it possible that I'm falling in love?"

Molly continues discussing all of this with her psychologist. Feeling completely safe there, she talks about her family, her friends, and Howard. As the psychologist asks questions and gives Molly feedback, Molly begins to see how dysfunctional her friends are and she receives validation for what she has always perceived as her family's cruelty. Sadly, she begins to see how the voice in her head has programmed her to be as rude and judgmental as her family, that she has learned and is repeating the same painful behaviors toward her friends that have been directed at her. Slowly, Molly begins to be aware of the negative self-talk that has created her own jealousy and abrasiveness. Discussions with her therapist about what really matters in life and in relationships is helping her believe that Howard's qualities are pretty incredible to find in one person.

"Howard really is a nice man," she tells her therapist. "I was rude to say he is bald. His hair is receding, but no more than for most men his age. I have been unreasonably critical and insensitive." Through therapy, she is able to put aside her critical nature and see Howard as a prize; she now recognizes that she is fortunate to have his attention.

Molly and her psychologist have discussed whether she should continue spending time with her friends or if she feels spending time *with them will inhibit her recovery. Molly explains that she feels her friends are basically good people but that they have just been deeply hurt, like her. She doesn't want to desert them and she believes that she can hold her own and not let them sabotage her growth. She is enthused about the changes that are taking place in her life and hopes she can pass along some hope to her friends.*

When Molly sees her friends, they continue to be full of questions and smart remarks. They have, however, discussed between them the change they have seen in her; she seems less agitated, less abrupt and sarcastic, and even happy. They tell Molly that they think it's time they meet her new boyfriend.

Molly's inner voice confuses her at times, especially because she has people in her life whose comments mirror her negative voice and because her interaction with healthier people is limited. Howard's presence in her life, however, helps her re-establish her equilibrium, so she can sort out what is and isn't the truth, what is and isn't appropriate.

Her relationship with Howard has also been an impetus for seeking therapy. She realizes that he is a quality person and she admires him very much. He comes closer to being a potential life partner than any man she has dated, and she doesn't want to sabotage that possibility by being unable to match his level of emotional health. Because of Howard's loving and supportive behavior toward her, she has been able to initiate a therapeutic relationship with a psychologist who is helping her more than she thought possible. As she grows and changes, so does her perspective about the future, and she now believes that she has the potential to have a better life than she had previously thought.

Jake

Jake searches the shelves of a bookstore for information on self-esteem. He looks through several books, selects two, and then sheepishly approaches the checkout counter. The people working there, however, are neither interested in—nor critical of—their customers' selections. They are just paid to do their jobs. Deidre had offered to go with him and to purchase the books for him, which he thought was very sweet, but Jake was determined to take full responsibility for doing whatever was necessary to once and for all get some insight into how to alter his irrational thought patterns. He knows that the voice he hears in his head is his mother's, repeating her critical comments and attacking him over and over.

There are times, although infrequent, when Jake can actually see the full picture, how his mother programmed him to question his manhood and worth and to be suspicious of a woman's declared devotion. However, at other times he is hooked back into believing her chastisement and to feeling hopeless. Right now, however, Jake is in a good space. He takes his change from the cashier and, with the books under his arm, leaves the store and walks to a nearby park where he plans to spend the afternoon reading.

That evening, after three hours of reading and reflecting, Jake initiates a conversation with Deidre about his thoughts, saying, "I'm really excited about what I read today. I know that this probably sounds crazy, but I have already gained a tremendous amount of insight about what low self-esteem is and about how it's affecting me. It's as clear as can be that I really do have low self-esteem. A part of me is embarrassed to say that as it seems so unmanly, but I've got to get past the humiliation, because it's true. I have low self-esteem."

Deidre knows how hard it is for Jake to say this and she is pleased that he can. She knew what he was doing that afternoon or at least what he had planned to do and she saw that he had come home with books, but she has refrained from asking questions for fear of upsetting him. Now that he has opened the door, she says, "I do understand how difficult it must feel to you, but having low self-esteem isn't any more your fault than if you had diabetes or thyroid problems. And it's wonderful that you are facing it. I'm so proud of you!" She reaches over and takes his hand in hers. "Do you want to talk more about it?"

Smiling back at her sheepishly, he responds, "Yes. Yes, I do want to say more, if you don't mind."

"I don't mind at all. I'd like to hear whatever you feel comfortable sharing with me."

"Well, first of all, I see that I am programming myself to be miserable. Not that I know what to do differently yet, but I can see that I keep my doubts and suspicions going by ruminating about my issues and by talking myself into really irrational thinking. Then I feel so frightened, miserable, and threatened that it comes out in defensiveness, rudeness, and unwarranted anger aimed at you, and for no legitimate reason."

"Wow!" says Deidre. "That's a lot to figure out in one afternoon, sweetheart. It sounds complicated to me."

"Well, it is and it isn't. But what I want to focus on right now is how reactive I am. You know, most of the time I'm not reacting to you or to anything I've just done but rather to old tapes I have in my head. I want to try to recognize this when it's happening and I want to ask you if you will help me with this. Do you think you'd be willing to do this with me, if I explain what I need from you?"

"Anything, Jake. I'll do anything that I can. How can I help?"

"Well, I'd like you to help me see when I'm overreacting. Then of course, once I'm aware that I'm doing it, it will be up to me to do something about it: shut my mouth, leave the room, go for a walk, whatever works."

"Would you want me to say something?" Deidre is sincere in wanting to help. "What could I say that wouldn't make things worse at the time? And would we have a signal between us for when we are out in public? What do you suggest?"

"Let me think about it," says Jake, "And another thing. I've decided to contact the psychologist that you mentioned who specializes in self-esteem recovery as well. I know from what I've read today that I can't do this on my own, even with your assistance. The books recommend that getting into therapy and a recovery program will make the process go faster. For now, I just want you to know what I'm going to be working on. I know I can't change these patterns overnight. I just hope you can be patient with me while I find my way."

"Of course, sweetheart. I want to support you and do whatever I can. You'll just have to give me some direction as to what would be helpful. Most of all, Jake, I want you to know that I love you and I'm proud of the steps you are taking right now. I also want to thank you for being willing to talk to me about this." Deidre has tears in her eyes.

"I love you, too," whispers Jake, choked up by her response. "I'm going to lick this for myself and for us. Thank you for being so supportive."

Deidre slides closer to Jake and pulls his lips to hers for a long, passionate kiss. Then they relax in each other's arms, both content with the dialogue they've shared.

Jake decides to take charge of his problem. Rather than continue to be miserable and blaming, he springs into action, determined to do whatever is necessary to work through his issues. With difficulty, he admits that he has low self-esteem and he tries to attack it in the same way he has tackled his career challenges: by getting information and then help from the appropriate resource, in this case a mental health professional.

His wife Deidre is supportive *and* cautious about treading beyond the boundaries he outlines. She had offered to help at the bookstore and he had declined her help. She had left him alone to do his research that afternoon. She didn't question him about it when he got home. Jake has stated that he has a problem and while she has offered assistance, she is letting him own the problem. When he wanted to share his findings, she was open but not pushy. When he asked for her participation, she readily agreed but gave him the space and time to give her further input about how that might occur. And in doing so, they shared a moment of intimacy, with Jake admitting to personal issues and talking about what he plans to do to tackle them and with Deidre listening attentively, verbalizing her support and encouragement, and stating her feelings for him. This is exactly what Jake needs to help propel and sustain his enthusiasm. As anyone knows who has been in therapy, there are stimulating insights and there are painful ones. Both have to be experienced in order to move beyond them.

Jake and Deidre have, at times, had an intimate relationship before, although at other times Jake's LSE has interfered with it. Now they have been honest and respectful and have shared their deep feelings for each other. Jake has admitted to imperfections that are uncomfortable to talk about, and Deidre has listened and praised him for his courage in doing so. Both have been vulnerable, open, and trusting of the other, the elements necessary for intimacy.

Jake is also beginning to recognize how his inner voice works and how it affects his life, though he is merely at the tip of the iceberg: If he remains open, if he continues reading and analyzing himself and his past, and if he gets into therapy, he will likely increase this awareness dramatically.

❧

Carey

Carey begins dating Dirk, and the two spend hours walking, talking, and hanging out at coffee shops. Bernice knows that her nephew is an unusually mature and sensitive young man or she would never have allowed this to happen. She also knows that he will watch out for Carey and be a good friend to her. Dirk has been at enough of the family gatherings that Carey has attended to know that she is reserved and naïve. He actually finds this refreshing compared to the girls he has known.

Dirk is also in college but unlike Carey, he has a lot of friends who gather at the same places near the campus, so the couple is seldom alone when they go for coffee. Carey likes the variety and the stimulation of being around other college students. They seem excited about life, even when they moan and complain about their classes or professors. She also likes the attention they all give her. They like and respect Dirk and so accept her as one of the group.

Afterwards, she and Dirk stroll through the campus and end up at his dorm or the library. Dirk is in premed so he has to study a lot. After seeing each other for two weeks, Carey and Dirk decide they want to see more of each other and start studying together in between classes. Otherwise, they mostly spend time together on the weekends since Carey's job requires her to work nights. Occasionally, they also have lunch together.

From the beginning, Carey and Dirk are attracted to one another. And soon after they begin dating, they begin to have some physical contact, although it is a process that takes some time to work out. At the end of their initial date, Dirk kisses her—a first kiss for Carey. Feeling awkward and out of her element, Carey is nevertheless thrilled. When his tongue enters and explores her mouth, she is startled but quickly adapts to the wonderful sensation and kisses him back. Dirk can tell that Carey is inexperienced, but just how much so he doesn't know; he tells himself to slow down. He also speaks to her quietly and directly, "Carey, do you feel comfortable with what we are doing? I like you and don't want to offend you or be too pushy."

In his mind he can hear his aunt's words to him, "You treat her with respect, you hear me?"

"I like you too, Dirk. I'm okay. Actually I do like it. Is it okay for you?"

Inside, he feels like laughing. He has never had a girl ask him if he is enjoying kissing her. He almost always likes kissing girls. Instead, he says, "Yes, it is great. I like it a lot."

After that, the couple usually spends some of their time together kissing, and each time Dirk moves a little beyond their last encounter. He kisses Carey's neck, her eyes, her ears, and from the nape of her neck down to the first button of her blouse, but no further.

Then one evening when their kissing is heating up, he runs his hands across her breasts, cupping one in each hand. Carey moans and doesn't resist. But when he begins unbuttoning her blouse, he feels her become tense. "Is this okay?" he asks. "Should I stop?"

"I think it's okay. It's just that I've never done this before. Aren't there some things we should talk about?" she then asks a bit anxiously, and then barely audible, "Like about safe sex?"

Dirk knew from the beginning that Carey is inexperienced not only in sex but in other areas as well. His aunt implied as much, and so he tells himself, "I should be the one bringing this up. I should be taking the lead in talking about this with Carey. She is probably very scared and doesn't know what I'm thinking."

Then to Carey, he says, "You're right. We should talk about this. We should talk about our relationship, about what we both feel comfortable doing with each other. And we should definitely have a clear understanding about safe sex before we get very far down that road."

"Are you sure?" asks Carey nervously, *"Is it okay that I stopped you and said that?"*

"Of course, Carey," Dirk responds softly. *"I've just never been with a woman like you. I like it that you want to talk about what we are doing."*

Carey lets out a perceptible sign of relief and buttons up her blouse. She is thankful they are in his car where it is dark because she knows her face is beet-red.

Dirk starts the car and they drive to her apartment. When they get there, he walks her to the door. But before he kisses her good night, he says, *"Carey, I don't want you to be embarrassed about what happened tonight and I won't either. Besides, I'm the one who owes you an apology for putting you in the position where you had to speak up. I'm sorry for that, Carey. I also don't want you to think I'm upset, because I'm not. My aunt told me you were special and I agree with her. You are special. And the next time we get together, we will discuss more of the issues and boundaries that are important for our relationship. You can count on it."*

"Thank you, Dirk," Carry says quietly. *"I accept your apology and I want you to know that I think you are special too. I don't know why you want to be with me, but I'm so glad you do."*

They kiss and say goodnight, and Dirk returns to his car. Afterwards, both are left with their thoughts. Dirk is thinking about what a fresh and direct way Carey has of communicating and how there is no subterfuge or manipulation with her. Carey is thinking how fortunate she is that so many wonderful people have come into her life and wonders how this could happen to someone so inadequate and unworthy. She begins to worry about how she can keep Dirk interested, fearful he will tire of her and fearful that she has so little to offer. She also begins to ruminate and to remember how badly she felt only a few months ago. She knows she must be prepared for the worst.

With her level of naïveté and her lack of experience, Carey has amazingly found, as her first boyfriend, a mature young man with healthy self-esteem. In addition, in spite of her own low self-esteem or maybe because of her fear of making a mistake, she has been motivated to initiate an intimate conversation with this new boyfriend. This relationship has the possibility of growing into a deeper one, if Carey can quiet her inner voice. The voice has settled down with her growing comfort in the emergence of her wonderful new life, her new coworkers, and Bernice and her family.

As is often the case, when stress is lowered and the LSE sufferer is surrounded by accepting and affirming people, LSE goes into a sort of remission. Even under the best of circumstances, however, low self-esteem never just goes away, but it does subside and can become inactive for periods of time. Only through a distinct process of recovery can a person get permanent control over this difficult problem; otherwise, it remains just below the surface, activated by a stressful moment, by rejection, by a harsh word or reprimand, or by some other negative feedback, real or imagined.

Now Carey's negative voice is activated. Something important is happening in her life. Someone significant has come into it. But Carey isn't used to having life go so well. She's sure it won't last. Surely it's just a matter of time before Dirk sees that she isn't good enough for him. This is how the inner voice can sabotage a person's life, for some LSE sufferers in Carey's situation would run away from this wonderful possibility. They would become so fearful and certain that they would ultimately be rejected that they would give up now rather than face whatever might come.

Jarrod

As a result of Jackie and Jarrod's problems, he is often depressed. After they have had their "make-up" session of sex, Jarrod feels happy for a while; then his inner voice takes charge, reminding him of why they had sex and of the things that Jackie does that upset him. He spends hours and hours going over and over past arguments, replaying the terrible words exchanged. At first his thoughts are focused on how poorly Jackie treats him and what that means. As his thoughts become more irrational, he sinks further into depression.

Eventually he realizes that nothing ever changes: they argue, they cut each other up with their words, Jarrod storms out, and Jackie initiates sex to appease him. They don't resolve any of their more serious disagreements; they just keep rerunning the same tape.

Jarrod tries to think through each step of their arguments. He outlines them on paper, trying to see what he could do differently to get Jackie to see how selfish and insensitive she is. He makes plans as to how he will respond differently the next time. Recognizing that his conversations with Jackie are primarily negative and therefore, he assumes, discouraging to Jackie, he decides that he will be more positive and supportive while focusing less on the negative.

That same day, Jackie calls unexpectedly to tell him that she is going to be late getting home and that he should go ahead and eat dinner. Taken by surprise, Jarrod answers with his usual sharp tongue: "And who are you having dinner with this time?" (Not "Okay, I'll see you later," or "That's fine. When do you think you'll be here?")

Jackie hears the tone in his voice and is immediately enraged. "Here we go again. Don't do this, Jarrod. Grow up and get a life."

"I thought I was supposed to have one with you, but I guess I was mistaken," he snaps back.

"I don't have time for this, Jarrod. Goodbye," says Jackie and she hangs up.

Now Jarrod is depressed. Jackie has gotten in the last word and left him hanging. He actually felt better while they were arguing rather than having her hang up on him. For a while he mopes around the house, finally fixing himself something to eat, and then sitting down at the table with a cup of coffee and his plate. As he does so, he finds himself staring at the papers lying there, the papers that he had written out just that morning, the papers that had led him to decide that he would talk differently to his wife. He had planned to be less defensive and more understanding. But now he realizes that he has failed at his first opportunity to put his plan in place. He wonders if he can really do this. Maybe he is going to have to seek help.

Jarrod sees that he and Jackie have established a destructive way of communicating. He also recognizes that they eventually make up after their fights, generally using sex to do so, and he makes a plan to change his reactions. But putting his plan into action proves to be much more difficult that he has anticipated; he finds that just wanting to change these patterns doesn't make it happen.

Because he hasn't thoroughly thought through the whole process, Jarrod isn't prepared for an unexpected phone call that instantly triggers his irrational reaction. His intentions are good, but his reactions are habitual. He will have to make a more specific and detailed plan and prepare himself several times each day—especially before he expects to interact with Jackie—if he is to be successful.

Jarrod's idea to change his reactions is a good one; however, limiting his responses will not sufficiently change the patterns that he and Jackie have developed. Jarrod is not dealing with the core issue of his low self-esteem and the irrational thoughts that accompany it. Until he can work through his past and see how this has affected his thinking, any changes he makes will only be superficial and temporary. His plan may alter the intensity and severity of the arguments, but these results will neither last nor resolve the issues that he and Jackie are so divided on.

Additionally, Jarrod's intentions seem altruistic, but in fact, are as manipulative as Jackie's use of sex. His real motivation is to change Jackie, to get her to see her own problems. He admits that he participates equally in their arguments, but he also thinks that the basic problems are hers.

Mandy and Willa

Mandy and Willa decide to eat the pizza while it's hot and to save Mandy's dinner for the next day. While they eat, Mandy shares about her frustrating day and Willa shares about her busy and exhausting one. Together they put away the food and clean up the kitchen. Then they settle down in front of the television to see if there is anything interesting to watch. Willa soon gets bored and because she's so tired, she announces that she is going to bed to read. Still feeling upset from her day at work and wanting to experience some emotional closeness with Willa so that she will feel better, Mandy decides to join her.

Coming out of the bathroom naked, she notices that Willa doesn't even look up from her book though Mandy knows she sees her. Climbing in beside her, Mandy moves close enough to be touching her partner. Willa looks over at Mandy, smiles at her briefly, whispers, "Hi," and then turns her attention back to her reading.

Mandy's level of sensitivity is now high and becoming more so every second. She scrutinizes Willa's every action, word, and movement. She wonders if something is wrong, if Willa is still upset about their argument. Wanting to feel secure and safe, she slides even closer to Willa, trying to cuddle. Willa doesn't respond. Then Mandy slides her hand over to touch one of Willa's breasts and Willa says, "Don't, Mandy. I just want to finish my chapter and then get some sleep. I'm really tired."

Mandy is immediately distraught. After being tormented all day at work, she now feels rejected by her partner. Immediately she becomes depressed and rolls over in bed with her back to Willa.

"Mandy, don't make a big deal out of this. I'm just tired," says Willa.

"Okay," says Mandy weakly, fighting back tears. She doesn't believe Willa. Instead she is convinced that Willa is angry and is punishing her. Her self-talk is running rampant, telling her that Willa doesn't really love her. In fact, why would she expect that she did? Mandy's inner voice gets more and more irrational and her depression deepens.

The moods of LSE sufferers can fluctuate from contentment to depression in a matter of seconds if their inner voice tells them one moment that all is well and in the next moment that they are being rejected, ridiculed, humiliated, criticized, or manipulated; whether or not this is really happening. Willa hasn't done anything to justify Mandy's mood-swing from feeling insecure to full-blown depression, except that Willa fails to meet Mandy's unstated emotional needs and expectations. Mandy's inner voice tells her that Willa knows what she wants and needs and that if

Willa loves her she will want to meet those needs. This way of thinking doesn't give Willa the right to attend to her own wants and needs, in this case, to finish reading the chapter in her book and then go to sleep. Mandy doesn't include Willa in the decision. She doesn't even ask a question, but instead, throws out cues that Willa is supposed to recognize and then take action to respond to, but only in the way Mandy wants. Unaware of what she is actually doing, Mandy is communicating that Willa has no choice but to do what Mandy expects of her.

If Mandy had instead said to Willa, "I'm feeling a little down tonight. Do you think we could cuddle a little before we go to sleep?" maybe Willa's response would have been different. If she had directly asked Willa if she was interested in being sexual and had given Willa the freedom to say "Yes," or "No," she might not have gotten depressed. But often LSE sufferers set themselves up by having a hidden agenda rather than bringing their needs out in the open. Often they have expectations and then their questions are really demands of the other person and not questions at all, for if they were truly questions the other person should have the right to freely say "No."

Mandy is too embarrassed to state her feelings and wishes so that Willa can freely and truthfully respond to them. Instead, she sets up a situation wherein she expects Willa to anticipate her needs; this is a test of Willa's love and devotion. When Willa doesn't recognize—or chooses not to respond to—Mandy's indirect requests, Mandy goes into a tailspin and interprets it as a lack of caring. So self-focused is Mandy that both of the partners should to be thinking of her needs and her needs alone that she doesn't consider that Willa is exhausted and has ever said so.

Darren

Darren is unaware that he is slightly depressed most of the time, though he is aware that he has suffered from severe depressive episodes in the past, usually after a relationship ended or following an incident where he felt he did something inappropriate in front of others. As a result of these situations, he has gone through life fearful and has tried to protect himself from possible ridicule or rejection by not doing anything except his ordinary routine. His inner voice constantly reminds him to be quiet in groups lest he receive negative feedback, or, worse yet, be ignored. He isn't aware of his depression, only his fear and anxiety.

One day, Darren's coworker, Sam, tells him that his wife's cousin, Katherine, is coming to town for a visit and they would like her to meet Darren. If he's interested, they would like him to come for an informal barbecue on Saturday afternoon. Katherine is about Darren's age and also has never been married. Sam explains that she is a receptionist for the front office of a cheese factory where she has worked her entire working life. Sam likes Darren and working beside him for years has known that Darren is alone and lonely. From what he knows of both of these people, Sam thinks that the work histories, education, and level of relationship experience of the two are probably similar, though Katherine has more friends and has been more social.

Darren hesitates, considering the invitation. His first impulse is to decline but he immediately realizes that if he doesn't accept the offer, Sam will know why. He will understand that Darren is too afraid to come because Katherine is going to be there. With this in mind, Darren thanks Sam for the invitation and graciously accepts. Sam says to dress casually and come by about 1:00.

All that Saturday morning Darren is nervous, but he tries to calm his fears. "What can possibly go wrong?" he asks himself. "It's just a little get-together and I know and like Sam's wife and kids, so I won't be with strangers. Katherine is just here for a visit, after all.

They just want her to have a good time. Besides, the food will probably be good and otherwise I'll be sitting here alone."

Arriving right on time, Darren is met at the door by Sam's oldest daughter, who tells him that everyone is out on the back patio. Though Darren has been there before, she leads him to the door and shouts at Sam to tell him Darren has arrived. Darren smiles awkwardly as he comes out of the house. Out of the corner of his eye he sees the two women but he focuses on Sam, who is approaching to greet him. The two chat briefly and then Sam guides Darren over to where the two women have stopped arranging the table to look up at the visitor. Looking first at Sam's wife, Darren says, "Hi," and then he looks over at Katherine, who is being introduced by Sam. The two strangers look at each other sheepishly and quickly break eye contact, with Darren commenting on how good the steaks smell and Katherine returning to her project. Inside though, Darren's inner voice berates him, "You jerk! Why didn't you talk to her for a minute? Why didn't you ask her if she was enjoying her visit or something?"

Sam says, "I'd better go check the steaks," and he starts to walk towards the grill.

Trying to retrieve the moment, Darren turns back to the women and says, "The table looks nice. Are those flowers from your garden?"

Both women look up and Sam's wife says, "Thank you, Darren. Yes, I usually have a lot of flowers for just this purpose. I love to have fresh flowers in the house and on the table while they are in bloom."

"Her garden is around the side of the house. It's quite beautiful. She keeps it immaculate," chimes in Katherine. "She has a vegetable garden too."

"Wow, that must take a lot of your time," says Darren, trying to keep the conversation going.

"Why don't you show him, Katherine?" suggests Sam's wife.

Katherine starts to blush and without looking at Darren says softly. "Sure, if Darren would like to see it."

Both of them know what is happening, but Darren tries to act nonchalant and enthusiastically he says, "I would. Let's take a look."

With that, the two of them walk across the lawn and around the corner of the house. As soon as they are out of sight, Sam looks over and winks at his wife and mouths, "Good going!" She smiles back.

Once alone, Darren and Katherine begin to relax. Both knew they were being watched and manipulated by two caring people, but knowing their intentions were good didn't decrease the awkwardness of the situation. As they wander down the paths between the flowers and vegetables, they share information about their work and their summer plans. Darren learns that Katherine has arrived two days before and is going to be here two weeks. He wonders if they will see each other again. They continue talking until they hear Sam's voice calling the kids to come out to eat and then they stroll back around the house.

While Katherine is busy uncovering salads and desserts, Darren takes a good look at her. She isn't particularly attractive, he thinks, but then maybe it's time he admitted that he isn't either. She is tall like him and slim. He has always wanted to date attractive women, but he reminds himself that his attempts to develop relationships with such women have never gone well. He likes Katherine and finds her easy to talk to. She seems to live a simple life just as he does, and when he had mentioned some of the things he liked to do, he learned she did as well.

Darren's damaged inner voice again tries to persuade him that he is going to fail, but he fights off the irrational thoughts that will surely make failure a reality. He reminds himself of some rational points as well as the distorted ones, for example, realizing that Sam is presenting him with an opportunity to meet someone he might like and that he wouldn't invite Darren to meet Katherine if he thought it would be a disaster. He also tries to squelch his inner voice by purposely telling himself that it is just a barbecue with people he knows and reminds himself not to make more out of it than that.

As a result of their inner voice, LSE sufferers often feel so inadequate that they strive to attach themselves to people who are out of their league. Thy want to be with people who are very attractive, even if they are not, people who live more exciting lives, who are popular and well-known, who dress sharp and have cars and homes that are beyond what they could afford for themselves. As teenagers, girls with LSE want to be with the captain of the football team, the homecoming king, the track star, or the guy with the flashiest car. Boys who suffer from LSE want only to date one of the most popular girls, girls who are thought to be extremely attractive, or a cheerleader. When these LSE sufferers get older, they continue to focus on external criteria rather than looking for people who share their values, interests, and lifestyle.

Being associated with attractive, popular, successful and highly respected people, those with low self-esteem feel better about themselves temporarily, as though by association they will be respected and seen as attractive and important. This is all smoke and mirrors, of course, because such a relationship can never be an equal one if one feels less adequate and less worthy than the other. Furthermore, a person's low self-esteem doesn't go away just because he has a beautiful woman on his arm or because she is the current girlfriend of a jock with a red sports car.

In the past Darren has fallen into this trap and in the process has sabotaged himself. Additionally, he has always wanted to date women much younger than he is, but his life doesn't include any of the trappings that would automatically attract younger women.

He has a good job but money is still tight; he lives a moderate but simple lifestyle, not a flashy one; he has a nice home but can't afford most luxury items; he isn't highly educated; he doesn't have any particularly appealing interests or hobbies; and he couldn't be called handsome.

Now he has met Katherine, who seems, as far as he can tell, to be friendly, pleasing enough to look at, easy to talk to, and evidently a very nice person, at least according to Sam. But can Darren change his expectations to something more realistic? Can he see beyond the surface to what really constitutes a potential friend or more? Can he let go of the nonessentials that he has always considered so necessary and instead look at the quality of the person? Can he look at the picture instead of just the frame? Darren will have to fight and eventually alter his inner voice if he is to have a chance at happiness, if he is going to change his self-defeating pattern of expecting perfection and ending up with nothing.

Oliver

Within 10 days of Jenny and Oliver's last fight, Oliver receives a phone call at home. He hasn't arrived yet and Jenny answers the call.

"May I speak to Oliver?" a woman's voice asks, sounding breathless.

"No, he isn't home from work yet. Can I take a message?" asks Jenny.

The woman on the other end hesitates and then says, "Are you his wife?"

"Well, no," Jenny answers. "Who is this?"

Ignoring the question the woman asks, "When do you think would be a good time to call back?"

"This is a strange conversation," thinks Jenny. "May I ask who is calling?" she asks for the second time.

Another pause, a sigh, and then the voice says, "This is his mother."

Jenny is shocked. She doesn't know what to say; Oliver's mother is calling after all these years.

"Are you still there?" asks the woman.

"Yes," says Jenny, almost too shocked to answer. "I'm still here. You say you're Oliver's mother?"

"Yes, and you are?" asks the other woman.

"We live together," says Jenny, "We just haven't gotten married yet." Then she adds, "I am not sure that I should be talking to you. I don't know how Oliver is going to feel about this. He should be home about 5:30. I suggest that you call back around 6:15."

"All right," says the woman. "I understand. I'll call at 6:15."

Jenny slowly sets the phone down. "What should I do now?" she thinks. "Should I tell Oliver that his mother called and is going to be calling back? Will he refuse to take the call if I do?"

But then Jenny decides that she has to tell him, that regardless of what she wants for Oliver, this is his decision to make and that first and foremost, she must allow him to make it.

Jenny is very nervous. She can't imagine how she would feel if her mother had abandoned her and was now calling after all these years. She wonders what Oliver will do, how he will react. Then she remembers that they are supposed to go to her parents for dinner. She calls her mother to tell her they can't make it, stating that everything is fine, and that she will explain tomorrow. Her mother is respectful of Jenny's boundaries and doesn't push her for more information

Pacing back and forth in front of the living room windows, Jenny waits for Oliver. Every few seconds she looks at her watch although it's a few minutes before he could possibly arrive. She just doesn't know what else to do with herself. She doesn't like being the keeper of this information. She is worried about Oliver.

When Oliver steps in the front door, Jenny walks toward him trying to look pleasant. They kiss and Oliver looks at her with concern. "What's wrong, Jenny? What's the matter?"

He can see on her face that something has happened. She isn't her usual relaxed and upbeat self, always so happy to greet him at the end of his workday.

I've poured us each a glass of wine," Jenny says. "Let's sit down on the couch. I have something to tell you."

This is not unusual. Jenny often has a bottle cooling and they frequently start their evening together with a glass of wine before dinner. Oliver takes the glass she hands him and they both sit on the couch facing each other. Jenny sets her glass down and takes his hand. Now Oliver knows something serious has happened. Jenny looks very worried. "Is she going to leave me?" he wonders. "What is it, Jenny? Tell me."

"Okay," says Jenny. She swallows and takes a big breath. "Oliver, a phone call came for you about 20 minutes ago. The woman said she is your mother."

Oliver stares at her. "Had he heard her right?" he asks himself. Then, he says, "Would you repeat that? Did you say she said she was my mother?" Oliver is incredulous.

"Yes, Oliver, that's what she said." "And," she looks him in the eye, "she's going to be calling back at 6:15."

Oliver quickly looks at his watch. It's 5:50. His mother whom he hasn't seen since he was a child is going to be calling him in 25 minutes. How often he has thought about receiving such a call, although not for the last few years. He had given up that dream long ago. Now the time has come and feelings are overwhelming him: sadness, longing, anger, hate, confusion. Looking like a lost child, Oliver reaches for Jenny and they hug in silence for several minutes.

An irrational inner voice accompanies LSE to some extent in all sufferers. Oliver's LSE was created by his mother's abandonment and his father's emotional instability, and his inner voice has told him over the years that others, especially women, are not to be trusted. This has resulted in ambivalent feelings toward Jenny, the one person who has really loved him. He has spent years fighting depression, overreacting to Jenny and others, and being defensive and withholding. Much like what happens in a near-death experience, many of these incidents now flash before his eyes. A part of him doesn't want to talk to this woman who claims to be his mother; he wants to punish her; he wants her to go away. But an even stronger part of him yearns to hear his mother's voice and he knows he will talk to her. Still, he wonders how he will react when she calls, when he actually hears her voice.

Mark and Bobbi

Mark and Bobbi both have an Inner Voice, as does everyone. Their inner voices critique the behavior of others and themselves but not in a critical way. Rather, their inner voices are primarily positive and only occasionally critical. For instance, Bobbi's inner voice says to her, "This book I'm working on is coming right along. I think it's going to be very good" or "I think I look good in this color and I should find more clothes in a similar shade."

Mark's inner voice may say to him, "I have got to get this article finished. I have some important details here that will be interesting to the public" or "I'd better give Bobbi a call and let her know that I can't meet her until later in the evening. I know she'll understand that I have to get this article written" or "I think I'd like to apply for that Asst Editor position. I guess I'll talk it over with Bobbi this evening and get her opinion" or *"I hate it that I got that speeding ticket this morning. I need to start getting up earlier so I don't have to rush to get to the meeting. Oh, well, I deserved the ticket. I was speeding."*

Additionally, because neither of them has an Inner Voice that continually demeans, criticizes, or condemns them, neither of them has suffered from depression that has interfered with the relationship. Also, neither has any physical problems that get in the way of any activities or responsibilities that either of them has.

◆ A note of comparison with those with healthy self-esteem

Those who have healthy self-esteem also have an inner voice, though theirs is not disproportionately negative. Instead, their inner voice is much more closely in touch with reality, giving them both negative and positive feedback that is generally accurate or at least the best that their intellect and senses can perceive. They do not have the negative memories of neglect, abuse, and abandonment that propel the negative inner voice of the LSE sufferer.

People with healthy self-esteem generally don't suffer from depression unless they have a chemical imbalance, a chronic type of depression. They may suffer from melancholy feelings when tragedy strikes, but they do not react to everyday disappointments, rejection, or criticism by becoming seriously depressed because their inner voice does not distort or inflate the facts the way the inner voice of the LSE sufferer does. Instead, those with HSE have a more rational way of thinking about the events of their life. They know that everyone suffers disappointment, loss, and unmet expectations; and they do not personalize them as the result of their own inadequacy or unworthiness. Rather, they realize that they do not have the necessary skills for some endeavors or that they may simply make poor choices at times that they later realize were not in line with their talents. They are also better at laying blame at the feet of the perpetrator. People with healthy self-esteem also freely take risks, make changes when it benefits their lives to do so, feel worthy and deserving of success, love, and prosperity.

RECOVERY

Medication is not the answer to overcoming low self-esteem though it may be a useful temporary tool if the person is too depressed to take the necessary steps toward recovery. Medication may also be helpful for those who have been so severely abused that their anxiety prevents them from doing the recovery work they need to do to heal their wounds. Keep this in mind because therapists will often steer the LSE sufferer toward working on the depression or anger problem, as a way to overcome low self-esteem. This is a faulty method, because they are treating the symptoms rather than the core issue, which is LSE.

Learning to control the inner voice is the real goal in recovering from LSE. And while that might not sound too complicated, it is a most difficult task to accomplish. Keep in mind that regardless of when you first become aware of your LSE symptoms, low self-esteem forms in childhood. The truth is that at whatever age a person begins the recovery process, that age measures the number of years their lives have been under the power and control of the negative inner voice. In other words, their inner voice has had that many years to influence every word and every decision they have made. It will take time to alter this, but it is, indeed possible and many have recovered to such an extent that their LSE no longer controls their lives and only rarely provokes irrational thoughts. Unfortunately, 100% recovery is impossible for there is no way to permanently erase the memories of neglect and abuse, but recovery is possible to the extent that the LSE has few negative reverberations that affect our lives.

QUESTIONS TO CONSIDER

1. When was the last time you felt depressed? How often do you feel depressed? Write down your answers.

2. In what situations do you get depressed? Write down your answers.

3. How long do your depressive episodes usually last?

4. What methods have you tried to get yourself out of depression?

5. Which have been most effective? For instance, does it help to spend time alone? To call a friend? To read a book? To do an activity with others?

6. Are you aware of your negative inner voice, your negative self-talk?

7. How often do you think that you make negative statements to yourself about yourself?

8. Do you ever confide in others about your perceptions as a means to validating your inner voice?

9. Do you feel you have anyone in your life that you could talk to about your thoughts?

10. Do you think you have low self-esteem? Have you thought so in the past?

11. Have you ever tried to get help in overcoming your low self-esteem? If so, what was the result?

12. Are you willing to do more to overcome your low self-esteem? If so, what do you think you would be willing to do?

Chapter 5

Repeating the Past

Cheryl and Tom

Cheryl and Tom have been married for two years. When they were dating, Cheryl, who responds to her LSE by being quiet and submissive, thought that she and Tom were as close as any two people could be. She realizes now that that was only because he was managing to control his temper for the short period they knew each other before they got married. Now she sees he had fooled her.

Once they got married, he changed. Whenever he doesn't like something she says to him, he uses his temper to intimidate her into backing down and overlooking his behavior. Additionally, Cheryl had not realized that Tom drank so much; but events since then made it apparent that he had curtailed that behavior as well, hiding his drinking by only drinking excessively with others or at his home when she wasn't around. Now he has a can of beer nearby most of the time.

Cheryl doesn't like it that Tom stops by the bar on his way home and she has told him so. Tom may care what she thinks, but alcohol is his master; it is controlling his life. And he doesn't want to hear about it from Cheryl. When she brings it up and does so quietly, he rages at her, frightening her back into submission. Cheryl cannot believe that she has made this mistake, for her own father was an alcoholic. She sees now that she has replicated her parents' marriage. Like her mother, she defers to her husband, having dinner ready late enough so that he has time to go to the bar first, only occasionally confronting him and then with no authority, and giving up on her complaint when he gets angry. Like her mother, Cheryl has become emotionally abused; she isn't willing to consider, however, that he would ever strike her. When she watched her father beat her mother, she had vowed to never be with a man who mistreated her. Now she is with Tom who emotionally abuses her, stomping on her feelings and letting her know that she is no longer a priority.

Sadly, Cheryl realizes that what she took as closeness and intimacy when they were dating was really great acting on Tom's part. From her perspective, he had carried out an Oscar-winning performance, while she had been the ignorant and needy girl too mesmerized by his good qualities to recognize his bad ones. Certainly there had been red flags. She had seen him fly off the handle a couple of times at his brother, and he had always suggested that they go to dinner someplace where he could have a drink.

At this point, their fights have become increasingly bitter and frequent and Cheryl is beginning to be afraid of him physically. In the past, she would never have believed that Tom might hit her; now she isn't so sure. She has tried everything she knows to do, suggesting they go to counseling, suggesting he get help for his drinking, trying to talk to him about why he drinks. No matter what she tries, the end is always the same: rage and bitterness, followed by silence.

Cheryl decides there is only one thing left to do: She must leave. She was mistreated by her father, and now she is disgusted that she has allowed it to happen with a husband. She has seen several women in similar situations who have stayed, ruining their lives. She is determined that she will not be one of them; it is time to stand up for herself. She always told herself that she would never be like her mother, but she finds she has become a carbon copy of her anyway.

Cheryl begins thinking of whom she might contact, where she might go. She has about $20,000 in a savings account from before they were married, so she knows she isn't destitute. They agreed when they married that this would be her money and she decides she won't take anything out of their joint savings. After much thought, she calls her friend and college roommate, who lives in another state. She feels that if she is going to leave, she'd better put some distance between her and Tom. She wants to go somewhere that he can't find her because his reaction will be rage and humiliation; Tom has often said that no one humiliates him and gets away with it. Having his wife leave him will be a sledgehammer to his ego, and it will definitely activate his own low self-esteem.

When Cheryl calls, her friend welcomes her with open arms, saying, "How soon can you get here?"

Next she calls an attorney and sets up an appointment for the following day. Finally, she calls her brother, the one family member she can trust, the one person who has encouraged her to get out of her marriage for over a year. She knows he will support her, will help her get her things together and into storage, and will keep telling her she is doing the right thing when she begins to falter. She decides she won't tell her parents until the day she leaves town and that even then she won't tell them where she is going. They can contact her on her cell phone if they need to.

Cheryl and Tom are perfect examples of LSE sufferers repeating their pasts. Cheryl swore she would never be like her mother, that she would never be with a man who mistreated her. Then she jumped into a marriage with Tom after such a short dating period that he was able to be on his best behavior, camouflaging his true self. Although she was familiar with the behaviors that often go along with alcoholism, Cheryl ignored signs that there might be problems. In addition, Tom only revealed as much about himself as he thought would be impressive—or at least acceptable, so Cheryl didn't see the real man she decided to marry.

Tom comes from an abusive, alcoholic background, where his parents were divorced. Cheryl has only met Tom's mother, who lived alone, held a full-time job, and owned her own home. She has always been very nice to Cheryl. Tom has never talked about his father only sharing that he and his mother had had a messy divorce and that he hadn't seen his father in years. He didn't tell her that his father had once been in jail for robbing a liquor store and had been falling-down drunk the last time Tom had seen him.

Both Tom and Cheryl have grown up in alcoholic homes. Both were verbally abused and neglected by their fathers. Both wanted a better life but didn't know how to make better decisions. Both wanted to be different from their parents but have replicated their behavior just the same.

This is one of the complexities of LSE. The person with LSE has in some way been mistreated in her early years, yet this mistreatment is all she knows. She doesn't know what steps to take to make her life turn out differently so all too often she simply repeats what she knows, unconsciously mirroring the life of the parent she identifies with.

Noisy and Quiet Reactors

People with low self-esteem often act—and react—in extreme ways. Some are so motivated by fear that they tend to hold in their opinions and their responses, trying to be invisible so as to avoid criticism, ridicule, or any other negative attention. They want attention but their experience is mostly one of painfully receiving feedback that focuses on their weaknesses or failures. They don't know how to get positive recognition so they avoid trying altogether. They become Quiet Reactors, responding to questions, confrontation, or comments with as few words as possible and always looking for a way to escape the situation.

Quiet Reactors are all too willing to defer to others their responsibility to be open and honest about their feelings or to problem-solve. Instead, they are so consumed with irrational thinking and so bound by fear of rejection that their feelings take precedence. Preoccupied with themselves and with their own needs and concerns, they refuse to deal with problems directly and in a timely manner, wanting to postpone or ignore any interaction that might be negative. After many such incidents where their partner has had to repeatedly initiate resolving problems and then been turned away, the partner's patience tends to wane and instead of remaining long-suffering, the partner becomes critical, pushing the LSE sufferer even further into depression and withdrawal.

Some partners are willing to probe their Quiet Reactors for answers as to what has upset the LSE sufferer, but many are not. And even those who are willing tire of it after a while, seeing the LSE sufferer's behavior as wimpy, selfish, immature, and even disgusting. Even Quiet Reactors themselves are not very tolerant of this behavior in others, for it's difficult to have a relationship with a person who is so withdrawn or self-absorbed that they are not readily available to deal with life's frequent challenges. Additionally, people tend to be intolerant when they either consciously or uncon-sciously recognize in others those negative characteristics that are true of themselves as well.

Unlike Quiet Reactors, who are more likely to be introverts than extroverts, Noisy Reactors are quite the opposite. Their voices can often be heard above the others in the room. Like Quiet Reactors, they crave attention, but Noisy Reactors try to get it by pushing themselves, their knowledge, their ideas, and their energy onto others. They may jump into conversations before they have fully grasped the drift or, in their enthusiasm and need to be noticed, they interrupt others or talk over them. They may also try to get attention by dressing in unconventional and flamboyant clothing, or by being the clown of the party. Like Quiet Reactors, Noisy Reactors have not learned the social skills that readily elicit the acknowledgment and respect they so desire. They may even watch others to see what they do to get noticed and then try to mimic what they've seen. But because this behavior is forced and unnatural to them and because they do not know when or where to use these behaviors, their attempts to be funny or clever only look stiff, out of place, or strange.

Noisy Reactors can be intimidating when they are respond-ing to confrontation. Even when challenged in a gentle and sensitive way, the Noisy Reactor usually responds with defen-siveness, anger, and blaming, unlike the Quiet Reactor who is prone to assume responsibility for the problem—whether or not it's her fault—and then shrink away in shame. The Noisy Reactor seems to know only these ways of reacting. He cannot cope with hearing that he has done yet another thing wrong, has disap-pointed someone, or has failed to do something that was expected of him. His immediate reaction is to protect himself from more abuse by justifying his actions and deflecting the blame elsewhere.

Just as Quiet Reactors can become annoyed and intolerant of others who have low self-esteem, so too Noisy Reactors can become impatient and critical of their fellow LSE sufferers. Thus when two people get together who both have low self-esteem, the smallest disagreement can erupt into a volcano or a standoff of silence, with no one listening and both distorting what is being said. At these times, each is caught up in their own issues, their own irrational thinking, and neither is very sensitive to the other. Until one or both of the pair gets into recovery, these relationships are often full of chaotic and destructive behavior.

Both forms of reacting are equally destructive to the person doing them. Both alienate him from others, and both are ineffective in helping him get what he wants. These reactions are a part of how LSE sufferers continue to sabotage their lives.

Jackson

Jackson is frightened but so relieved to finally have his problem out in the open and so thankful that the person he revealed it to has responded so well. "Brianne must truly love me," he says to himself. "She didn't even hesitate to be right there beside me once she knew the truth."

"Still," he thinks, as he gets ready to keep his doctor's appointment, "she may change how she feels, depending on what the doctor tells me after the tests."

As Jackson drives to the medical clinic, he becomes aware that he is sinking back into his negative thinking, and he tells himself that he has to break this habit of looking at everything through such clouded lenses. Since he and Brianne talked, he has been more aware of how long he has had this problem without doing anything about it. He credits this to his negative attitude and to feeling that he is hopelessly inadequate. He realizes that if he hadn't met Brianne, he would still be repeating his past behaviors of running away from the unknown at the first sign of difficulty.

Jackson is finally taking some action to alter his destructive habit of coming to conclusions without corroboration and then acting on his faulty deductions. Up to this point, his problem—and his assumptions about the problem—have run his life. If he had talked to a professional or friend in the past, his life might have taken a different path. His problem might have been resolved or, if not, he might have gotten an understanding of other options for changing the result. In other words, there are other remedies for erectile dysfunction that he could have considered. Things are only changing now because he has taken the risk to be truthful with the woman he loves.

Jackson is a Quiet Reactor. When women have rejected him in the past, he has shrunk away in silence and shame, wishing he could avoid ever seeing them again. In each instance, he didn't even return their belongings or care if he got his own back if it meant that he could circumvent a meeting. Instead, if one demanded that he return her things, he would call and leave a message while she was at work suggesting that she leave his things somewhere he designated and that he would leave hers there in exchange. This way he could avoid even talking to her again.

Jackson is going to take the needed medical tests to determine his condition, after which he will confer with the doctor and get recommendations for treatment. In the meantime, Brianne will be there to support him and Jackson will be doing his best to quiet his inner voice and to communicate with her.

Hopefully, the results will prove a means to helping Jackson change his perception of himself and, ultimately, his life.

Molly

Molly decides that she would, indeed, like her friends to meet Howard. But first, she knows she must explain some things to him. She feels it is time for her to describe her family, her childhood, and her friends; there is so much about her that he doesn't know and if this information is going to change his opinions or feelings about her, she wants to know now. She wants Howard to know about the baggage she carries from her past and that she has not always been as consistently nice a person as she has become with his influence.

That evening Howard comes to her home and after getting them each something to drink, she tells him that she needs to talk to him. He can tell she is serious and says, "Okay. What is it, Molly?"

"Howard, I need to tell you about the background I come from and what my family is like. They aren't very nice people."

Howard nods and says, "I'm interested in anything you want to tell me, Molly, but you needn't feel that you have to tell me anything you don't want to."

"No, Howard, I think you need to know more about me before you get in too deep," Then, leaving out the part about how her family had cackled when she talked about him, she describes her mother, father, and sisters, and how angry, bitter, and rude they are. She tells him about her abusive childhood and how she fears she will be just like her mother and siblings as she gets older.

"I'm so sorry that you had such a sad and painful childhood, honey," he says using this term of endearment for the first time. "But

you could never be like the women you are describing. You are much too honest, too sweet, too conscientious, and too sincere. There is nothing about you that could even resemble them."

"Oh, Howard, you are so wonderful, but I have been like them. I was becoming them before I met you. I have friends who talk to each other in the same ways and I have often joined in. I'm embarrassed to tell you this, and I've changed the way I'm interacting with them now, but hard as I tried to resist, I was on my way to being exactly the same as my family. But being around you, I feel so different. I feel respected; I feel worthwhile and cherished. I don't want to be that old way anymore. Your kindness and support brings out the best in me, Howard."

"It's understandable, sweetheart, that you would pick up the behaviors that you saw and lived with as a child," says Howard softly. "I can't imagine you being anything other than how I see you today. You may be a little rough around the edges coming from that environment, but all that matters to me is that you feel good about yourself today and in the future. I don't care about, nor do I need to know, everything you feel you have done wrong in the past. As far as I'm concerned, it doesn't matter. You know I've been married, and I'll tell you, it wasn't a pretty marriage. I'm sure you've had other relationships but we don't need to focus on the past, and we don't need to do today what we've experienced in the past. And if you feel you are a better person today because of our relationship, then thank you; I know that the same is true for me as well. You make me want to be the best I can be; you make me a better man."

As Molly had hoped, Howard is very understanding and nonjudgmental. She thanks him for these fine qualities and then goes on to tell him about her friends. Then she says, "My friends would like to meet you. I can't guarantee how they will behave and if you don't want to, I will understand."

"No, of course, I'd like to meet them. And don't worry, I won't be offended if they say or do something that you think is rude, so don't

*feel like you have to coach them ahead of time or feel you have to pro-
tect me. I think it's a great idea. What do you suggest we do with
them? Dinner? An activity?"*

*"How about pizza and bowling?" she chuckles, then says, "I don't
even know if you bowl. Do you?"*

*"Well, I haven't in a long time, but I'm game to try. Let's do it—
and soon."*

Molly is fearful of repeating her past, of growing old and finding she has become as bitter as the other members of her family.
Being aware of this possibility, however, she is more likely to face
the issue head on. She is open to recognizing the ways she may be
duplicating their behavior and so, if she stays cognizant of it, she
will likely avoid the same outcome. She is a Quiet Reactor, but
Howard is also quiet and sensitive, and he draws her out when she
seems deep in thought, mulling over all that is changing in her
life. He frequently asks what she is thinking, asks if there is anything she wants to talk about, and he is a good listener. If she
actively pursues learning about low self-esteem, she will be able to
see even the subtle ways in which LSE sufferers mimic the attitudes and behaviors of those whose influence created their LSE in
the first place.

Molly has her insight on her side. Unlike her sisters, she has
known that her family is dysfunctional; she has experienced their
cruelty and their bitterness; she has felt their disappointment and
their envy. She has also known that she doesn't want to be like
them, that she doesn't want to repeat her past, but until Howard
came into her life, she didn't have anyone with whom to compare
their behavior so as to actually see how to be different. Now
Howard consistently models mature, sensitive, and caring behavior, which helps Molly to have both an incentive to change and a
sense of direction.

Jake

Like an addict coming off of drugs, Jake's emotions fluctuate. One minute he is excited to know that he is finally able to identify his core issue. The next he is angry that he has this problem and feels as though he'd like to strangle his mother, even though she is no longer alive. He thinks of what he could do that would be symbolic of expressing his anger at her for leaving him such a legacy. "Maybe I will pile gravel on her grave," he thinks. "How could a woman be so disturbed as to purposefully take her bitterness out on her own child, hoping his life will be as miserable as hers had been?"

But Jake recognizes some differences. At least he doesn't think that he has her ruthlessness or her desire to hurt others. At least he has made something of his life. He is determined to no longer let his past control his present or direct his future. He has met other challenges and he is convinced he can be successful in this one as well. He does regret, however, that he has been too stubborn to do this sooner. Then he faces the truth: "I thought I was too damaged to be fixed. What has changed my mind?" he asks himself. "I guess it's Deidre. She means too much to me to let this problem ruin what we have. I guess I just haven't felt until now that what I have is too important to lose."

Jake has turned his anger on himself, but he is now turning it directly toward his mother, where it belongs. Children, even adult children, have difficulty blaming their parents for what was obvious poor parenting and even deliberately destructive behavior toward them. Instead, they believe that the parent wouldn't have mistreated them if they hadn't in some way deserved it. Once an adult realizes that he has LSE, he also begins to recognize why he has it and who did what to him to cause it. There is in this process a defining moment for the LSE sufferer, when he must either point the blame toward his persecutor or continue to view himself as incompetent, inadequate, unworthy, or unlovable.

Jake wants never again to sink into depression as he has in the past. He has been a Quiet Reactor, sulking and withdrawing when he is upset. He has moped and stewed over distorted thoughts and irrationally based scenarios. He has refused to talk about what he was feeling, leaving it up to Deidre to drag his thoughts out of him, rather than taking the initiative and responsibility of sharing his feelings and concerns with her. If he now wants to alter his depressive pattern, he needs to take responsibility for sharing his feelings on a consistent basis, sorting out which feelings are related to situations and behaviors in the present and which are feelings related to his past. He will have to be accountable for learning to do this rather than placing blame on Deidre where it is not deserved or warranted.

Carey

Carey is naïve and has little experience in relationships. As a result, she is often more frank and outspoken than most people who have learned to soften or mask their true thoughts and feelings. She is unaware of the games people play in relating to others and she doesn't know how to be anything but forthright, which Dirk finds unusual but charming. He thinks that Carey's sincerity and genuine desire to be honest are two of her many excellent qualities. Never before has he been able to fully relax with a girl, knowing that what she says is what she means.

Carey is equally enamored of Dirk; he is such an enigma to her, so totally opposite from her father and her older brothers. Carey has often wondered if she would ever date or get married, and she probably would have disregarded the possibility altogether if it had not been for her younger, sensitive brother, Joey, and two male teachers who enabled her to see that all men were not such jerks.

Now Carey realizes that her life is different from what it was less than a year ago. She has friends, college, a job, an apartment, and a boyfriend; most importantly, she feels loved. She realizes that her worst fear of replicating her past is unlikely, that becoming her mother is not going to happen. For, unlike her mother, Carey has already formed rela-tionships with healthy people; she is self-sufficient and she is dealing with life's challenges as they come.

Carey has not developed some of the bad habits she might have if she had had more interactions with others. She is not competitive, jeal-ous, sarcastic, or rebellious, instead, she is socially inexperienced causing her to feel anxious and look awkward. She learned to stay out of the way of her older brothers and her father, but she had her brother, Joey to spend time with. With both of them introverts by nature, they talked deeply about their feelings, their interests, their futures. They seldom argued or even disagreed but, instead, formed a camaraderie that they both knew would last forever. Quiet Reactors, both of them, their reactions were mostly internal and ones that others might never notice. Still, they each recognized when the other was depressed and did their best to bolster each other when necessary. Carey tried to take some responsibility for her younger brother's care and felt rewarded for her efforts. Together they seemed to assess their home situation with a detachment that served as a shield from the some of the verbal and emotional abuse they experi-enced. They had each other with whom to process the events at the end of each day. They pushed and prodded each other in their schoolwork and intellectual achievements, celebrating together when one or the other scored high on a test or got a positive comment from a teacher.

They explored nature together, read and discussed books and television programs, even attended an occasional school function together. Neither had other friends. At school Joey was the target of bullies because he was small. Carey hadn't been able to make friends though she had tried. She and Joey just had each other.

In many ways, Carey seems very mature for her age, mainly because she had to fend for herself emotionally while growing up. Many girls would not have bounced back this way from a home such as the one she grew up in, but Carey knew early on that her life was in her hands. And while she didn't see into the future as far as marriage, she did know that she was smart and that she could learn faster than most of her peers. She not only excelled in school but she devoured every book and magazine she could get her hands on, and on a variety of subjects. The confidence she gained from her passion for information and her relationship with Joey now helps her in new situations and has impressed Dirk.

Carey thinks about what she wants in her relationship with Dirk. She knows that this weekend they will have a very important talk. She wants to be clear in her own mind about how she feels and what her limits are. She decides to talk to Bernice, even though she is Dirk's aunt, as Bernice is the only adult whose input she respects and trusts.

Carey is a Quiet Reactor. As Dirk has easily recognized, it is unlikely that Carey will whine and carry on if she doesn't like what is happening. Instead, she regularly and directly says what she feels needs to be discussed. She doesn't mince words, though she is sensitive and thoughtful in her remarks. For the most part, Carey is more assertive than most Quiet Reactors; this is largely true because she has decided she doesn't want to make any major mistakes in her life as the result of her naïveté.

Jarrod

Recently Jarrod has seemed to get some insight into how he is contributing to those ridiculous and confusing fights with Jackie during which they both spin out of control and become rude and abrasive. He sees how they are both so busy being defensive that they act as though they don't care for each other. He is determined to change his part and to treat Jackie the way he wants to be treated. Mostly, however, he is thinking that if he is nicer to her and doesn't get defensive, she will quiet down and listen to what he has to say. Mostly he is thinking of what he can do to get what he wants.

Jarrod decides to see a counselor to get some help with his domestic situation. "Maybe a therapist can help me figure out how to help Jackie see what she is doing," he thinks.

Jarrod and Jackie are both Noisy Reactors. In fact, they are instant reactors. They leap before they look, and they bark and bite at the same time. In other words, they talk before they think and their words are simply reactions to the other person rather than responses that they have given any thought to. They both get defensive before they even hear the other out. Neither considers the content of the other's complaint and neither considers the other's feelings. Instead, they are both so focused on having their own needs for security met that they ignore the other.

This is not an intimate relationship, and unless one or both of them can become more stable and less self-focused, it is unlikely this relationship will change—and it is doubtful that it will last. Jarrod plans to seek counseling, but it is yet to be seen how dedicated he will be to the process or how determined he will be to take responsibility for his behavior if Jackie doesn't make changes.

Both Jarrod and Jackie are repeating their pasts. Both have come from dysfunctional homes, Jackie from an abusive one and Jarrod from one where he was neglected. Neither of them has seen appropriate modeling of how to balance love and responsibility between partners, and neither knows how to build intimacy. Even their sexual relationship, which is often fulfilling, is based on deception and manipulation. Jackie uses sex to defuse the tension following arguments, and Jarrod uses sex to convince himself that Jackie really loves him.

Mandy and Willa

Willa is becoming more and more aware of how her behavior towards Mandy has been much like what she experienced in her childhood home. There, her parents often argued, spewing out rage and hatred at one another. These fights usually ended up with her father hitting her mother or her mother throwing things at her father. Fortunately, they never seriously injured each other because they were usually too drunk to deliver a good punch or hit their target.

One Saturday morning Willa drives to a nearby park to walk and write in her journal, telling Mandy that she needs some time by herself to think. With the sun beaming down through the trees, Willa is reminded of her safe place, the cove of trees that she had gone to when she was upset or fearful of her brother, the place where she had been able to find solace when life at home became unbearable. This feels like déjà vu; here she is again walking, sitting, and writing under a leafy umbrella, trying to understand her life and remain motivated to do what she can to improve it.

Above all, Willa wants to alter the direction of her life; she wants to change the patterns that she watched and is now repeating. She was recently amazed when she recognized that she was doing the things she so abhorred in her parents and her brother.

Willa has been discussing her difficulties with her therapy group, and they are a big support to her, and they provide a place where she must be accountable. She realizes, though, that she must have a more specific plan to work on her LSE at the same time that she is trying to change her behavior or her efforts may go unrewarded and her goals unmet.

Willa is a Quiet Reactor to such a point that she has been an avoider, removing herself from any environment where trouble was brewing. She realizes that she is going to have to learn to stand her ground and face the issues between Mandy and her if they are going to be resolved. She knows that she needs to become more assertive, something she has never practiced doing, but something she decides she must learn to do now.

Again, having a household in which both partners have LSE is double trouble. Both have their issues, which are similar yet different. Both have suffered from some form of abuse, neglect, or mistreatment and, as a result, both are needy. Neither has experienced a healthy family and so they have no picture in their minds of what one should look like or how it can be established. Their only frames of reference may be the few times they visited in the homes of friends or relatives or the artificial relationships they have seen on television or in movies, neither of which depict reality.

However, the couple now has a chance that they didn't have at first. That opportunity to save the relationship comes with

Willa, who has recognized what is happening. She sees not only that she is reacting to her past and repeating what she learned there, but she also sees that she has low self-esteem, a problem that if left unchecked will ruin the love she and Mandy have for each other.

If one of the two can begin to recover from LSE, there is a much better chance that the other will as well. If one of the two takes responsibility for her actions, there is a much better chance that the other will recognize the change and want the calm assurance she sees developing in the other. Only time will tell, but with at least one person trying to break the cycle of irrational responding, arguments may be defused and both will have less of a need to be defensive.

Darren

After dinner at the barbecue at Sam's, the four adults do the dishes together, with Sam and his wife teasing each other and tossing an occasional pickle or carrot stick at the other, and with Darren winking at Katherine over the playfulness of the other two. They all laugh and have a good time. Then settling down in the living room, they talk for several hours. Though he has tried to postpone the moment, Darren knows it's time to go home. He rises, thanks Sam for the invitation and his wife for the dinner, and then turns to tell Katherine that he has enjoyed meeting her. Before he can begin, however, she stands up and says, "I'll walk you out to the car."

"Okay," he says, pleased but blushing all the same.

Turning back to his hosts, he bids them goodbye, then opens the door for Katherine.

Walking side by side with Katherine toward his car, Darren says, "I had a great time today and I'm really pleased to have met you."

"I'm glad to meet you too," she responds enthusiastically. "Will I see you again while I'm here?"

"I'd like that if you want to," Darren says. "What are your plans for the week?"

The two agree to go to lunch the next day and Darren drives home. His heart is beating rapidly. He doesn't know what to think. "Was she really interested in seeing me again? Or was she just trying to please Sam? No, I think she likes me," he thinks in amazement. "And I like her too. Wouldn't you know it that I would finally find a woman with so much in common, but who lives halfway across the country? Just my luck!"

However, what Darren also knows is that he feels like he has fit in, that he had a good time with Sam's family, that he was able to relax and be himself, a rare occurrence for him. He feels they responded to him more positively than people sometimes do. He also knows that he feels something special for Katherine; there is something between them that he hasn't felt before. He is happy that he will be seeing her again the next day.

Later that night Darren starts thinking about his past relationships and the reasons each one ended. In each case, the woman he was dating had voiced complaints and in each case, he now has to admit, he hadn't listened to her concerns. Instead he had gotten defensive and argumentative. He has thought about this off and on for several years— how these relationships had ended—but before now he couldn't admit that it was because he had been too frightened and insecure to hear negative things about himself. Suddenly he is fearful that he will repeat his pattern. He thinks about how lonely he has been. Each time before, he missed the woman for a long time afterwards. Now he thinks, "I may have another chance to be happy, but only if I do it right. Only if I'm willing to listen and change, if necessary." Darren falls asleep with the realization that he has more soul-searching to do.

❦

Oliver

Oliver breaks out in a sweat. He can't imagine what he will say or how he will react when his mother calls back. He looks at Jenny questioningly, and she leans toward him and puts her arms around him, drawing him to her. "I love you, Oliver. I'll be here with you, right beside you if it's what you want."

"Yes, please stay with me. I don't know what to do, what to say to her. Did she say where she was calling from?"

"No, she didn't," answers Jenny, "and I didn't think to ask. Do you think she might be here in town?"

"Jenny, this feels like a dream or a nightmare. I don't know which, but it's surreal. What should I do?" he asks.

"I can't tell you that, Oliver. That is up to you. I'd only suggest that you don't do anything rash right now. See what she has to say and then give yourself time to digest it. Keep the doors open, if you can, until you've had time to think and decide what you want to do."

"You're right, Jenny, I don't have to decide anything right now. I'll just see what she has to say and why she has called." Oliver pauses and then says, barely above a whisper, "I may cry, Jenny. I feel like crying now."

"Oh, Oliver, of course you do. Who wouldn't? You haven't heard from your mother since you were a child. You've suffered greatly because of what she and your father did, and now she seems to be re-entering your life. It's a shock. I can't even begin to imagine how you must feel, but you don't need to hide your emotions from her. It's okay to let her hear how you feel and it's nothing to be ashamed of."

Oliver looks at his watch again, something he has been doing about every 30 seconds. Trying to fortify himself, he pours another glass of wine, but before drinking it, he goes into the bathroom and splashes water on his face and then stares in the mirror mouthing to himself, "My mother. My mother."

Returning to the living room, he sees that Jenny is holding the cordless phone. He sits down beside her and takes a gulp of wine. They sit hand in hand on the couch and Jenny opens her mouth to say something when the phone rings. Oliver jumps, startled by this ominous ringing that he knows could signal a change in his life, reuniting him with the woman who abandoned him or, at the very least, dredging up the emotions he has tried so hard to bury and that he doesn't want to relive.

Oliver takes a big breath and picks up the phone. Bringing it to his ear, he clears his throat and says, "Hello, this is Oliver."

Oliver's life has been greatly affected by the abandonment, first by his mother and then in essence by his father too. Since then, he has had difficulty trusting others, including Jenny whom he loves and who loves him. He has been unwilling to make a commitment to her because he doesn't trust that she won't do what his mother did. And fearful of being an irresponsible parent, Oliver has denied himself the opportunity to have his own children. What he doesn't realize is that he has repeated his past by not being willing to be fully committed to Jenny, the very thing he has despised in his parents.

Also, like his parents, he has been a Quiet Reactor. He doesn't rant and rave when Jenny asks for a commitment; instead he finds a reason to put her off, saying it isn't the right time. Oliver's parents never fought openly or loudly. His mother had been unhappy but evidently she hadn't told her husband, as he seemed completely surprised when she left them. Oliver's father had been self-absorbed and he didn't have a clue that his wife was seriously discontent.

Now Oliver's life is being shaken up again. Two differences now exist, however. He is an adult, fully capable of taking care of himself and he has the love of a wonderful woman at his side to support him.

Mark and Bobbi

Like those afflicted with low self-esteem, Mark and Bobbi are also repeating their pasts. The difference is that Mark and Bobbi come from healthy environments where people were kind and supportive of each other, where children received affection and were treated with respect, and where parents were healthy themselves. In their homes no one drank excessively, no one was on drugs or in trouble with the law, and neither parent was having affairs. Their parents were middle-class people: Mark's father was a barber and his mother was a kindergarten teacher; Bobbie's father was a horticulturist and her mother gave private piano lessons. They were devoted parents, encouraging each of their children to take school seriously and to become involved in extra-curricular activities. They were socially active with other families, and the parents all had individual interests as well. They brought their children up to be independent, secure, and ambitious.

Like his parents, Mark has other interests besides his career and his relationship with Bobbi. He belongs to a chess club that meets once a month, he goes golfing occasionally with friends, he belongs to an athletic club where he regularly works out, and he volunteers as a big brother to two siblings who are without a father.

Bobbi also has her own interests, including the love of gardening that she picked up from her father. An introvert, she enjoys visiting nurseries and working in her own garden. She also belongs to a book club and volunteers to read to children who are terminally ill.

Mark and Bobbi are indeed repeating their pasts, but they the lucky because they have a background worth replicating.

Mark and Bobbi are neither Noisy nor Quiet Reactors because they "act" consciously rather than react to what others say to them. Most often they respond to others in the manner of mature adults, listening to what others have to say, considering the content of the message, and then choosing how to answer.

One day Bobbi is irritated with Mark about a statement he made in front of several couples at a dinner party and she tells him so, "Mark, I would like to talk to you about something. Could we talk about it now?"

"Sure, Bobbi, what is it?"

"Well, I'm feeling irritated with you. That comment you made about me at the dinner last night was very embarrassing. It bothers me that you would say what you did in front of other people."

Mark lowers his eyes while nodding his head. He is reviewing in his mind the statement she is referring to. Then he looks up at her and says, "You know, Bobbi, you're right. That comment was completely uncalled for. I'm very sorry I embarrassed you. It was thoughtless of me. Please forgive me for being so insensitive."

"I forgive you, Mark." Then she grins, winks at him, and says, "But don't let it happen again." Then she adds, "Seriously, though, I appreciate your response right now. Thanks for being understanding and for acknowledging that my feelings are important.

All couples have disagreements, times when one or the other is thoughtless or insensitive, times when they make mistakes or forget commitments. That's life. The problem is not that they do these things, though it affects their partner at the time. The main issue is what they do when they are confronted about their behavior. Mature healthy people take responsibility for their behavior.

They do so by apologizing and acknowledging the feelings of the other person, then by trying to do whatever is necessary to not repeat the behavior. When the other person sees that they respond in this way, they feel respected and loved. When they do not get this type of response, they tend to question how trustworthy, dependable, and sincere the other person's commitment is.

◆ A note of comparison with those with healthy self-esteem

Those who do not struggle with the memories and scars of having lived in dysfunctional environments do not have a negative past to duplicate or from which to recover; thus, this characteristic of LSE doesn't apply to them. People with healthy self-esteem are likely to look back at their pasts and have positive thoughts and fond memories. Most of what was modeled for them was normal and appropriate behavior, providing them with a foundational knowledge about loving and caring for others, raising children, problem-solving, and working together. They are much better prepared to handle life's challenges, life's inequities and disappointments, and life's benefits.

They may tend to be noisy or quiet people, but this can be attributed to their inherent nature and whether they are extroverts or introverts, rather than to being dysfunctional. Introverted households are generally more quiet and calm while extroverted families tend to include more boisterous laughter and interaction, more chatter, and more physical activity. In either case, this is not due to dysfunction, and neither is better than the other.

RECOVERY

Memories can never be erased, but they can be seen through a different perspective. The LSE sufferer can begin, through recovery, to realize that what she has experienced was not the result of anything she did or deserved. Obviously, no child deserves to be abused, ignored, abandoned, or mistreated. Instead, what has happened to these LSE sufferers is the result of unhealthy individuals, whether they were the perpetrators of these destructive acts or the caregivers who failed to protect the child. These adults may well be LSE sufferers themselves.

Both the perpetrators and those who didn't protect the child may have been mistreated and abused. However, this does not excuse them for replicating these hurtful behaviors. For once we become adults, we can no longer blame others for who we are today, only for what they did to bring us to this point. From there we must take responsibility to recover and through that process become the best we can be. Adults who were hurt as children cannot hide behind the tragic truth of having been abused or use it as a justification for equally inappropriate behavior toward others.

We do not have to repeat our pasts, yet most LSE sufferers do so, until the results of their self-sabotage and destructive behavior toward others become apparent and they decide to do what they can to recover from what was done to them.

Noisy and Quiet Reactors are just that: reactors. What they need to do is to focus on what others are saying to them. Then they need to allow themselves time to digest what is being said before they respond. They need to consider the validity of the other person's words and statements and examine themselves to see if they are acting appropriately to those around them rather than reacting as a means of defending themselves or warding off attack. Thus Reactors need to become Actors, responding from their own thoughtful choices and volition rather than as a defensive pose.

QUESTIONS TO CONSIDER / THINGS TO DO

1. In what ways do you perceive that your thinking and behavior has been the result of the dysfunctional environment in which you grew up? Write down your answers.

2. Do you think that this behavior has been detrimental to your life? If so, list as many ways as you can of how your life has been negatively affected by these specific thoughts and behaviors.

3. What have you done to alter any negative or self-destructive behaviors that have followed you from your early environment?

4. Do you feel you've been successful in your efforts?

5. List the victories you have had in your recovery.

6. List the specific behaviors you have been able to change as a result of your efforts.

7. What else do you think you could do to continue your recovery process?

8. Do you have a timeframe for moving to the next step of your recovery process?

9. Are you a Noisy or Quiet Reactor?

10. How has your mode of reacting affected your life?

11. Are you aware of how you might learn to change from being either a Noisy or Quiet Reactor?

Chapter 6

Floaters and Paddlers

Kendra and Jerry

Kendra's husband expects sex with his wife every night. He openly states that he can't sleep if he doesn't have sex-it's his "sleeping pill; he says. Of course, this means that Kendra must be available; she isn't given the choice to say "no" to this ritual. For years, she has conformed to his expectations, convinced it is her responsibility as a wife. At least that's what he pounded into her by ranting and raving early on in their marriage, when she tried to refuse to cooperate with this. Not understanding intimacy and without knowledge of what a woman could have in a good sexual relationship, Kendra was nevertheless distraught. She tried different tactics to get out of accommodating him: she would stay up feigning work that had to be done until she thought he would be asleep. But of course, he couldn't sleep! She tried the excuse that one of the children wasn't feeling well and she wanted to be available in case she was needed. She even began just spreading her legs when he got into bed and letting him do as he wanted; she didn't participate, just lay there-but he didn't care-he got what he wanted. After all, he wasn't doing it for her.

Nothing she tried worked. He wouldn't listen to her and he didn't care about her feelings. He just berated her for not getting her work done during the day, for being overly protective of the children, or trying to upset him. Beaten down over time, she decided giving in was the easiest way to cope with the situation.

Now, eleven years and four children later, Kendra has started to believe that her husband's demands are inappropriate. For years she was so isolated at home raising the children that she didn't even have anyone to confide in, but even if she had had such a confidant she would have been too embarrassed to talk about such private matters. Jerry had refused to let her work until their financial situation required she do so. Now, however, six months after taking a new job with a large corporation, she has found that women frequently share their feelings about sexual activity with one another-something that shocked her in the beginning. When she actually developed a blossoming friendship with a coworker and confided in her about her husband's expectations, the coworker said, "What a jerk! I'd tell him to take care of himself, to go masturbate. Or tell him to get sleeping pills. I wouldn't let him use me like that. You don't have to put up with this behavior."

Kendra was shocked. "You mean a wife doesn't have to do this for her husband?" she asked.

Kendra has low self-esteem. She grew up in a family that ascribed to a repressive and dogmatic religion. The adults in her family and at her church told her what to do, what to think, how to dress, how to spend her time, and with whom to associate. They frequently criticized her behavior and when she had an independent thought or disputed their views, told her that her rebellious attitude and actions were "of the devil." They drilled into her head that she had better obey them or be punished by God.

Growing up, Kendra was depressed, fearful, and unhappy. She wanted to leave home but had nowhere to go and no means of escape. Then she met Jerry, a smart-alecky kid who drove a fast car and liked to party. Whenever she had the chance, she tried to be where he might see her, and when he finally noticed her and asked her out for a ride, she jumped at the chance, knowing she would be grounded for a month and forced to do penance if her family or a church member ever found out. Jerry was smooth; he told her how beautiful she was and how attracted he was to her. He wanted sex but Kendra was too frightened and began to cry. Realizing she was a virgin, Jerry quit pressuring her, but unaccustomed to not getting what he wanted, he vowed to make her his own. Every opportunity he had from then on, he spent with her. She was so flattered and felt so loved for the first time in her life that when he said "Let's run off and get married," she screamed, "Yes." After all, this was her ticket to freedom. She wasn't able to see Jerry for who he was, a smooth-talking and selfish person, who saw her as an object that would enhance his life. All Kendra could see was that Jerry didn't criticize her all the time like those at home; little did she know that was because he was on his best behavior. He was on a mission to capture her.

When children grow up with rigidity and constant criticism in a closed environment that fosters fear of punishment, they become insecure and anxious, never knowing when they may say or do the wrong thing. Following the rules becomes crucial to survival, and enjoying independent thoughts or pursuing individual goals and dreams must be avoided. In this repressive environment, children don't feel safe and don't feel adequate about venturing out into the world by themselves. Consequently, they are prime targets for any person who wants to dominate others; they are vulnerable to someone who claims to love them.

Who could resist feeling for the first time that you have found someone who loves you? Who in Kendra's situation would be capable of making a good choice for a partner? What would the criteria be? It is most probably that she would be attracted to anyone who didn't do the hurtful things that she experienced at home. This is the rebound effect, finding someone who doesn't have the bad traits that we are trying to escape. There is no clarity to evaluate the new person on his strengths and weaknesses. There is only the ability to see that what's before us looks and feels better than what now exists. Thus when we jump from one situation to another, we generally don't use good judgment.

In Kendra's case, as in the case of most people who suffer from low self-esteem and who are from abusive and repressive environments, finding a person to run to seems to be the modus operandi, the standard procedure used to escape. The problem is that Kendra jumped from one oppressive situation into another. Once Jerry convinced her to marry him, he no longer had to be the good guy; he no longer had to act as though he cared about her or her feelings. Instead, she could now become the person who fulfilled his dreams, much like she was supposed to fulfill the expectations of her parents.

In this marriage, Jerry keeps Kendra home, not allowing her to have a job. Alienated from her family and the only people she knew growing up-her church community, Kendra is very isolated, especially after she gets pregnant and begins having children. She's too busy and tired to do anything except care for the children, attend to Jerry's needs, and manage the home. This is how Jerry likes it. When he wants to show her off, he takes her out to dinner or to the occasional company picnic or party, where he stays close by, once again keeping her from forming relationships with others.

The Difference between Floaters and Paddlers

Because of her low self-esteem, Kendra has become a Floater. While she has the power to change the circumstances of her life, she is unable to recognize that possibility. Consequently, she stays stuck in an abusive relationship with an unhealthy man who is not only damaging her but whose actions are modeling poor behavior for his children and likely charting the course for their futures in the process.

Floaters tend to go along with whatever is happening in their lives at the time, repeating their mistakes without insight or thought as to how they might do something differently. They tend to accept the circumstances of their lives without awareness that they can alter their path. They are too fearful of rejection and failure to risk change, even if their present situation is unpleasant or unsatisfying or doesn't help them reach their goals. In fact, Floaters readily give up their goals and resign themselves to disappointment, assuming that they just aren't as worthy or competent as others and that life is more difficult for them. Personal growth is not a concept that Floaters consider or understand. Instead, they play it safe by not looking beyond the normal and mundane concerns of daily life. They tend to be spectators rather than participants, reading and talking about what others are doing, avoiding thinking about or sharing their own feelings.

Floaters often have poor communication skills because their lives and personal involvements are so limited. With little experience in talking about issues and feelings, Floaters are often seen by others as boring and rigid, impeding any efforts to develop intimacy. Jerry has never really considered Kendra's merits objectively. He chose Kendra because she was attractive, available, and because she fit his purposes for a wife: submissive, dependent, gullible, and motherly.

Unlike Floaters, who tend to live simple, predictable, and even mediocre lives, Paddlers are LSE sufferers who are more introspective and have one or more people or groups in which they can discuss personal issues. They may also read books and attend seminars or go to hear speakers on subjects about personal growth and relationships. Using this input, they set personal goals and actively work to meet those goals in the hopes of becoming more in touch with their feelings, more astute concerning the dynamics of their relationships, and more aware of how their pasts are affecting their present lives. They are curious and involved outside their family environment; they are participators, not just watchers or people who get their information from television. They are generally involved in one activity about which they are very passionate.

Paddlers are not to be confused with all people who are highly successful or skilled in their careers. These successful-looking people are LSE sufferers who have become overachievers but who still haven't dealt with their fear of rejection and their belief that they are less adequate, unworthy, or incompetent than others. Instead, Paddlers strive to understand themselves and why they do what they do; they are concerned about their own personal growth and the needs of those they love. Paddlers take charge of their lives rather than relying on others for their decisions and direction in life. When they need help, they seek it; when they don't like specific circumstances in their lives, they try to find solutions. They are proactive, making plans, setting goals, overcoming obstacles, and actively working to improve their situations and their relationships. They are LSE sufferers who are determined to overcome their low self-esteem rather than allow it to destroy their lives.

Jackson

Jackson meets the doctor and they talk for a while. The doctor is straightforward with Jackson and treats his erectile dysfunction, his impotence, like any other medical issue, which helps curb Jackson's anxiety and embarrassment. He lays out the plan for Jackson, describing the necessary tests and encouraging Jackson by telling him the problem may be easily corrected. He also indicates to Jackson that his impotence may have been worsened by his anxiety. The doctor says that the entire problem may even be due to anxiety since Jackson has no difficulty getting an erection but can't maintain it. He tells Jackson that anxiety is the main cause of impotence. He also tells Jackson that some counseling may be necessary and asks him if he would be open to therapy as part of the recovery equation.

Jackson is extremely relieved and hopeful. He tells the doctor he will do whatever he recommends. The doctor then does a physical exam, after which the two discuss the rest of the process and set a date for Jackson to return to discuss the findings.

Jackson has promised to call Brianne on her cell phone as soon as he leaves the doctor's office, so once he returns to the car, he does that. She has been anxious for Jackson, knowing how sensitive he is and how embarrassed he will feel talking to the doctor. Jackson's first words to her are "Well, I'm done. I liked the doctor a lot; he was very encouraging and he made me feel less nervous than I was at first."

Brianne is pleased to hear his voice and to see that he is excited rather than upset about the appointment. "Oh, Jackson, I'm so glad. And I'm proud of you for doing this. I know it must have been hard." Brianne responds in her usual upbeat way.

"Thanks, Brianne. And thank you for your support. I couldn't have done this if it hadn't been for you." Then he thinks, "No truer words were ever spoken. Left to my own devices I would have lived my life never knowing if this problem was reversible. Now at least I'll know."

"But honey," says Brianne, "what do you mean when you say the doctor was encouraging? What exactly did he say?"

"Well," says Jackson, "He said that I shouldn't worry, that he thought this was likely a malfunction that could be corrected. And he said it might all be due to anxiety and that what I may need to do is go to counseling. I told him I would do whatever he recommended."

"I'm so proud of you, Jackson. I really respect what you are doing, that you are taking charge and seeking the help you need to get past this. And remember, I'm in your corner and I will continue to be here if you need me." Brianne speaks with a strong conviction that Jackson can hear.

Jackson has up until now been a Floater. In each instance, he has run from his problem rather than seek help. He has not had the insight that comes from introspection and a focus on personal issues; therefore, he has not seen the pieces of his life and how they have come together to form an overall picture. An LSE suffer, Jackson has determined that his impotence is merely a sign of how inadequate he is. It has never entered his mind that his inability to maintain an erection might actually be reversible or something other than a physical problem.

If Jackson is able to work this issue out, he will likely see the necessity of taking charge of the rest of his life so as not to repeat the years of agony he has suffered unnecessarily. This is an example of the power of intimacy, of being truly loving and of being loved in a way that permits a person to be vulnerable, knowing that the other will not turn away or even flinch when he admits to some failing or crisis in his life. And in response to his partner's commitment, he also knows that if the roles were reversed that she too could bare her soul and he would stand solidly at her side.

There are a variety of reasons that a person with healthy self-esteem might be attracted to one who has low self-esteem, but in this case, it is that Brianne sees Jackson's potential and his spirit. She sees the parts of him that are of high quality: his integrity, his curiosity and willingness to try new things, his gentle and caring spirit. She has come to view him as highly trustworthy, sincere, loyal, and dependable. She likes his sense of humor. Basically Brianne first saw the true inner Jackson and then later realized that he was wounded, not cruel, not uncaring, not deceitful, just wounded. She saw too, that in spite of his wounds, he was a person of value and she decided he was a keeper.

Molly

Molly makes plans with her friends to go bowling the following Saturday afternoon. In spite of a few catty remarks, they all seem pleased that she and Howard want to spend part of their weekend with them.

Molly and Howard arrive first and they reserve a lane, rent their shoes, and find bowling balls. Then Howard pays the bill for all of them. Molly's friends arrive a few minutes later. They come in the door talking and laughing and then become silent as they approach Molly and Howard. As Molly introduces Howard to her friends, he smiles broadly and shakes their hands. Then Molly tells them to get their shoes and bowling balls, saying that Howard has already paid for everything. Her friends are shocked and pleased. They look at Howard, say "Thank you," and think that maybe he isn't so bad after all. While the couple is waiting for the others to join them down at the scoring table, Molly leans over to Howard and whispers in his ear, "Well, you are sure getting off on the right foot. I think they are impressed."

As they begin bowling, Molly's friends are quiet, but as the evening goes on, Howard manages to find a way to get them to open up by focusing on each one individually. He asks questions about their work and then shows a genuine interest in the answer, occasionally sharing something about himself. He is so charming that not one of them can resist his magnetism. Adding to their acceptance is the fact that Howard isn't a good bowler and yet when he throws a ball and only hits one or two pins, no one laughs louder than he does. This and his other appealing characteristics help everyone relax and feel like friends. Afterwards they go to eat pizza and when the bill comes, Molly's three friends insist on picking up the tab, something she can't remember them ever doing. When they part, they are all happy and vow to get together again.

As they drive home, Molly says to Howard, "You are really something, you know that, Howard? In one evening, you won over my friends and transformed their behavior. They weren't nearly as sarcastic or rude as they normally are. You really brought out the best in them."

Howard is very pleased, "You know, a little kindness goes a long way for people who haven't had much of it. I liked your friends,

Molly. I think they are okay, they seem wounded to me and they act a bit tough, but I like them. I'm glad we did this."

"Thank you, honey," she responds, "Thank you for being so accepting of my friends."

Howard turns toward her in the car and after making eye contact says, "Anytime, sweetheart, anytime."

Molly is a nice person. Despite her background, she is sensitive and kind. She could have dropped her friends when she got involved with Howard, but in spite of their rude and offensive behavior, they are her friends and she wants them to meet Howard, she wants to continue to include them in her life. She probably also wants to see how he will react to her friends since in many ways, they are much like her family. If she and Howard stay together, she will eventually have to arrange a meeting with the family as well. She sees after the evening of bowling that Howard makes a good impression most everywhere he goes, though she still thinks her family will be tough to charm.

Molly has tried to make changes in her life, though she hasn't known the most constructive ways to accomplish her goals. She hasn't had people around her who have helped to lift her up; rather, she has been surrounded by people who have had equally unhappy lives. Yet inside, Molly is a person with high standards. She felt guilty when she joined in with her friends in their crude behavior and is pleased that she doesn't engage in that anymore. For years Molly was a Floater, but as of late she has changed her behavior towards her friends and has entered into therapy. Feeling cared about and hopeful for her future, she is motivated to learn what has caused her to feel so inadequate that she was willing to settle for one-night stands rather than work towards developing the skills that might make it possible to develop an intimate relationship. She is beginning to blossom and her world is opening up before her. She has new enthusiasm, a new relationship with a man she admires, and friends who, she sees, have potential. She is becoming a Paddler.

Molly is an enigma. One the one hand, she once was willing to settle for any man who would have her; her expectations were very low and she was going down the same path as her sisters. Then when she met Howard, she suddenly became picky and her expectations were that the man in her life should have a perfect body. Now that she is getting in touch with how her past has affected her thinking and her behavior, she sees that she was ridiculously rigid and that, more importantly, a person's appearance is really irrelevant. If she had chosen *not* to date Howard because of her shallow views, she would have lost the opportunity to have the healthy relationship she now has with a truly wonderful man.

Jake

Jake follows through on his commitment to call the psychologist that Deidre had told him about, and he sets up an appointment for the following week. In the interim, he has a couple of days in which he feels his jealousy raising its ugly head. He and Deidre go to a movie one evening and while standing in line he notices three different men give her the eye. He has to admit, however, that she did nothing to solicit their interest and she did nothing to reciprocate it. His wife is just a beautiful woman and a head-turner. He feels anxious to start therapy and to get some help with his irrational resentment. He hates feeling the way he does and knows he has ruined many an evening for the two of them because of his responses. Determined to get it off his mind, he turns to Deidre and starts a conversation about the actors in the movie. Sensing what is going through his mind, Deidre slips her arm through his and snuggles up to him, letting him know that she can tell he is try-ing to respond differently than he has in the past. He smiles knowingly at her and thinks, "What did I do to deserve this wonderful woman?"

Jake has been a go-getter in his career, largely because his LSE prompted him to prove his worth, but he has actually remained a Floater. Though he has had chronic problems with jealousy and insecurity and has lost relationships as a result, he has continued to repeat these self-defeating behaviors without seeking help. Jake has just allowed life to happen and has tried to cope with his disappointments and failures by spending more time at his work. He has given little or no thought to changing or to considering that thinking and the behaviors that follow are the root of his problems. Instead, he has accepted his broken rela-tionships as how life just is, comparing their short-lived status to those of friends who have also gone through more than one divorce.

Not until now, when the stakes are higher than any he has faced, has he been willing to focus on his feelings of being sexually ineffective and on the woman who told him so. But now Jake wants to expel his mother and her hateful words from his mind. He wants to cast off the chains of shame and guilt that she purposely placed on him for her own purposes. "My mother was a sick woman," he says to himself, "full of bitterness and spite. But in some ways, I'm like her. I make Deidre suffer for my unhappiness and my insecurity. This is what I have to change. I don't have to continue to be what my mother wanted me to be—a man who feels less than a man. I don't have to let her illness ruin my life."

Jake seems determined to become a Paddler; in fact he has already begun paddling. He did this when he bought reading material, when he confided in Deidre, and when he called to get a therapy appointment. He was paddling when he asked Deidre if she would help him and when he stood with Deidre in the ticket line and chose to start a conversation rather than continue ruminating about the men who were ogling her. Whether he stays with it will be up to him. Whether he recovers from his LSE will depend upon his determination and perseverance, but right now Jake seems motivated and a good candidate for recovery.

Jake has also had unreasonable expectations. He was attracted to—and married—a beautiful woman; yet he gets very upset when other men notice her or when she seems to be enjoying their attention. If it weren't for his low self-esteem, Jake might feel flattered that other men see his wife as so attractive and that such a beautiful woman wants to be with him. Instead, because he doubts his own virility, he finds the attention of others and her responses threatening.

Unreasonable Expectations

Another stumbling block to developing healthy relationships for those with LSE is that they tend to have unrealistic expectations of their partners, largely because they do not voice these expectations but keep them hidden to see if their partner will read their needs and try to meet them. This is a test. The LSE sufferer doubts that he is of value, doubts that he is deserving and lovable, and so he frequently tests to see if his doubts are true. This is, however, an inadequate test, and one his partner is sure to fail because the agenda is hidden; the partner has no way of knowing what the expectations are or what is required to meet them. The LSE sufferer, however, thinks that his partner should know; in fact, he believes that she does know, and concludes that she is purposely ignoring his needs because she doesn't love him and doesn't care about his feelings. Mandy repeatedly tests Willa and feels devastated when Willa doesn't pass the test by responding as Mandy wants her too. Then her inner voice convinces her that Willa must not really care or she would have responded differently.

An LSE sufferer may also throw out clues to her partner in an attempt to see if her partner really loves her. She thinks she makes her wishes and expectations obvious. Then she watches to see if her partner picks up on these clues and tries to please her. It he tries to do so, she interprets his action as a sign of his love and devotion. If he does not, and her expectations go unmet, she may become severely depressed, convinced that she is being duped by a partner who does not truly love her. Thus self-doubt created in childhood creeps into the lives and relationships of LSE sufferers and distorts their thinking in the form of distrust which then permeates their thinking about their partners. They feel they must test their partners to see if they can be trusted. This type of communication is counterfeit and is not a recipe for intimacy. (For more on testing and the unreasonable expectations of LSE sufferers, see *Breaking the Chain of Low Self-Esteem*, pp. 213-231.)

Some LSE sufferers have few expectations of others. Like Ellen, they have given up their dreams, have accepted the way others mistreat them, and have resigned themselves to lives of loneliness and misery. They don't strive to improve themselves or to change much in their lives because they don't feel equipped to know how to change and they don't feel confident that they can take care of themselves.

Both the LSE sufferer whose expectations are too high and the one whose expectations are low or non-existent will have difficulty ever attaining an intimate relationship.

Carey

On Saturday afternoon Carey and Dirk decide to get a pizza and take it to her apartment so they can eat and talk without interruption. Dirk picks her up and they drive to the pizza parlor, both trying to make small talk and obviously aware of the subject they plan to discuss. They slip into a booth while waiting for their order and Dirk decides to break the tension by broaching the subject, "Are you nervous about our talk?" he asks.

Carey smiles sheepishly and nods.

"Well, if it helps any, I'm a little nervous too," he adds, "but I think it will be okay. We're just going to talk. We don't have to make any decisions, unless we agree on something. I'm not going to pressure you in any way, Carey."

"I know that, Dirk, but thank you for saying so," she responds, beginning to relax. She is glad he has brought up the topic.

They get their pizza and cokes and head to Carey's apartment. When they get there, they place the food on the coffee table and get paper plates. Then, they remove their shoes and with pizza in hand sit at opposite ends of the couch.

After taking a few bites, Dirk begins. "I like you a lot, Carey. I enjoy our time together and I think you are wonderful. I want you to know I consider this relationship to be a serious one for me. I'm very interested in being sexual with you, but I won't push you and I want to know how you feel about me."

Carey nods at Dirk, finishes chewing, and sets her plate on the coffee table. She looks at Dirk and says, "I really like you too, Dirk. You are my first boyfriend, so I don't know how I'm supposed to feel at this point, but I didn't think someone like you would ever want to date me. You are so good to me, so respectful. You've included me with your friends and they are so nice to me too. You've opened up a whole new world for me. I feel so lucky to have met you."

"Thank you, Carey. That's very sweet of you to say."

Carey takes a long drink and continues, "I've given this a lot of thought and I'm glad I had this week to do it. I love it when we kiss and when you touch me. I think I'm ready to go further, but I'm embarrassed to have to ask you to be patient with me 'cause this will all be new to me."

"Of course I'll be patient, Carrie. I remember my first time. I was nervous, clumsy, and not very sensitive, I have to admit." They both chuckle.

"And about safe sex?" Carrie asks.

"I will have condoms with me for whenever we decide to do this," says Dirk.

"And I am now taking birth control pills," says Carey. Actually after their talk, Bernice sent her to see her own doctor to get a prescription.

"Okay," acknowledges Dirk. "That's good."

"Is this weird, having this conversation?" asks Carey.

"Well, it is the first time I've had a conversation like this in advance, but I think it's the right thing to do and I admire you for initiating it. This seems right to me." Dirk puts down his plate, leans forward, and gives Carey a quick kiss and then sits back, sighs, and reaches for more pizza. "This is great pizza," he says smiling. "Probably the best I've ever had. How's yours?"

Carey smiles back, "The best," she nods.

Carey is a Paddler and has been one most of her life, even if she didn't make visible strides with her LSE until she met Bernice. She has tried to improve herself and attempted to figure out what she was doing wrong when she didn't fit in at school, even though she didn't gain the insight to understand what the problem actually was. When social opportunities have presented themselves, she has tried to take advantage of them and has managed to make friends even though these situations were very difficult at the time. In spite of her background, she has developed an intimate relationship with her younger brother, with Bernice, and now with Dirk. She is making careful, thoughtful decisions and not running blindly into the unknown.

Carey had reasonable expectations for knowing she could take care of herself, but her experience and successes have far exceeded her expectations for a social life and for a romantic relationship. As with many LSE sufferers, she hadn't expected much personally and is amazed by the turn of events in her life. She now has a new family and friends, and she sees life as full of opportunities that are within her reach.

Jarrod

Jarrod begins therapy and is confronted by the therapist because he seems to want to talk about Jackie more than about his own behavior and feelings. The therapist allows this for a couple of sessions because Jarrod seems genuinely interested in improving their relationship and is telling his story about their interactions. And when she points out to him that they need to focus on his issues, he says, "Oh, yes, of course, I just wanted to get some insight from you into why you think she is doing what she does." When the therapist says that she has no way of knowing that, since she's never met Jackie or talked to her, Jarrod backs off.

Then the following session, he pulls the same maneuver, first talking about his efforts to be more considerate and the nice things he is doing for Jackie, like taking her to her favorite restaurant for dinner or suggesting that he barbecue for some of her friends. Soon, however, the conversation turns back to Jackie, with Jarrod trying to get the therapist to give an informal diagnosis of his wife. He acts as though he is only concerned, but Jarrod truly believes Jackie is the problem and he wants some information he can present to her to get her to see that as well. As a professional, the therapist isn't taken in by Jarrod's manipulative behavior. Instead, she tells him that she thinks he has low self-esteem and needs to look at himself rather than at Jackie. She gives him a book to read.

The next time Jarrod comes in, he says he has read part of the book and he concurs that he does have low self-esteem. They discuss a technique for recovery and he goes home with an assignment. The following session, Jarrod comes in excited about what he has learned and accomplished in actually maintaining appropriate behavior; these seem to be significant steps toward recovery and the counselor tells him so.

Then Jarrod again begins to ask questions that indicate he is expecting immediate changes in Jackie's behavior as a response to his. If he changes, shouldn't she see it and do the same? Shouldn't she be able to see the mistakes she is making, how poorly she is treating him? Again, Jarrod has shown his hand, his real motivation, which is to get Jackie to see the error of her ways. He is using therapy to try to develop strategies to affect her behavior rather than to recover from his own core issues.

Again, the therapist confronts him about his motives for being in therapy, repeating her earlier message that he is the client, that his recovery is the focus of therapy. Finally Jarrod realizes that he isn't going to be able to get the therapist to say whatever it is he wants her to say so that he can have a label for Jackie.

"If only she understood," he thinks, "that Jackie is the one with the problem and would help me fix her, everything would be great. Sure maybe I have low self-esteem, but that doesn't amount to much. It's no big deal. The problems in our marriage are due to Jackie's selfishness."

Jarrod is a Floater and it doesn't look as if that is going to change. For that matter, Jackie is a Floater as well. Both are accomplished in what they do, Jarrod at his job where he has risen to vice president of a company that makes tennis rackets and Jackie as an organizer of charity and community functions and now a volunteer consultant. Jackie is more social and has many friends. Jarrod has two men with whom he fishes, but neither of them has taken an interest in personal growth, or in improving their relationships with their mates, or in trying to understand how their pasts have impacted their lives. Jackie reads a lot, but only to gain insight for her working relationships; Jarrod seldom reads more than the newspaper. Neither one is introspective or has spent time trying to understand why they do and think as they do. Both have poor communication skills when it comes to working through personal issues, even though they are equally good communicators and problem-solvers in their careers, where their interactions are more impersonal and center on business issues.

Both Jarrod and Jackie also have unrealistic expectations of each other. Jackie too frequently expects Jarrod to eat dinner alone while she is socializing at a restaurant with her friends. Afterwards she is likely to come home excited and bubbly about her time with these other people while she gives him little encouragement or verbal support. Jarrod also has unreasonably high expectations about what Jackie should sacrifice for him. If only this couple could learn to compromise and each take responsibility for the ways they are contributing to their domestic problems, they might be able to reach an amicable solution, especially if they would address their self-esteem issues.

Floaters can either be very social or more solitary. They can be successful in their work but not be effective in their close personal relationships, especially those in which they are expected to be responsible to another person and considerate of that person's feelings. Many people have both a public and private persona, rather than an authentic self that is who they are in all settings. Such is the case with many people who suffer from low self-esteem. They think that who they really are is less than acceptable, so they carefully present themselves as who they think others expect them to be. Both Jackie and Jarrod have public masks that don't necessarily represent their true characters or even who they see themselves as. They put on a public face that looks appealing but that changes when they come home and let down. They feel that they shouldn't have to put on airs at home, but they don't realize that the face they present to their loved one is not very attractive and not very conducive to developing intimacy. In this way, they give their best to strangers and acquaintances while expecting their mate to accept what's left over.

Mandy and Willa

Mandy is in a very sensitive emotional state. She has been having self-esteem attacks regularly, usually stemming from expectations she has of Willa that go unmet because Willa isn't aware of them. For instance, Mandy remembers that their clothes will be ready at the cleaners tomorrow, but rather than remind Willa, she waits to see if picking up the clothes is important to Willa. Since most of the clothes are Mandy's, she wants to see if Willa will think the clothes are a priority and one she has logged into her memory bank. When Willa comes home without the clothes, Mandy is extremely disappointed and says to her, "Why didn't you get the clothes at the cleaners? You know they were supposed to be ready today."

"Oh, I forgot. I'll pick them up tomorrow," says Willa.

"What if I was planning to wear one of the outfits tomorrow? Why can't you be more responsible?" says Mandy, angrily.

"Is it really that important, Mandy? Why are you making such a fuss? Do you have some special event tomorrow at work that you needed something specific for? You have lots of great clothes."

Now Mandy feels embarrassed and put down. "Willa doesn't respect my feelings," she says to herself as she leaves the room and goes upstairs.

Willa is perplexed. "Now what?" she asks herself in frustration. "What did I do wrong now?" She follows Mandy upstairs and finds her sitting on the bed looking forlorn. Sitting down by her, she asks, "What's wrong, Mandy? Did I do something to upset you?"

Mandy is afraid to say anything. Part of her knows that she has been unreasonable and now she is embarrassed. She is upset with Willa but doesn't want to admit she reacted this strongly to such an unimportant event. Of course she didn't need the clothes. It was just her way of checking out Willa's commitment to the relationship, but that sounds ridiculous now too. She doesn't know what to do.

Sensing what is happening because she has done the same thing herself, Willa puts her arms around Mandy. "It's okay, Mandy. I love you. Let's just forget this and go rent a movie; then we can make dinner and spend the evening together. Maybe we'll get a sexy movie," she says flirtatiously.

"Okay," says Mandy weakly. "I love you too, Mandy. I'm sorry."

"Forget it, Mandy. Let's go." She grabs Mandy's hand pulling her off the bed and the two of them go down the stairs and out the front door.

As an LSE sufferer herself, Willa understands what is happening with Mandy. Rather than ridiculing her, she lets Mandy know she understands, affirms her love for her partner, and helps her overcome her embarrassment. She truly loves Mandy and knows how much it hurts to have these self-doubts.

Willa is a Paddler. In spite of her surroundings, at an early age Willa began journaling her feelings and thoughts about what she was going through. While unable as a teenager, to get help, she felt that someday she would do so. On her own, she developed an important skill; she learned to draw by reading art books and practicing. In her hiding place she read many other books that advanced her knowledge and understanding of the world, so that when she now sees the need for personal growth, she not only seeks out a group she can afford but is persistent in attending and putting into practice what she is learning.

Mandy, however, is a Floater. She has made one attempt to seek professional help, but she felt it was not useful and didn't stay with it long, and she hasn't done anything beyond that. The changes Willa is making may inspire Mandy to look at her own behavior, but ultimately Mandy will need to take charge of her own LSE and the irrational thinking and unrealistic expectations that accompany it if she wants to maintain her relationship.

❦

Darren

The day after the barbecue, Darren picks up Katherine and they go to lunch at a nice chain restaurant that he has been to once before. Darren doesn't get out much except to a few chain restaurants and so he doesn't know any special place to take her. Katherine seems fine with the choice; they order their food and then they talk for a while. Darren seems nervous; he is fearful that he will do something or say something to offend Katherine or cause her to dislike him. It had been easier the day before when other people had added to the conversation.

After lunch they go for a walk through a large city park. At one end is a lake and they sit under a tree and watch the boats and the water skiers. His head tells him that this is an impossible relationship because they live so far apart, but his heart tells him that he has met an exceptionally nice woman.

At one point Katharine begins to talk about her background, her difficult childhood, and the years of therapy, both individual and groups that she has participated in, trying to work through the issues that have plagued her. She asks Darren if he has ever been in therapy and he shakes his head.

Katherine goes on to say that she reads self-help books and attends growth-oriented workshops whenever she can. Darren doesn't know what to say, so he just listens and nods his head. He is surprised to hear that she has been in therapy and for a long period of time. He thinks of therapy as something for losers, or disturbed or severely depressed people. He can't imagine why Katherine would have found it necessary. "After all," he thinks, "I came from a family that had a lot of problems, but I haven't had to go to therapy."

Darren is totally unaware that he is a prime candidate for therapy; he is so lacking in insight that he doesn't even know it.

Darren doesn't have much to contribute to the conversation. He doesn't even know what questions to ask. Katherine is aware that he hasn't shared much about himself at all, and she decides to ask him about his family and childhood. Darren shares facts with her about where they lived, what his parents did for a living, and a little about the coastal town he grew up in. He doesn't share anything personal or make any interpretations about his childhood environment. He thinks that such information should not be talked about to someone he hardly knows, but in reality, Darren doesn't have a clear picture of the dynamics of his family and is unaware of how dysfunctional they were. He has just accepted the way they were as a matter of fact, not as anything he could do anything about and he has had no reason to analyze their behavior. He has no idea of how his childhood has affected him and how it has made him who he is today.

At the barbecue, both Darren and Katherine thought that they had a lot in common. Now they aren't so sure. Darren likes her, but he feels as if he is listening to a foreigner when she talks so unabashedly of her feelings, of going to therapy, and of her efforts to learn more about relationships. "Doesn't she realize that when she shares about being in therapy that she is saying that she didn't know what other people already know?" he thinks. "Isn't she embarrassed to have to get help from a professional in order to live her life?" This is how naïve Darren is.

Katherine thinks about what she sees and senses about Darren and she decides that he is a man who has likely been as hurt as a child just as she was. She thinks that he is also extremely shut-down emotionally and out of touch with his feelings. She wonders if he is open to exploring more about life than he has to this point or if he is so stuck that he can't get out of his rut. She decides she will wait until she has spent more time with him before she broaches this subject.

Katherine brings up the topic of exercise, something she knows Darren does. He has said he likes to ride his bike and often rides to work. He also walks often and belongs to an athletic club where he works out regularly. She asks him about his exercise program and they talk about what they have each found helpful and they laugh about the exercise machines that they think are unbearable.

The two go to a movie and while standing in line to get their tickets, they hear the people behind them talking about a political issue that has been in the papers. Quietly Katherine says to Darren, "Did you hear what they were saying? I can't believe that people are so gullible."

Darren shares her opinion and nods, then says, "I know what you mean. It's too bad people are so misinformed." They continue talking about aspects of the coming election until they get to the ticket booth.

After watching the movie, Darren takes Katherine home so she can attend a birthday party for Sam's wife. On the way home, they discuss the movie and talk about their opinions of it. On both this subject and politics, Darren has been more forthcoming and not nearly as nervous.

Darren is clearly a Floater and Katherine is just as obviously a Paddler. While Katherine has been interested and involved in many avenues of growth, Darren has mostly not been. Instead, he has remained on the sideline, watching others participate, fearful and disinterested, with rigid and outdated beliefs about what is appropriate in communication and in relationships. He limits himself to discussing factual information except when the topic is not controversial or when he already knows the opinion of the other person.

Can two people who have conducted their lives so differently ever meet in the middle? This is what Katherine contemplates while Darren is left bewildered about who she is and how she so openly talks about subjects he was taught were too personal to share and no one else's business.

Oliver

"Hello, Oliver," says a woman's shaky voice, "this is your mother."

After a few seconds of silence, Oliver replies weakly, "Yes, I know. Hello."

The woman's breath catches as she tries to talk. "Oliver, I know this must be a shock to you. I can understand if you do not want to talk to me, but I'm hoping you will. I would like to have the opportunity to talk with you."

Oliver is silent. His heart is racing. He is trying to recognize her voice and thinks maybe he does. He hardly hears her words.

"May I continue?" she asks.

Again, Oliver is silent until he realizes that she has asked him a question. "Yes, go on," he says.

"Thank you, Oliver, thank you," says his mother. Then she says, "I know I have a lot of explaining to do. I am not going to make feeble excuses for what I've done to you, but I would like to answer your questions and to try to heal some of the pain I've caused you. I know I have no right to come back into your life after all these years," she takes a big audible breath and says, "but, I'd like to communicate with you, if you agree."

"Where do you live?" asks Oliver, with the first full sentence he has been able to form.

"I live in a suburb of Baltimore," she answers quickly, encouraged that he has interacted with her and hoping he will continue to talk to her or at least listen.

"What do you do there?" asks Oliver, bitterness in his voice. He is wondering if she has another family there, but he can't bring himself to ask.

"I'm not working right now. I have an apartment there. I live alone," she adds, anticipating what he wants to know. "I've never had other children, Oliver. You are my only child."

This shocks Oliver. He had always envisioned her with several other children and imagined them each getting the attention from his mother that he should have received. Now he thinks that the picture is different from what he thought, though he doesn't know what it actually looks like.

"I want you to know, Oliver, that I've thought of making this phone call hundreds of times, but I have just never had the courage to do so. I also want you to know that I'm aware that I don't deserve anything from you or expect it." Oliver can hear her beginning to cry. "If you feel it would be in your best interest to continue to speak with me, that is what I would like. However, if you feel that it would be in your best interest to have no more interaction with me, I will respect that. And, Oliver, you don't have to answer me right now."

"Okay," he replies.

"What I suggest," she says softly, "is that you take time to think about this and maybe give me a time when I could call you again to get your answer. Would that be okay, Oliver?"

"Yes, I think that's a good idea," he says, getting his full voice back. "Maybe you could call me again in two weeks."

"Two weeks, yes, I think that will be fine, Oliver. Should I call about this same time?

"Yes, this time is good."

Jenny is whispering something to him and Oliver adds, "May I have your phone number?" He doesn't know how to address her, what to call her.

"Certainly," his mother answers and she give him the numbers. Then, she says, "Is there anything else you'd like to say or ask me right now, Oliver?"

"No, I don't think so," says Oliver.

"Okay. I'm so pleased to hear your voice, Oliver. Thank you for talking to me. I will call you in two weeks."

Oliver sits as if paralyzed, overwhelmed by the enormity of the moment. Jenny sits quietly beside him and takes his hand. They sit in silence for several minutes; then Oliver begins to tell her what his mother said.

Oliver is a Floater. He has been deeply hurt by his mother's abandonment and his father's withdrawal into a depressive mental illness. He has almost blamed his father more than his mother, because he reasoned that his father knew that he was all Oliver had and still he became so self-absorbed that he left Oliver parentless and homeless, until relatives took him in.

Since his parents abandoned him, Oliver has tried to cope with life and has often acted in ways that were more related to his feelings about his parents than about what was going on in his own relationships at the time. He has done nothing to try to reconcile his feelings or his reactions, instead believing that his thinking was logical and based on reality. He has over-generalized from his parents' behavior as though what they did is the way everyone reacts in a relationship or in a family. Without realizing it, he has been so hurt that he has worked harder at protecting himself than trying to work through his pain. He has, indeed, been a Floater.

Oliver has also had unrealistic expectations of Jenny, viewing her as a woman who will likely be as disloyal as his parents were. This has been hurtful to her and has created an unnecessary distance between them. In doing this, he has denied himself the opportunity to experience intimacy with the woman who loves him.

Mark and Bobbi

Neither Mark nor Bobbi is a Floater or a Paddler. Those terms only apply to people who suffer from low self-esteem. Instead, both are very involved in life and in social issues. Their work demands that they understand or at least strive to understand people. As a freelance writer, Mark is always considering the motives and intentions of the people he writes about. He has read many books on psychopathology and other books on mental health to get insight into why people think and act as they do. As the author of children's books, Bobbi is very interested in how children think and learn so as to discern how she can best teach life's lessons to them in a way they can understand. She too reads books on self-esteem and other areas of personal growth.

The couple frequently read together in the evenings and often get into discussions about what they are learning.

◆ A note of comparison with those with healthy self-esteem

Those who are not encumbered with the memories and scars of childhood that form low self-esteem are free to learn what they need to learn, to find the resources that will enhance their lives, and to be introspective without the constant guilt and remorse that LSE sufferers must cope with. They are not shackled with self-doubt so that they can freely relate to potential partners without fear of replicating their parents' marriage; in fact, they may want to have a relationship like their parents. While those with healthy self-esteem still experience disappointment, failure, frustration, and unexpected tragedies, they can do so with confidence and feelings of worth, and knowing that they deserve the good things in life.

People who have HSE generally do not have unrealistic expectations of others, or if they do, they have them about one or two specific issues rather than as a blanket way of thinking in which expectations are frequently idealistic and beyond reach. Instead, the majority of expectations of those with healthy self-esteem are reasonable and doable. In addition, people with HSE express their expectations, discuss them, and compromise, if necessary; this is the opposite of the hidden agendas of LSE sufferers.

People with healthy self-esteem are neither Floaters nor Paddlers because these terms only apply to LSE sufferers and to the ways they react to their LSE. People with HSE have all levels of motivation and introspection but are usually more enlightened about feelings and the effects of behaviors on others because they have freely communicated about such things throughout their lives.

RECOVERY

Many factors play into the ability to form an intimate relationship, even among people who are emotionally healthy. Add to that the many open wounds that LSE sufferers live with and that refuse to heal without treatment, and the probability of achieving intimacy is even more remote.

There are steps that LSE sufferers may take to "improve" their low self-esteem. While these steps are the theme of many books that address LSE, they are only band-aids to put on the wounds. They are not designed to end the pain and alter the damage that has been done to those with low self-esteem, and they are not designed to correct the problem. They are relievers, not cures. They do not lead to recovery but only provide temporary and partial relief.

As the stories here demonstrate, awareness is the first and most crucial step to altering the destructive role that LSE plays in lives. Until a person knows that he has a problem, he will not seek information or help. Until that person can pinpoint that the problem is, in fact, low self-esteem, the less likely he is to know what information and help he needs and where to find it. Awareness is always the first step in correcting a problem or in perfecting a skill.

For recovery to occur, LSE sufferers must become Paddlers. They must branch out, finding ways to expand their knowledge and their understanding of how healthy relationships function. They must be willing to wade through the sludge, the painful memories of the past, for the purpose of pinpointing what the significant negative influences were in their lives. Then, and only then, can they quit pointing the finger at themselves and, instead, point it where it belongs. This is necessary to overcome guilt. They must then be willing to look at how they have taken the negative messages and behavior directed toward them in the past and translated them into distorted thinking about themselves that now result in self-defeating behaviors and lowered expectations. Finally, they must have the courage, determination, and persistence to do whatever is necessary to alter this self-sabotaging lifestyle.

QUESTIONS TO CONSIDER / THINGS TO DO

1. Has anyone ever told you that you have excessive expectations? If so, who was that person? What is your relationship to that person? Write down your answers.

2. Do you believe that your expectations are excessive?

3. Do you feel your expectations have negatively impacted a relationship you are in?

4. What, if anything, have you tried to do to change these excessive expectations?

5. What, if anything, has seemed to be helpful?

6. If nothing proved to be helpful, have you considered doing anything else?

7. Do you consider yourself a Floater or a Paddler? Write why you think this is so.

8. If you are a Floater, do you now see the need to become a Paddler?

9. List possible things you could do to begin paddling.

10. Do you have family, friends, or acquaintances who you think are Paddlers? If so, are they people you feel you could approach to talk to about what they are now doing or have done?

11. Make a personal commitment to begin paddling today. Read a book, join a support group, get into therapy, attend a workshop on relationships, or start journaling. Take small steps on a continual basis and you will soon find that you will have greatly improved you life.

Chapter 7

Developing and Maintaining Intimacy

Davida and Sammy

Davida and Sammy dated for three years before they married. Within six months, Davida was pregnant.

One of seven children from a poor home in New York City, Davida was nevertheless the product of healthy, hard-working parents who loved and nurtured each of their children. Sammy came into her life when he stood across the counter from her in the deli where she worked throughout high school. The deli wasn't a place he frequented, but he had seen Davida go in there several times and he wanted to get a closer look. She was a sophomore then and he had graduated with honors the year before. He was a handsome young man with a twinkle in his eye, and the two were instantly attracted to each other.

Sammy hadn't fared as well as Davida in his home environment. His father had frequently been unemployed and depressed; his mother had been diagnosed with ovarian cancer when he was young and died when he was 11. Sammy was alone much of the time and, feeling unloved and insignificant, he developed LSE. He was also

235

angry about the life that fate had handed him. Acting out his feelings, Sammy developed a reputation as a wild kid; he got into trouble with the law a few times, though only for minor pranks. After receiving increasingly discouraging feedback for his antics and with the encouragement of a discerning teacher to focus more on his studies, Sammy straightened himself out. He began getting good grades, he got a job, and he started mentoring younger boys who had also lost a parent. When Davida and Sammy met, he worked at a grocery store three blocks from the deli, where he was considered a first-rate employee and a hard worker.

After they met in the deli, the two young people began seeing each other regularly. They would take their breaks at the same time and eat their lunch together or go for long walks. After work, Sammy would walk Davida home and often stay for dinner with her family before jogging back to his father's apartment.

This was the first relationship for both of them, and they were open and honest with each other. They had nothing to hide, no past relationships that they were rebounding from, no breaches of trust from other boyfriends or girlfriends to cause them apprehension. They talked about everything and they talked for hours. Without the hang-ups most people have, intimacy came easily. They also waited until Davida was a senior and 18 years old before they consummated their sexual relationship.

Davida's family was delighted with Sammy. He had quickly become a member of the family and seemed to fit in well. Davida's siblings all looked up to him, and her two oldest brothers often played basketball with him at the YMCA.

In August after Davida's graduation, the two held their wedding at a community church; then they settled into a small apartment just blocks from work and the homes of their parents. Both continued their jobs and the couple were happier than they ever thought possible. As a wedding gift, Sammy's employer gave him a sizable raise and made him assistant manager of the store.

Sammy and Davida discussed having children, which both of them wanted, but they decided to wait two years before trying to get pregnant so they could save up some money. They agreed to use condoms and conscientiously did so. Life was perfect until one night in September, when the condom broke. Both were upset, Sammy especially, since he didn't know anything about being a parent and wasn't ready to be one. He certainly hoped Davida hadn't gotten pregnant.

As fate would have it, however, she was pregnant, and nine months later she gave birth to twin boys. Davida was elated; her mother was also happy but she was concerned. Newlyweds with two little babies wasn't a good start in her eyes, and her fears were soon confirmed. Not only was Sammy now faced with the responsibility of being a father, but also it was obvious that Davida would not be able to continue working with two babies to take care of.

As the weeks went by, Sammy became resentful. He felt like he had when he had lost his mother; he felt alone. Feelings of inadequacy permeated his days. Davida was kept busy, even with the help of her mother, and by the time Sammy came home from work, she was usually too tired to notice he was there. The evenings were taken up by the children's needs, and the young parents were frequently awakened in the night by one and then both babies crying at full volume.

Sammy and Davida began to snap at each other. Both were exhausted most of the time and their patience ran thin. Sammy's low self-esteem, formed by neglect and what felt like abandonment when his mother died, was coming back in full force. He felt unloved and insignificant as he had in his youth.

Each of the couple was coping as best they could, but both felt cheated. And there didn't seem to be any reason to verbalize it to each other, which might have been helpful, because each one felt that the circumstances of their lives were beyond their control. Their perfect relationship was floundering. The intimacy once developed was not being maintained; in fact, it was evaporating.

⚜

With intimacy, there are two challenges: developing it in the first place and then maintaining it through stress, through life's transitions, through periods of illness or tragedy, while meeting career and family demands. Try as we may, situations often occur that are beyond our control and that interfere with intimacy.

Of course, the development of intimacy must come first, but many couples let their guard down once they've come this far. They start to take their intimate relationship for granted as if once they've found it, they can't lose it. However, this isn't so. Intimacy can dissipate much faster than one would imagine unless it's fed and nurtured.

Davida and Sammy's situation swelled rapidly out of control. Neither was prepared for what happened. They hadn't had much time together before they had to begin planning for the babies, including Davida's morning sickness and her changing body and needs. Sammy wasn't prepared to see Davida's ever-expanding body. He was only 20 years old, with the limited wisdom of youth. He didn't have any sisters or other family members who had been pregnant. He had always thought the pregnant women that he saw in the store and on the street were pathetic to look at. Now his young wife was looking the same way and she waddled when she walked. He was embarrassed to look at her or to be seen with her. He felt scared and inadequate, and once again he wondered why things kept happening to him.

The situation that Davida and Sammy faced was not of their choosing and the unplanned birth of not one but two babies put a crimp in their plans and devastated their finances. The situation was even more difficult because of their age. Furthermore, Sammy was not aware of his low self-esteem; he wasn't aware what it was that affected him. Consequently, he personalized the situation, telling himself that the reason this had happened was due to some inadequacy in him, though he couldn't explain that irrational thought or recognize it for what it was.

Low self-esteem can contribute to the difficulty in establishing an intimate relationship, and it adds to the confusion and inability to maintain that intimacy when difficulty arises. Low self-esteem produces many irrational reactions that are self-destructive to the lives of those afflicted. Most of these reactions ultimately interfere with any opportunity to develop or re-create intimacy. Thus, recovery from low self-esteem is a critical goal for anyone who suffers from it. And it is far better that we deal with it before we have destroyed something important to our life.

Jackson

When the test results are compiled, Jackson meets again with the doctor, who reiterates that the most common cause of impotence is anxiety. He goes on to say that Jackson's test results show no abnormalities or physical reasons for his erectile dysfunction and that he is convinced that Jackson's difficulty in maintaining an erection is due entirely to anxiety and stress. Jackson responds with a loud sigh of relief.

The doctor then asks him if he has any idea what has caused him to be so anxious. Jackson shares that he thinks his anxiety stems from his childhood, and he describes the dysfunctional environment in which he grew up.

The doctor nods his head, "I can see why you might feel inadequate and be anxious about developing a sexual relationship. Once you've had your first failure, your apprehension would certainly have been much greater the second time. I think that each time you have been with a woman, you got so nervous that you lost your erection, leading to even more anxiety the next time. Do you think that might be accurate, Jackson?"

Jackson nods as he hears this. "Yes, yes, I think you're right,"

"Do you have any questions right now, Jackson?"

"No, I don't know what to ask."

"Are you interested in a woman now?"

"Actually, I am in a relationship. I didn't mean for it to happen, but I have fallen in love with a wonderful woman and she loves me. I tried to end it when I knew I couldn't avoid sex any longer, but before I could break up with her, she confronted me. Rather than have her think I was married or in trouble or something, I told her the truth. I still can't believe I did it, but I did. I told her and she was wonderful. She wasn't the least bit judgmental. In fact, her reaction was totally supportive and understanding. If that hadn't happened, I probably wouldn't be here today."

"Wonderful, Jackson. You will have support in this process. Well, I want you to relax. I firmly believe that this is going to be okay. I want you to get into therapy. If you have someone you want to see, that is fine. Otherwise, I have several names I can give you."

Jackson has met a wonderful woman and formed an intimate relationship. Finally with the encouragement of someone who cares about him, he has been able to verbalize his problem. This has led to his seeking a medical opinion that has proven to be far less threatening than he had anticipated. The doctor suggests that his problem may not be too difficult to overcome, especially because he has a partner who is mature and understanding. Brianne is patient and encouraging, and she will stand by Jackson, without unreasonable expectations and without judgment. Additionally, Jackson will now be seeing a therapist to address his anxiety. Hopefully the person he sees will recognize that his anxiety is but a symptom of his core issue: low self-esteem. Hopefully, Jackson will be successful in reversing his sexual dysfunction, and he and Brianne will go on to have a close relationship that includes not only emotional and verbal intimacy but sexual intimacy as well.

Molly

Molly has plans to meet her friends for dinner a few days after the bowling party. She wonders what they are going to say about Howard. She hopes they won't be as cruel as they sometimes are when they are jealous of the other person's good fortune. She tries to prepare herself to detach from their behavior if it is negative and to remain kind and amicable. She is determined to be the quality of person that she wants to be. She doesn't want her behavior to be controlled by what others say and do, as has often been the case.

Molly enters the café just as her friends are being seated. They see her and wave to her to join them. When she is seated and they have all greeted each another, one of the women asks, "Well, how's the boyfriend?"

Molly smiles warmly and answers, "He's just fine, I think. I haven't seen him for a few days as he's been out of town, but I've talked to him."

"I'm sure you have. How many times a day does he call you, Molly?" asks the other woman.

"Oh, only each evening," responds Molly, keeping her voice light.

"Well, I, for one, think he's a nice guy," says Dan. "I had a good time with you guys, bowling and eating pizza. He's very friendly and funny though not too hot a bowler." He chuckles. "He may be a little overweight, but he's not fat, and I don't think his hair has receded any more than mine."

Dan's comments are followed by a few seconds of silence. Molly is stunned; the others seem to be reflecting on his remarks as if making a decision.

Then Molly says, "I'm so glad you had a good time, Dan. Howard really liked you too. In fact, he told me that he really enjoyed all of you and had a fun time. He suggested we all get together at his house for a barbecue."

Her friends seem not to know what to say. The women glance at each other and then at Dan, who nods at them and smiles, as though reminding them of something that has earlier been discussed. Then one of the women says, "Hey, that sounds like fun.

The other woman agrees, "Yeah, I could go for that."

This group is not accustomed to getting invitations and certainly not from a man they have spent time with, even if he is Molly's boyfriend. Molly is pleased and knows that what has happened here is more than she expected and about as much as her two women friends can manage to give her. She wants to hug Dan. He created this positive mood and the others followed suit. She is also amazed that Howard had this effect on her friends. "He is truly remarkable," she thinks.

Molly feels like she is floating much of the remainder of the dinner, but she tries to follow Howard's example of focusing on each of her friends. Individually, she attempts to show an interest in— and be supportive of—what is going on in their lives. At times they get into their critical and negative routine, but Molly doesn't join in when they do. She just busies herself with her food. They part with her promise to set a date for the barbecue and a last-minute shout from one of the women in the parking lot, "Maybe Howard has some single friends."

"Maybe," Molly shouts back.

Molly is happier than she can ever remember. She is beginning to understand herself. She is recognizing the dysfunctional patterns of behavior that she has developed as a result of her upbringing. She has a wonderful and sensitive man in her life and she sees hope for her friends. She has a psychologist who is helping her see the entire picture of her life. "Can life really be this good?" she asks herself.

Looking down the road three years, we see that Howard and Molly move on from emotional intimacy to physical intimacy, and then get married. Now they have an 18-month old boy and a baby girl.

Molly still sees her psychologist regularly, just not as often. She and Howard have worked at having a relationship with Molly's parents, but they do not allow the grandparents to baby-sit their children. Molly has explained why they don't feel comfortable with this. At first, her parents were so enraged that they didn't call Molly for six months. Finally realizing that she and Howard were not going to relent, they decided they would have to accept these conditions in order to see their daughter and their grandchildren. Molly doesn't see her sisters and their families except at Christmas when she and Howard attend dinner with the entire family.

Molly still spends time with her friends. One of the two women friends was in a serious car accident, and Molly and Howard were both at her bedside at the hospital as well as major contributors to her care afterwards. They see her often and she has become more of a sister to Molly than her own ever were. Having become much more emotionally healthy but unable to work a full schedule, this friend is now a principle caregiver to the children, enabling Molly to work part-time. Dan has been in and out of two relationships in the past three years, with no success in making them last. He and Howard have become friends and now both belong to an athletic club where Howard subsidizes Dan's membership. Molly's other friend is in an abusive relationship and they seldom see her. Molly keeps hoping that her friend will get her life straightened out, but she knows there is little she can do until her friend asks for help.

Why is it that Molly has developed in such a different direction from the other members of her family of origin? How is it that she has chosen such a different path, that she has been able to focus on the positive situations in her life and has pursued them rather than the negative options that she could have continued to engage in? What is it within people that gives one the strength to pick herself up and go on while another does not have that courage or resilience?

Many influential people, experience statements and thoughts enter into a person's personal development. Each can have a profound effect on that person's willingness, insight, and motivation to overcome low self-esteem. Some need much more encouragement than others. Some need a nudge; others are so self-motivated that getting a glimpse of what could be is enough to start them on the road to recovery. Molly has that inner resource, that inner strength, that inner understanding of right and wrong that propels a person forward, so that when the opportunity to receive support presented itself, she grabbed it and moved forward, becoming a better person in the process. She has matured and become a much healthier person because she wanted it enough.

Jake

Jake gets very involved in his therapy. As he does, his awareness of the destructive effects of his irrational inner voice grows. He also becomes more conscious of how easily his negative thinking is evoked and how distorted it can become in a matter of seconds. He finds it unbelievable that for so many years he has been seeing the responses and behaviors of others through such distorted lenses. This background has given him a view of life that is subtly skewed, slightly off-center, and irrationally based. He begins to recognize how once a person accepts one distortion as truth, all of the thoughts that follow are at least as distorted, if not more so. In fact, the second thought is generally more skewed than the first because the basic premise was wrong to begin with. Thus, each thought that follows the first distortion builds upon it and becomes more negative and less factual.

For example, if Jake begins with the thought that Deidre is looking with interest at other men, this is a distortion. In all likelihood, considering his personal background, his next thought, which will build on the first one, is "She doesn't love me anymore."

If he accepts that thought as true, the next might be "It's because I'm not satisfying her sexually" followed by "I'm going to lose her" and "I can't live without her" and "My life is over." All LSE sufferers do this, though most are not aware that these thoughts are distorted. At the time, this stream of thoughts seems perfectly logical.

LSE sufferers frequently go through a process like this although with differing circumstances fueling their thoughts. Once set in motion, each new thought builds on the one before it, becoming more far-reaching and with increasingly serious consequences, even though no more information has been added to produce this increase in irrationality. Then, since our feelings are the result of our thinking, our emotions and the following behavior are the result of our irrational thoughts.

Jake is not only becoming aware of his distorted thoughts but he is also learning how to change this pattern of behavior by learning to discard or replace thoughts that do not rely on fact, truth, or history. Through therapy and the recovery program that he is involved in, Jake is becoming able to see the big picture of how he, not his mother, has sabotaged his life. And as a result of this recognition, which is profound, he is beginning to catch himself before he overreacts, before he mopes or withdraws, and before he becomes depressed. However, this process of becoming conscious of his thoughts and consequent behaviors will take time, as many of these behaviors are subtle.

He is also forcing himself to share with Deidre what is happening within him at the time it is happening. This is helping her to understand what he is going through and is drawing them closer together. She is proud of the way Jake is handling the struggle and tells him so. She sees the improvement in his attitude and reactions and tells him this as well.

Jake has come a long way. He has moved from being angry with his mother and blaming her for his lack of success with women to deciding to take responsibility for his own behavior. He has moved from projecting his feelings onto Deidre to being willing to examine those feelings. He has decided to seek help for his personal problems just as he has always done in his career. And, as a result, Jake has a whole new life before him. His perspective of himself and of others will likely never be the same. Barring some unseen circumstance, or Jake losing his determination, or the couple becoming complacent, Jake and Deidre will likely make it together, maintaining the lasting intimate relationship of two healthy people.

Carey

Carey and Dirk consummate their relationship but are careful not to make sex the focus of their relationship. They continue to spend much of their time together, and Carey continues to take college classes. Her perspective about her future is expanding, and she thinks that she is trying to decide what she wants to major in. Both Dirk and Bernice have tried to help her see the many options that are possibilities.

Carey and her brother Joey have talked regularly by phone since she left home. She felt like she was deserting him when she moved away, but she also knew she had to go or she would drown in the tidal wave of negativity she was experiencing. She has tried to buoy Joey up from a distance, knowing that he feels alone and is a target for her father's displeasure. Carey has checked with her employer and arranged for a summer job for Joey, so he will be coming to stay with her for several months before returning to his senior year in high school.

Carey is anxious for Joey to come so that he, too, can experience a different environment from what he has known and so he, too, can benefit from the friends and lifestyle she has established. She looks forward to having Joey and Dirk spend time together. She thinks the two have much in common because both are serious, sensitive, and deep thinkers. She knows that Bernice will love Joey and take him under her wing in the same way she did Carey. She hopes he might even decide to return there after he graduates.

We cannot predict what will happen in the relationship between Carey and Dirk. They are in love with each other, but they are also young. Each will have many opportunities, decisions, and challenges in the next few years. The most important factor for these two is that they are learning what a truly intimate relationship looks and feels like, something that, once experienced, they will always understand. The two may continue their relationship and decide they want to spend their lives together, or their lives may take turns that direct them down different paths. Either way, they are experiencing the wonderful feeling of being truly loved and loving another on the deepest level possible.

Joey and Carey will be able to continue their intimate relationship as brother and sister. She will be able to include him in her life, introduce him to her friends, and help him to experience a better way of life than he has had. Their time together will further cement a lasting relationship so that they will have one another to confide in and have one another for support throughout their lives.

Jarrod

Jarrod believes that Jackie is the real cause of the problems in their relationship. He sees her as selfish, as focused only on her feelings and needs, and as insensitive to his. He also believes that she wants the attention of others far more than she wants his. He has learned that he has low self-esteem and that distorted thinking accompanies LSE, but he only sees his behaviors as accelerating their debates, not as responsible for them. He doesn't recognize that LSE is a serious obstruction to healthy living and that his life had been negatively affected by it long before he met Jackie. Instead, he connects all of his setbacks and his misery to her behavior. He has convinced himself that if he could only get Jackie to see how inappropriate she is acting, how disrespectful of him she is, maybe she would see the truth and be motivated to address her problems. Then everything would work out between them and they would both be happy. This is his fantasy.

Jackie, on the other hand, sees the problems in their relationship as belonging solely to Jarrod. She sees him as insecure, which he is, and as being overly jealous without reason. She doesn't believe that she provokes him, only that he overreacts.

Jarrod and Jackie are at a stalemate. Their relationship cannot move forward until one or both of them accepts some responsibility for their issues and until both of them become willing to compromise. In all likelihood, this relationship will never change and while they may stay together out of desperation and fear of being alone, it is doubtful that they will ever have a healthy, satisfying, and intimate relationship.

Mandy and Willa

The kind of confusing interactions that Mandy and Willa experience would be perplexing to many people, especially those who have healthy self-esteem or those who have LSE and don't know it or what it means. These conflicts, however, are not bewildering to Willa. She has LSE and knows some about what that means. She has personal experience in overreacting and distorting the words and actions of others, and she knows that when an LSE sufferer responds and acts as Mandy does, it is the result of insecurity and self-doubt. Therefore, when Mandy moves into an irrational episode, Willa doesn't feel disdain. Rather she experiences empathy for Mandy; she knows how much pain Mandy is feeling.

Simultaneously, Willa realizes that she cannot give Mandy the sense of security she needs; she cannot erase Mandy's self-doubt. She can only let Mandy know that she loves her and encourage her to get some help. Willa understands that it is her responsibility to stay detached from Mandy's angry, blaming statements, that she must not get pulled into arguments that become chaotic and that only create more disillusionment.

Willa is determined to become healthy. She hopes that in time, Mandy will have the same vision and determination. She has also given thoughtful consideration to how long she should remain in this relationship if Mandy does not recognize her need for help. She knows that it will be difficult to continue being a positive and supportive partner if Mandy continues to attack her or test her loyalty and devotion. She decides that she must have a serious talk with Mandy to encourage her to get help with her self-esteem issues.

Whether this relationship continues depends on many factors, the most important of which will be Mandy's willingness to admit that she needs help. Second, Mandy must be determined to change, to persevere in her efforts to find that help, and to work through a recovery program. If this happens, the two will still have to face all the other issues that a couple must address, such as lifestyle, friends, finances, etc. They will have to see if they can develop an intimate relationship based on mutual respect, love, and integrity.

Darren

On Tuesday following their Sunday lunch and movie date, Katherine telephones Darren at work. She tells him she has been reading the paper and sees that a well-known political figure will be speaking that evening and wonders if he would like to go with her. He says, "Sure, but do you think we can still get tickets?"

"I just called," Katherine responds, "and they said that a few tickets are still available. Best of all, there is no reserved seating. So, I could run and get tickets and if we got there early, we could prob-ably get good seats."

"Great," says Darren. "What time do you think we should get there?"

They make their plans and Darren is jubilant. "She called me!" he says to himself. "How about that? She wants to spend more time with me."

Katherine has decided to try to broaden Darren's horizons. She likes who he is, she respects the standards and values he has expressed, and she thinks he is a quality person, although one who has not had enough experiences. His life seems far too narrow to her, and she wants to see if Darren is willing to branch out to other interests once exposed to them. She is pleased that he was receptive to her suggestion.

Again, we do not know where this relationship is headed. Katherine likes Darren and is not bothered by what he does or doesn't know, but she is concerned whether he will be open to new experiences and knowledge. She hopes that he is, and she thinks that with a positive and sensitive companion, he may open up and relax. She is willing to take the lead in this venture. If Darren continues to see the potential of this relationship and is willing to experience new things, he may also be more willing to take a look at the personal issues centering on his LSE. There is hope for this relationship to grow and blossom, but there is an equally strong possibility that it will dissolve.

Oliver

Oliver decides that he doesn't want to cut himself off from a relationship with his mother even though she has caused him years of pain and insecurity. She is, after all, his mother and she is reaching out to him. Even as he makes this decision, his mood fluctuates, but he is adamant about speaking to—and meeting with—his mother and at least listening to what she has to say.

Jenny is secretly thrilled with his announcement that he is going to have more phone conversations with his mother. She hopes that Oliver can finally begin to heal from the tragedy that he experienced so early in his life. She worries, though, that this could be equally hurtful if his mother rejects him again or makes excuses for her behavior. She clings to the fact that his mother has contacted him and that she seemed sincerely interested in how he would feel about her call.

At their second phone call, Oliver's mother says, "Oliver, there are some things I'd like to say about the past. Will that be okay with you, Oliver?"

"I guess so," he responds, knowing what is coming and wondering how she will say it.

" I know that I have no right to ask you to forgive me, Oliver, and I won't, but I do want you to know that not a day has gone by that I haven't regretted my decision. I was young and immature and I didn't know how to change the situation that I had so stupidly created. It was nearly two years after I left before I learned that your father had become mentally disabled. I felt heartsick and I then realized that I had likely destroyed two lives, both yours and your father's. I haven't known how to face you after I cavalierly and selfishly left you. I knew you were staying with your uncle and his family and I could only hope that you would be better off with more responsible adults than me."

She went on, "Oliver, I don't expect you to respond to any of this. I just wanted you to hear these words. I never stopped loving you and I will forever regret what I did to you."

"I hear you," said Oliver.

Then quickly, so as not to end their conversation on such a sour note, his mother began to ask questions about himself. "What line of work are you in, Oliver?" and "Tell me about Jenny. She has a very pleasant voice," and "Have you ever been married?" "Do you have children?" "Did you go to college?"

These were questions Oliver was able to answer, though in his heart he felt reluctant to give her the information she would have known if only she had stayed around and been his mother.

After a while, Oliver begins to open up with her and feels tears burning in his eyes. When he cries, she does as well. At one point Jenny reaches over and take his hand and he smiles weakly at her.

After two months of weekly phone calls, his mother comes to visit at Oliver's invitation. Together they look at photo albums, given to Oliver by relatives. They look at scrapbooks Jenny has helped him make from the box of pictures, report cards, and newspaper articles that he had saved. Jenny leaves them alone, only occasionally striding through the room as if on a mission but really to see that Oliver is all right. She brings them coffee and fresh-baked cookies, then fixes a light lunch for the three of them. Afterwards, Oliver suggests to his mother that they sit on the back deck for a while. He asks Jenny to join them.

For months, Oliver and his mother communicate by email, by phone, and with occasional visits back and forth, always accompanied by Jenny. Finally, on one visit, as he and Jenny are preparing to leave her apartment to go to the airport, Oliver receives her parting hug and turns to leave. Turning back, he says to the older woman, "I'll talk to you soon, Mother."

The woman stares at him, realizing what he has just said. Their eyes remain fixed on each other's. This is the first time he has called her "Mother," and it marks the moment at which Oliver has decided to forgive his mother. It is a turning point in his life and the both his mother and Jenny recognize it. A small smile spreads across the lips of all three adults, broadening into wide grins.

"Thank you," the older woman says breathlessly, too overwhelmed to say more. "Thank you, Oliver."

The following Saturday Oliver asks Jenny to marry him and she happily says yes. She has witnessed the change in Oliver over the months since his mother has re-entered his life. His heart has softened since he gradually let go of the anger and resentment he had held toward his mother.

Getting to know and understand his mother, then letting go of his anger and resentment has enabled Oliver to see how he has let his past skew the view he has of himself, how he has developed insecurity and self-doubt as well as an inability to trust others due to the bitterness he has harbored. Being reunited with his mother has freed him from anger and has given Oliver a new perspective of his past and of himself. His self-esteem is in the process of becoming inactive. This doesn't mean that Oliver's has overcome his low self-esteem, but it does mean that he is now happy and that he is surrounded by people who love him.

Jenny and Oliver became much closer during his reunion with his mother. He wanted to share everything with her and he yearned for her feedback. When Jenny willingly participated but stayed in the background so that he could begin to heal, he respected her for it and he began to see how much she really loved him and how wonderful she was. He was finally free to love this amazing woman and he didn't want to lose her.

Oliver and Jenny went through a lot together before they could grasp true intimacy. Jenny stayed by him but was reaching the end of her patience when Oliver's mother reappeared. Oliver was stuck in his rigidity, resentment, and distrust and would likely have let Jenny go rather than make a permanent commitment.

Then, the unexpected happened. Oliver's mother called after so many years of silence. Almost as unimaginable, Oliver was cautiously receptive and gradually opened his arms wide to both his mother and to Jenny. Now they will be married and his mother will be in attendance. Jenny and Oliver have achieved intimacy; however, as with all intimate relationships, they won't stay intimate unless they nurture it, so their work is not over.

Mark and Bobbi

For this couple, developing an intimate relationship came easily. Each one has been involved in other relationships and both have a clear picture of what they want and expect from a prospective partner. Mark and Bobbi feel fortunate to have found someone with similar values and someone who doesn't seem to be carrying any significant, negative baggage from their pasts.

The past experience of each one has made them aware of how a relationship can dissolve as quickly as it came together if it is not given regular attention. Consequently, they make sure that they have sufficient time to communicate, time for fun and shared experiences, and time for sex; they make their relationship a high priority. Preserving this priority status will be necessary to maintain this level of intimacy.

◆ A note of comparison with those with healthy self-esteem

Life is an ongoing struggle, especially for those who suffer from LSE and who have been abused, neglected, or abandoned as children. They are the walking wounded, limping along through life with distorted thoughts about their inadequacy striking them like arrows or bullets. Feeling like soldiers on the firing line and with negativity coming at them from any direction, they feel constantly in danger and in need of being on full alert. While they are not in battle in the literal sense of the word, those with severe LSE are as fearful as though they were.

LSE sufferers find even the daily challenges to be threatening while those with healthy self-esteem may get frustrated but otherwise take these inconveniences in stride. Those with HSE don't feel tense every day, fearful of what may occur. They don't feel they have to watch their words for fear of saying something that others will think is strange or stupid. Those with HSE basically accept themselves and expect that others will as well, while the opposite is true of those with LSE, who can personalize the behavior of an irritable store clerk, a driver who cuts them off while talking on his cell phone, a client who doesn't show up, or an unexpected bill that comes in the mail. Those with healthy self-esteem see these inconveniences as a part of life that is to be expected, and while they don't like these situations, they don't let them affect their moods or their behavior.

Jake has struggled with men looking at his wife and imagines her looking back because she is dissatisfied with him. Mandy gets overly upset and draws irrational conclusions when Willa forgets to stop at the cleaners or doesn't call ahead of time to tell her she is bring home a pizza. Jackson has sexual difficulties but doesn't seek help. These are responses of people who are confused about expectations and are plagued by a lack of self-worth.

People with healthy self-esteem would not react in these
ways. The man who has a wife others look at would feel proud and
pleased that she chose him. The woman whose partner forgets the
clothes at the cleaners might be miffed, but she would not connect it to a negative theory about the status of the relationship.
The man with sexual problems and healthy self-esteem would
seek help immediately. Those who have healthy self-esteem can
more readily cope with these irritations and issues because they
don't blame themselves or take responsibility for things they did-
n't cause or contribute to. Furthermore, they can keep these
incidents in proper perspective and not let them become issues
that threaten the relationship or their belief in their partners.

Another part of the ongoing struggle for those with low self-
esteem is that of maintaining intimacy once it has been
developed. Those with healthy self-esteem are more likely to see
the importance of working at a relationship and will be open to
doing so, but this requires a degree of vulnerability that those with
low self-esteem may find too threatening. For instance, when confronted, we need to be willing to consider the other person's
complaints, if we are going to maintain intimacy. We must be willing to both share our feelings and be sensitive to the feelings of
others if we are going to maintain intimacy. We must be willing to
be honest and trustworthy if we are going to sustain intimacy.
Those with low self-esteem find these behaviors very stressful and
threatening while those with healthy self-esteem do not.

RECOVERY

To recover from low self-esteem, a person must be willing to be vulnerable. He must be willing to openly look at his failures, his withdrawal and avoidance patterns, his anxiety, and his distorted thinking. He must desire recovery enough that to be willing to endure the pain of remembering, thinking about, and analyzing his past and be willing to take an in-depth look at how he is replicating his past. Recovery is an option and a recovery program is available. He may be required to sacrifice to do it, relegating energy, time, and money to the process. He may need to eliminate some people from his life and take risks in other areas. He must want it enough. Until he works through recovery, the struggle will be ongoing and his life will remain unfulfilled. He must want it enough.

QUESTIONS TO CONSIDER / THINGS TO DO

1. Are you now or have you in the past considered therapy?

2. If you have been in therapy, how many therapists have you seen?

3. If you have been in therapy, how many of these therapists recognized that your core issue was LSE and had a program for recovery?

4. What other diagnoses, if any, did they give you?

5. Would you now consider therapy?

6. Would you be willing to sacrifice sufficient time, energy, and money, if necessary, to get the help you need?

7. Have you read any books on self-esteem?

8. Have they been helpful?

9. Are you motivated to get help for your LSE? Do you want it enough?

Sexual relationships issues of those who have low self-esteem

Because this book cannot fully illustrate how LSE interferes with the sexual aspects of intimacy, I have added the following list of even more of the many ways that thinking and subsequent feelings of those with LSE negatively affect intimacy in sexual relationships.

- ◆ Demanding sex rather than requesting it because of unreasonable expectations

- ◆ Thinking that if our partner loves us, he will always be ready to have sex

- ◆ Using sex to gauge our partner's commitment (Is our partner willing to have sex whenever we want to?)

- ◆ Complying with sexual requests even when we don't want to in order to please

- ◆ Faking orgasm because we don't want to disappoint our partner

- ◆ Using sex to try to get our partner to overlook our behavior or to forget problems (believing that sex should make everything all right)

- ◆ Being unable to climax because of anxiety or feelings of inadequacy

- ◆ Being unable to ask for what we need to reach climax

◆ Feeling unable to be the initiator of sex

◆ Feeling too inhibited to be open to sexual experimentation

◆ Expecting that any form of affection should lead to sex

◆ Equating sex with love

◆ Experiencing impotency due to anxiety

◆ Experiencing extreme embarrassment about sex including talking about sex, being touched in sexual ways, and hearing or creating the sounds associated with sex

◆ Feeling to self-conscious to have our body seen during sex or to see the body of our partner

◆ Feeling unable to relax and to be playful during sex

◆ Feeling inadequate in general because of childhood memories of sarcastic remarks about our masculinity or femininity

◆ Feeling inadequate sexually because of memories of being told we were worthless like one of our parents and that no one would ever want us

◆ Becoming promiscuous or developing overtly inappropriate and flirtatious behavior as a result of being molested as a child

- Trying to please any man who shows us attention because we were rejected or abandoned by our father

- Passive-aggressively withholding sex to punish our partner for some perceived slight

- Feeling so insecure that we are jealous of our partner's relationships with other men or women

- Trying to make our partner jealous to see if she really cares

- Being overly fearful that we are not performing adequately and constantly questioning our partner about it

- Constantly needing affirmation after sex that our partner loves us

- Constantly questioning our partner as to how we compare to past sexual partners

Chapter 8

Getting the Help You Need

Tucker and Jill

Jill and Tucker's relationship has been eroding for several years, their communication becoming more stilted and hostile. Each accuses the other of being responsible for the arguments, and each is becoming more disillusioned with their marriage.

A college professor who teaches literature, Jill grew up in the city with parents who both worked. Her mother was a career counselor and her father worked at a home for troubled youth. Both of her parents were skilled in expressing themselves and both had healthy self-esteem. Their home provided a positive environment and a safe place to talk about feelings, ideas, dreams, and goals.

Tucker grew up in different homes after his parents both died in a boating accident. He was only 6 years old at the time. At first Tucker and his two younger brothers lived with his paternal grandparents. Six months after moving to their home, however, the grandfather was diagnosed with bone cancer. His health deteriorated rapidly and because Tucker's grandmother became fully responsible for her husband's care, the children had to move. Since

265

no other relatives stepped forward to intervene, the only option was to send the boys to a foster home. This time, however, they were split up, with the two younger boys going to one home and Tucker to another.

Now, not only had Tucker lost his parents, but his grandfather had become incapacitated, his grandmother was unavailable to continue caring for him and his siblings, and he was separated from his brothers. In addition, Tucker went from being with his parents, who were financially stable and living a typical middle-class lifestyle, to living with a family that was struggling financially, a family that had taken him in primarily to supplement their income. In his new home, conflict was common, often centering on unpaid bills and insufficient funds. There wasn't money for a second pair of shoes for Tucker; there wasn't money to go out to dinner or to a movie. Once again he felt deprived, not only of love and support but also of the things that he would have had if these tragic events had not occurred. Tucker felt cheated and resentful.

Tucker is an introvert: quiet, reflective, and reserved. In this new environment, he soon grasped the situation, including the fact that he was alone, that he had no parents or grandparents, that he was seldom able to communicate with his siblings. His foster parents were kind to him, but they were stressed with their own situation and more focused on their two children than on him. The woman tried to be sympathetic but as a part-time waitress with her own family to care for, she had little time to spend with him individually.

Tucker is very bright, and he knew this as a child. When he applied himself, he excelled in his classes. When he didn't like the teacher or felt that the teacher didn't like him, he rebelled, refused to do his homework at times, and even mouthed off. He visited the principal's office more than once. He never let his grades slip too far, however, because his academic achievement brought him attention, support, and affirmation.

When Tucker graduated from high school at 18, he received the trust fund that had been set aside by his parents. He had counted the days until he could get the money and move out on his own. He didn't hate his foster parents; he just didn't have feelings for them one way or the other. What he did hate was life! He hated what had been done to him: taking away his parents and the wonderful life they had had, separating him from his friends and then his brothers, allowing his grandfather to get sick and die of cancer, putting him with people who had so many problems of their own that he was just an extra body to feed and clothe.

Determined to salvage what he could, the first thing Tucker did the week he turned 18 was call his younger brothers. He had only been able to see them once or twice a year because they lived at a distance, but he had eventually taken a paper route to make money for himself and to be able to phone them regularly. In this important phone call, Tucker told them that the next week he would have his trust fund money and he would be moving to the city where they lived to find an apartment, get a job, and go to college. The brothers would be able to spend more time together and be a family again.

Tucker's brothers had fared far better than Tucker. They had lived with a loving couple who had no children of their own, who were financially stable, and who had showered them with love. Whenever he visited, this couple had always been very kind to Tucker, taking him and his brothers to the zoo, to movies, to sporting events, and other entertainment. There was always a variety of good food to eat there too, and Tucker was envious but pleased that his brothers had received affection and good care. At least he hadn't had to worry about that.

Tucker moved, got a job, and started college, renting an old house near campus and buying all the furniture he needed. Then he went shopping for clothes and filled his closets with new shirts, sweaters, slacks, and shoes. He bought a stereo and an armful of CDs. He was making up for lost time.

Then, during his second semester he met Jill, an equally bright student who had a positive attitude about life and the enthusiasm to go with it. Both young people were intense, philosophical, and thoughtful and they spent hours talking about books, their classes, and eventually their backgrounds. The two grew to be even more compatible as Jill found ways to expose Tucker to things he had missed. Together they went to sporting events, to gourmet restaurants, to the local museums and art galleries, to concerts, plays, and even the opera.

A year after Tucker graduated, his younger brothers did. Tucker and Jill rented a larger house, moved in together, and a month later were joined by the brothers, who also entered college. Tucker was happier than he had ever been. He was reunited with his brothers, they were all carefree students, and his life was rapidly evolving into something far beyond what he could ever have anticipated. When Jill graduated and Tucker had one year left, he proposed marriage and she accepted. They agreed to marry the following June after his graduation.

When they married, Jill's parents presented the couple with the down payment on a small ranch-style home, and as a result of his outstanding grades and, good recommendations from his professors, Tucker landed a good starting position at a company that provided excellent opportunities for advancement. Then he and Jill settled down to married life, adult jobs, and responsibilities. That's when the difficulties began. Unbeknownst to Jill, Tucker's trust was depleted and he had built up credit-card debt.

Tucker had felt deprived for many years and unconsciously he was trying to make up for it. Once he received his trust, he had spent recklessly, first buying a new car, an expensive watch, and a gold necklace. He had shopped at the finest clothing stores, wanting to have the latest styles, feeling that he never had enough of anything. Most of the time he had also picked up the tab for the many things he and Jill did, and he had showered her with flowers, jewelry, and gifts, which made him feel very grown up.

Some of this excessive spending had taken place before he met Jill, and when he seemed to always want to pay for their entertainment, she assumed he was well off financially. When she later learned of his background, she still was unaware of his financial limitations because he never told her the size of his trust; it was only after their marriage that she was shocked to learn that not only had Tucker gone through the $250,000, but he had been borrowing money from his brothers for several months and that he had accrued credit-card debt. She found this out when one of Tucker's brothers mentioned that his wedding gift was to forgive the $3,000 Tucker owed him.

Tucker had tried to fill the void he felt within him by accumulating things, unaware of the cause or implications of this behavior. Tucker has low self-esteem as a result of his difficult childhood. He feels a deep-seated need to make up for what he has lost and what he has missed out on. He has difficulty denying himself anything that he wants. Jill recognizes how deprived he has felt and feels bad for him. She also is concerned that he has so recklessly spent the entire trust from his parents and has so little to show for it. Then things get worse.

Jill gets the mail one night and finds a bill that says their account is overdue. Her first inclination is to think that Tucker has forgotten to pay it and she makes a mental note to ask him about it.

At the dinner table, she mentions it: "Tucker, did you pay the water bill this month?"

Tucker's head rises sharply, "I'm sure I did, Jill. Why do you ask?"

"We got a reminder today saying that the payment was past due. Are you sure you paid it?"

"Why are you interrogating me?" he snaps. " I said I mailed it, didn't I?"

"Yes, but why are you being so testy? I just thought maybe you forgot. But you are really overreacting so now I'm wondering if you are telling me the truth. Are you, Tucker?"

He says nothing.

"Don't lie to me, Tucker," she says, looking him directly in the eye.

Tucker stares back at her for a few seconds. Then he lowers his eyes and seems to concentrate on moving his food around with his fork.

Jill sits quietly, watching him, and then says, "Tucker?"

"Okay, okay," says Tucker defensively, "I didn't forget it. I didn't have enough money in my account to pay it."

"Why not, Tucker? You just got paid last week. Where did your money go?" Jill can't believe what she's hearing. Tucker first lied to her and now admits he really didn't pay the bills. "Who is this person I married?" she asks herself.

"Hey, don't talk to me like I'm a child. I just didn't have the money. Okay?"

"No, Tucker, it's not okay. I want to know where you spent the money and if there are more bills you didn't pay. Tell me, Tucker," she says forcefully.

"Okay," he says grudgingly." I gave my brother a couple hundred and I bought that new racing bike I told you I wanted. I forgot it was time to pay bills again."

"Tucker!" Jill exclaims. "How could you? You can't afford a racing bike right now. We have a new home. We need furniture. We have utility bills. We have the expensive wedding ring to pay for that you insisted on. What were you thinking? And why do you owe your brother money? Are you still borrowing from him?"

"Hey, don't get on my case, okay? I'm sorry I didn't get the bills paid. I just wanted that bike so bad and I just didn't think. I'm really sorry. I won't do it again."

"You're right that you won't do it again, or you'll have to start handing your paycheck over to me. And you'll have to take the bike back tomorrow, you know," Jill says.

"What?" Tucker yells. "I can't take it back. Do you want me to look like an idiot? It would be too humiliating. I can't do it," he says with tears in his eyes. "I've never had a bike. You had all these things when you were a kid. I never got them."

"Tucker!" she shouts. "This is not about a bike. This is about trust. I can no longer trust you."

"You're making a big deal out of nothing, Jill. Calm down," Tucker replies.

"Calm down? You want me to calm down when I just found out that my husband has lied to me?" she asks.

"Okay, okay, I made a mistake. I'm sorry. Really, I am. I just wasn't thinking."

"Tucker, I know you missed out on a lot and I'm so sorry for what you went through. But we are adults now and we both have to be responsible for our behavior. I hope someday you can have all the things you want, honey, but we don't have the money to do it right now." She pauses. "If you don't take it back, I will. It's your choice."

Tucker immediately storms out of the room shouting, "You're just like the rest of them. No one ever cared about me, not really."

Jill sits for some time at the table, quietly thinking. She knows that Tucker has, for four years, been spending large amounts of money and now she knows that he has continued doing so even after the money ran out. She hears him justifying his actions, saying he deserves it because he has been deprived. She can see that he has this empty black hole and is trying to fill it up. She feels very sad for him and worried at the same time.

Finally she goes out to the backyard where Tucker is sitting on the steps looking forlorn. She sits down beside him and remains quiet for a full minute; then she reaches over and takes his hand.

"Tucker," she starts quietly, "I know how hurt you've been. It's so tragic to think of a child losing his parents, then his grandparents, and then being separated from his siblings. If only you had at least had had a better foster home, it might have helped heal some of the wounds, but then you had that bad experience as well. I do understand the circumstances, Tucker, though I won't begin to say I understand how you feel or how difficult this has been for you. What I do know is that you can't make up for what you lost by buying things. We can only go on from here, living our lives as best we can, enjoying each other, enjoying new experiences from time to time, and trying to be true to ourselves and to each other."

"It's just not fair," Tucker says sadly.

"You're right, Tucker, it isn't fair. It is, however, the childhood you were dealt. You were deprived of a lot, especially the love and attention of parents, but it doesn't have to ruin your future, sweetheart."

"I know, you're right," he says. "It's just so embarrassing. Sometimes I'm like a kid in a candy store. I can't deny myself the things I want. Everything else goes out of my mind and I become so anxious that I can focus only on getting whatever it is I want at the time. I know this is really childish and immature, but sometimes I can't seem to do anything about it."

"Tucker, I want to ask you to do something for me—and for you," she says.

"What is it?" Tucker asks. "You want me to take the bike back. I will, though I don't want to."

"Well, yes, the bike has to go back, honey, but that isn't what I was going to ask. I'd like to see you go to therapy. Will you do that, Tucker? You need to talk to someone about all that has happened, *someone who can give you some insight and guidance about how to handle the memories, the pain, and the loss you feel. I think it would help, Tucker. I think you have low self-esteem. Who wouldn't if they had been through what has happened to you?"*

"Will this never end?" cries Tucker. "Am I going to be saddled with my background all my life? Can I never be free of it? I get so depressed at times and the things I buy make me feel better for a while."

"I know, Tucker," Jill agrees. "It's what a lot of people do. They spend money to feel better, but it doesn't last. That's why I want you to go to therapy, to deal with the problem so it won't affect the rest of your life, so it won't affect our life and our children's lives. I love you, Tucker. You can do this. We can do this."

"You really think it's the answer?" he asks.

"I think it might be," Jill replies. "I think it's worth a try and I'll even go with you if you need me to the first time."

"But how would I know who to see?" asks Tucker. I wouldn't know how to find the right person."

"We'll figure it out. We'll find someone who works with self-esteem issues. I'm so proud of you, Tucker, for being willing to do this. I'm so very, very proud of you," she says and she leans over and puts her head on his shoulder.

Tucker has had a very unfortunate childhood. One can only imagine what a child would feel like after suffering so much loss and being so alone. And it's understandable that a child who has had to take care of himself and who has felt so deprived would want to have and experience everything he could once he was free to do so. Tucker's anger propels him forward, providing him with the energy and the dogged determination to go after what he wants, knowing that others have never been there to provide it for him. Where others with LSE might have cowered and stepped out slowly and carefully when they got on their own, Tucker has attacked life, trying to soak up every opportunity and attempting to accumulate personal possessions to symbolize his success and self-worth.

The problem is he has been irresponsible in doing so. Whenever he starts to ruminate about his past and what he was deprived of, he begins to get anxious and angry and has a self-esteem attack. During the attack he gets so upset that he runs out and buys whatever it is that he thinks he missed out on and needs to have to calm himself down. Of course the joy of owning such things as the bike he never had doesn't make him feel better about himself and it doesn't replace his missed childhood. Rather this behavior gives temporary relief while slowly eating up his sizable trust fund and saddling him with credit-card debt.

Stimulated by the enjoyment of the moment, he has compromised principle for pleasure. Now he has to rein in his wants and learn to appropriately balance his impulses. As he gets into therapy and focuses on recovery from his low self-esteem, Tucker will be able to see how his irrational thinking that says he has the right to have everything he wants is getting him into trouble and is irresponsible behavior. With guidance, Tucker will be able to overcome his LSE.

RECOVERY

Most people who suffer from LSE cannot recover to the extent that is possible without professional help. They may be able to change to some degree, they may gain insight into their behavior, and they may develop some new skills, but most LSE sufferers are unable to alter their irrational thought patterns without an objective facilitator to keep them in touch with what's true, factual, or based on history, the three tests of what's healthy thinking.

Jackson spent years in agony over his sexual dysfunction and deprived himself of happiness until he was able to see he needed help. He saw a medical doctor who then directed him to therapy. There, if attention is given to his LSE and resulting anxiety, he will likely be able to correct the physical problem and continue a fulfilling relationship with Brianne.

Through the relationship with a wonderful man, Molly gains insight into behaviors and attitudes she wants to change in herself, but it is through therapy that she comes to understand her LSE and to finally work toward recovery. Molly is a Paddler, eager to learn and change. She will likely recover successfully from her LSE.

Jake's relationships haven't lasted long due to the insecurity he felt from being ridiculed by his mother. When Jake becomes aware that he is repeating his pattern of irrational jealousy and anger and is about to ruin his present relationship, he becomes a Paddler. He begins reading books, he analyzes his behavior, he admits to his LSE. Realizing that his efforts to control his jealousy haven't worked, he decides to go to therapy.

Carey, who came from a home where she was demeaned, ignored, and treated as insignificant, begins to change the way she has viewed herself, largely through the acceptance of Bernice, a surrogate mother who has re-parented her and guided her into other positive activities and relationships. She may one day decide to seek therapy to further understand the consequences of her early years, or her LSE may not be reactivated, if she remains in a positive environment. Her LSE is not necessarily gone, but the positive aspects of her life keep it below the surface where it is not negatively affecting her life for the time being. On rare occasions a person is able to recover from therapy on their own; Carey is very insightful and may be one of the few who can do so.

While Jarrod seeks therapy, he does so for the wrong reasons. He is trying to use the therapist as ammunition against his wife Jackie. If only he can get the therapist to say something negative about Jackie, he can throw those comments at her when they argue. Jarrod has LSE but isn't motivated to work on himself. Additionally, his wife has LSE and so their interactions are frequently so chaotic that neither one knows how to change the patterns. It is unlikely that Jarrod is going to overcome his low self-esteem because he is a Floater; he doesn't understand himself, his motivations, his fear and anxiety, or where it came from and he seems to have no desire to become enlightened.

Mandy and Willa are both LSE sufferers. Willa's immediate response to their problems is to suggest they both get help. She finds a support group and works hard to understand her LSE and to overcome it. She is a Paddler. Mandy is easily discouraged when therapy doesn't immediately bring results, largely because she hasn't found the right therapist. She continues her pattern of self-sabotage with little insight or motivation to seek further help. She is a Floater.

Darren is also a Floater. He is set in his ways, shutdown emotionally, and unaware of his self-defeating thinking and behavior. He has met a woman he is attracted to and who is a Paddler. She has actively pursued avenues of personal growth, including therapy, and she sees that Darren has avoided many of opportunities she has availed herself of. She decides to challenge Darren to a broader view of life; she wants to see if he will respond when encouraged to look at life differently. If he does, Darren may one day be willing to go to therapy. It's doubtful that he can overcome his LSE without help.

Oliver, is on the road to recovery due to the return of his mother and the steadfast love of Jenny. Though these two factors will not be enough for Oliver to grasp the broad picture of low self-esteem and how it is affecting all areas of his life, it has been sufficient to quell his distrust of Jenny and to give him a more positive perspective of live. He, too, is a good candidate for therapy, and the positive changes taking place in his life may free him up to consider such an option.

Most people, however, don't know how to select a therapist who is prepared to deal with their specific problem. This is even more difficult when looking for a specialist in self-esteem recovery, as there are few such specialists available.

The following pages are designed to help you evaluate:

1. if you need therapy

2. how to find the therapist you need

3. what to expect from therapy

Personal Reasons for Getting Into Therapy

If you are undecided about whether therapy might help you to work out the problems you are having in developing or maintaining intimacy, the list below might be helpful.

Therapy is recommended if any of the below statements are true:

1. If you know you have low self-esteem and haven't been in recovery.

2. If you were abandoned, abused, neglected, or in other ways mistreated as a child.

3. If you feel unworthy, unlovable, insignificant, or in competent.

4. If you have difficulty knowing whom and when to trust.

5. If you are too fearful to try new activities, learn new skills, or enjoy new experiences.

6. If you are frequently anxious or depressed, or if you suffer from self-esteem attacks.

7. If you frequently feel that others are laughing at you, berating you, or treating you with disrespect.

8. If you are aware that your thinking is at times irrational and distorted.

9. If you frequently feel angry and resentful.

10. If you are overly self-conscious.

11. If you are too fearful to ask for advice, information, or help with a decision or conflict.

12. If you frequently feel rejected by romantic interests.

13. If you've been told by more than one significant other that you are insensitive, abusive, or consistently defensive.

14. If you have difficulty being alone.

15. If you have difficulty making friends.

16. If you lack confidence in your interactions with others.

17. If you have not been able to maintain relationships.

18. If you are unable to ask for what you need, tell others when they hurt you, or state your opinions and ideas.

19. If you want to become a Paddler.

20. If you want to become assertive rather than passive, aggressive, or passive-aggressive.

21. If you avoid social situations.

22. If you lack a support group.

Reasons Why Therapy Might Help When a Significant Other Cannot

Therapy is especially important for those with LSE because they need someone who can be objective, someone who is emotionally neutral and who can stand back and see the self-defeating patterns of the LSE sufferer. Because of the irrational behavior of LSE sufferers, the feedback that they receive as adults is often as painful as what they experienced as children, the pain that caused their low self-esteem in the first place.

One of the main things that those with low self-esteem need is a person who understands what LSE is and how it affects their life. They need a support person who can see what is happening when they, and they need someone they trust to gently guide them in becoming aware of how they are contributing to their own problems. They do not need more criticism or disapproval. Only with this type of feedback and support can an LSE sufferer feel safe enough to admit to and discuss his irrational thinking and distortions. Only with the assistance of a person who is sensitive and understanding of the patterns common to all LSE sufferers can the afflicted person feel the respect that she deserves, respect that was not shown her when she most needed it—in childhood. Only those who are familiar with all the aspects of LSE can be objective in the midst of the confusion that arises in the lives of LSE sufferers.

Second, a therapist has the skills to tenderly confront the LSE sufferer when necessary, often with humor, helping the client see that what he has thought is so terrible about himself is just the behavior of a person trying to cope, not an indictment or condemnation of him as a bad person. This is a significant issue for LSE sufferers; they tend to equate the displeasure of others or confrontation by others as a statement that they are a bad person, that there is something innately wrong with them. A therapist should have the skills to address this in a way that's far less threatening than when the LSE sufferer speak to herself, enabling her to hear and digest the information and suggestions for change without being defensive.

Third, a therapist can demonstrate respect for the LSE sufferer through his understanding of the problems the client is dealing with. The person who has low self-esteem is very sensitive to any indication that others disrespect him or are silently disapproving of him. A therapist can present a sharp contrast to this type of behavior.

Fourth, a therapist can point out the progress of the client, which can be very encouraging to the LSE sufferer who is otherwise easily discouraged and depressed and cannot recognize his own improvement. A therapist can point out the subtle changes and, in doing so, help the client see that he is gaining in insight and behavior change. An LSE sufferer can never receive too much support when he is striving to make changes because altering life patterns is very difficult and fraught with setbacks.

Things to Consider When Selecting
a Therapist

Choose only a therapist who specializes in self-esteem recovery work. A thorough understanding of the development and effect of low self-esteem is essential for a therapist to be effective in helping a client to recover. Unfortunately, most therapists are not equipped to do this because they follow the diagnostic manual of the mental health community that views LSE as merely a symptom of many other disorders and not a valid disorder itself.

Choose only a therapist who will interact with you, offering guidance, making suggestions, and providing explanations. Interview your potential therapist before you start and ask in what ways he participates in the therapy process. Let him know that you want a therapist who freely interacts with you.

Stay in therapy only if you feel comfortable with your therapist. This does not mean that you should quit because your therapist confronts you or because you find it difficult to share intimate details about yourself or your past. Therapy can be uncomfortable, especially in the beginning when you are unfamiliar with the therapist, when you are uncertain of the process, or when you are feeling vulnerable. After a while, you and your therapist should develop a connection and you should begin to feel more relaxed and even excited about the work you are doing there. If that doesn't happen or if you feel the therapist is disrespectful or demeaning, seriously consider finding a new therapist. Try not to overreact, however, or to run at the first feelings of discomfort.

What to Expect in Therapy

Don't expect to be comfortable immediately. You will be in a new situation and with a new therapist for the purpose of sharing your personal problems. In time you will become more at ease as you build trust and you become more familiar with your feelings and reactions.

Your therapist may find it necessary to confront you about some irrational thought you have expressed, but she should do it gently. Try not to be defensive; she is only there to help you.

Quit therapy if you do not feel you are being supported. This does not mean you should quit the first time that you and the therapist don't see eye to eye, but if you feel the therapist is repeatedly disagreeable or discouraging, look elsewhere for support.

Don't expect to recover from LSE overnight. Remember that low self-esteem is a complex problem, one that is ruling your thinking. You have practiced this way of thinking for most of the years you have been alive and it will take time to alter these well-formed patterns.

Expect to feel a level of dependence on your therapist, especially in the beginning. As you become more confident, develop more skills, and gain more insight, you will also become more independent.

Group therapy is also an option, especially if you cannot afford individual therapy and if the group facilitator specializes in self-esteem recovery work.

ꕥ

Tucker and Jill

Tucker has promised to get therapy and begins his search for a therapist. He first calls around in his own area, talking to therapists to see if they know of anyone who specifically works with self-esteem issues. Not one of them is able to give him a referral, however, one of them says she has recently read a book by a specialist on self-esteem who does phone therapy, but while she remembers the title, she can't recall the author's name at the moment. She says that in areas of expertise where there are few experts, phone therapy is often available. He goes to the Internet and using the book title, finds the specialist in another state. He calls and interviews the psychologist and decides to give phone therapy a try.

Together, he and the therapist review his background and the hurtful elements of his life. He likes it that he has homework to do, books to read, his thoughts to record, and behaviors to try out and practice. They talk about low self-esteem, how it is formed, and how it affects the millions of people who suffer from it. He feels better knowing he's not alone, that others have gone through similar and even worse circumstances than he has.

His therapist assigns him two books to read and both he and Jill bury themselves in these informative books. Then he is given a workbook to delve into. All the while, he is making his weekly phone sessions and he begins to recognize a change in his thinking. He is becoming aware of his dysfunctional thinking.

When summer comes, Tucker and Jill decide to take a vacation and they choose to go to the city where his therapist lives, to visit the area and to have several sessions eye-to-eye with the psychologist he has been working with. He feels that a bond has developed and he yearns to see the therapist in person.

After the vacation, Tucker continues working on his issues. He has learned how his irrational thinking is responsible for his mismanagement of money and the way he gives himself permission to buy what he wants rather than what he can afford. He also has to face the fact that he must now consider Jill's opinion before making large expenditures, and the two of them work out an agreement to do this.

Tucker and Jill spend hours talking about their childhood experiences and their feelings. Intimacy has been re-established. As the months go by, Tucker rarely has a self-esteem attack or reacts irrationally. He is able to catch his distorted thinking before he puts it into action; he is able to make better choices for his life.

Tucker will never forget his painful childhood; he will never fully get over the loss of his parents at such an early age. He will, however, be able to live his life unencumbered by those memories rather than trapped and controlled by them. The process of recovering from his low self-esteem is allowing Tucker the freedom to love Jill, to be a person of integrity and loyalty, to be a person focused on the present and less on the past. Tucker is well on the road to recovery. Tucker and Jill are happy and have developed an emotional, verbal, and physically intimate relationship.

To contact the author:

Phone: 503-330-2830
Fax: 503-625-1545
Email: mjsorensen@TheSelfEsteemInstitute.com

To order more copies:

To Addresses within the US:
Send $18.95 USD   No Shipping Charge

To Addresses in Canada:
Send $26.95 plus $4.95 shipping and handling USD

Send all orders to:

Wolf Publishing Co.
16890 SW Daffodil St.
Sherwood, OR 97140

Or use your credit card by ordering through
www.TheSelfEsteemInstitute.com

For other destinations, please email us first at:
mjsorensen@TheSelfEsteemInstitute.com

Large quantity discounts available

Also available in bookstores nationwide